RELIGION OF THE FIELD NEGRO

Religion of the Field Negro

On Black Secularism and Black Theology

Vincent W. Lloyd

FORDHAM UNIVERSITY PRESS

New York 2018

Copyright © 2018 Fordham University Press

All rights reserved. No part of this publication may be reproduced, stored in a retrieval system, or transmitted in any form or by any means—electronic, mechanical, photocopy, recording, or any other—except for brief quotations in printed reviews, without the prior permission of the publisher.

Fordham University Press has no responsibility for the persistence or accuracy of URLs for external or third-party Internet websites referred to in this publication and does not guarantee that any content on such websites is, or will remain, accurate or appropriate.

Fordham University Press also publishes its books in a variety of electronic formats. Some content that appears in print may not be available in electronic books.

Visit us online at www.fordhampress.com.

Library of Congress Cataloging-in-Publication Data available online at http://catalog.loc.gov.

Printed in the United States of America
20 19 18   5 4 3 2 1
First edition

CONTENTS

Introduction — 1

I. CORNERSTONES

1. Cone — 21
2. Baldwin — 39
3. Mbembe — 60
4. Derrida, Agamben, Wynter — 76

II. QUESTIONS

5. What Is Black Tradition? — 97
6. What Is Black Organizing? — 113
7. For What Are Blacks to Hope? — 131
8. For What Are Whites to Hope? — 147

III. EXEMPLA

9. The Revelation of Race: On Steve Biko — 163
10. The Racial Messiah: On Huey P. Newton — 181
11. The Postracial Saint: On Barack Obama — 198
12. The Race of the Soul: On Gillian Rose — 216

Coda: The Birth of the Black Church — 233

Notes — 239
Bibliography — 267
Index — 281

Religion of the Field Negro

Introduction

"There were two kinds of slaves," Malcolm X lectured in a Detroit black Baptist church.[1] The house Negro identified with his master: "Whenever the master said 'we,' he said 'we.'" When the master was in danger, the house Negro rushed to protect him. The house Negro enjoyed the comforts that come with proximity to power: better housing, better food, and better clothes. In return, the house Negro managed the other slaves, keeping them "passive and peaceful." These other slaves, the masses, were field Negroes. Living in flimsy shelters, eating castaway food, and wearing old clothes, the field Negro felt only hatred toward his master. Field Negroes were constantly looking for opportunities to escape. According to Malcolm, the field Negro was particularly intelligent; nonetheless, the revolutionary impulses of the field Negro were repressed by the anesthetic preaching of the house Negro.

Across town from Malcolm, civil rights leaders including Adam Clayton Powell were speaking at the Northern Negro Leadership Conference. The conference organizers had shunned black nationalists, and in protest Rev. Albert Cleage organized a Northern Negro Grass Roots Leadership Conference at the same time.[2] It was there that Malcolm was speaking, to the masses rather than the liberal elites. Indeed, by the end of his speech Malcolm's account of the house Negro developed into a full-throttled attack on Martin Luther King and other leading civil rights leaders, just months after the March on Washington. Malcolm portrayed these leaders as instruments of the white liberals who were invested in maintaining the status quo and who saw the cultivation of black elites as a means of managing the hostile, unruly black masses.

Identifying himself with the grassroots, Malcolm argued that divisions among the masses should be set aside in favor of unity based on a common enemy, "the white man." At Bandung, colonized peoples from all over the world— "black, brown, red, or yellow," but all ultimately subsumed under the label "black" in Malcolm's speech—realized that their struggles had a common cause in the white man. Malcolm suggests that the same conclusion ought to be reached in the United States: "You don't catch hell 'cause you're a Methodist or Baptist, you don't catch hell because you're a Democrat or a Republican, you don't catch hell because you're a Mason or an Elk. . . . You catch hell because you're a black man." Malcolm does not say exactly what he means by "black"; it is clearly not a physical description. Its meaning seems to be defined by a common enemy. While Malcolm is quite explicit about who that enemy is—he has "blue eyes and blond hair and pale skin"— Malcolm's real target is the system of white supremacy, a system in which all whites are complicit.

Once Malcolm has established that he stands with the masses, he shows how the politics of the masses, of the field Negro, differs from the politics of the elite, of the house Negro. The latter want racial integration by nonviolent means. Malcolm cuttingly reduces this to the desire to "sit down next to white folks on the toilet." "That's no revolution," he concludes. The field Negro seeks a genuine revolution that is dramatic and violent, a radical transformation of the ways of the world rather than accommodation with a white regime. Ultimately, what the field Negro seeks is "land."[3] This conclusion derives from the analogy with resistance to colonialism: colonial overlords were being pushed away and land redistributed. What Malcolm seems to mean, in the U.S. context, is not literal land but rather sovereignty. The genuine revolution will only be complete when the sovereignty of the white regime is rejected and the sovereignty of blacks is established—when blackness is expressed in a way that is irreducible to the terms set out by whiteness. What this might look like remains vague in Malcolm's rhetoric, but it is the motivating goal of his militancy. And house Negroes stand in the way.

According to Malcolm, the house Negro is the preacher who praises peaceful suffering while cashing checks from the powers that be. The field Negro embraces "good religion," "old-time religion," "the one that Ma and Pa used to talk about." This is religion aligned with black revolution. It commends intelligence and obedience, but it also commends resistance to those worldly forces that would cause suffering. While Malcolm says he finds this religion in the Qu'ran, it is also the religion of an amorphous black tradition (of "Ma and Pa"), as well as the religion of those Methodists, Baptists, and other Christians who are oppressed; it is the religion of the black masses. In an interview the same year, Malcolm asserted, "A Muslim to us is somebody who is for the black man; I don't care if he goes to the Baptist Church seven days a week."[4] Malcolm repeatedly singles out his host, Rev. Cleage, as an exemplary Christian minister whose religious commitments are aligned with the masses. At the time, Cleage's theology was radicalizing; five years later, in 1968, he would publish *The Black Messiah*, the first book of black theology, released a year before James Cone's *Black Theology and Black Power*. Just as Malcolm had pointed out that "Christ was a black man," Cleage retold the Christian story from the perspective of contemporary black oppression.[5]

On Malcolm's account, then, the religion of the field Negro is unified by its opposition to white supremacy and its alignment with black revolution, even if the particular form this religion takes varies widely, from mosque to church, Baptist to Methodist—and perhaps outside of an institutional context altogether. If the revolution claims black sovereignty, the God of the field Negro is similarly sovereign, irreducible to the terms of the white world. To worship that God means to struggle against white supremacy: to challenge the idols (from objects to ideas) that whites elevate to sacred status in order to consolidate their hold on power. In his speech, Malcolm is careful to avoid attributing positive content to God. All he says about God is that God authorizes the struggle against oppression. It is the house Negroes who claim to know who God is, who claim that God wants blacks to follow the rules of the white world and wait patiently for incremental change. The white world puts the black preacher on a podium next to "a priest, a rabbi, and an old white preacher," all of whom promise that racial justice is right around the corner. The house Negro works with the racial and religious categories that are given by the white world; the field Negro seeks a new set of categories, scrambling the old divisions and allowing for an effervescence of new concepts emerging in light of political struggle.

The black masses had the capacity to effect a revolutionary transformation of American society, but house Negro preachers were always holding them back—and so the house Negro became Malcolm's prime target. On their own, the black masses would naturally rise up against white supremacy, so if Malcolm could outwit the house Negro, the revolution would surely follow. The critical work involved in challenging the house Negro is difficult and painful but essential. Malcolm holds up as exemplary a nine-year-old Chinese girl who shot an "Uncle Tom Chinaman"—her father. In Malcolm's view, it is only with such violent breaks, turning away from familiar comforts and toward an as-yet-undetermined vision of blackness, that white supremacy can be countered. In religious terms, conversion is necessary: away from the religion of the house Negro, toward the religion of the field Negro, embracing the worship of a God irreducible to worldly, white terms.

Where Malcolm's contemporaries occupied the role of house Negro with their liberal Protestant preaching, today this role is occupied more often than not through an embrace of secularism. By secularism I mean the exclusion or management of religion by the powers that be. For the secularist, there is nothing beyond the ways of the world; they must serve as our starting point. We can explore, reinterpret, or wallow in these ways or use them as a basis for imagining new ways, but we must not delude ourselves into believing that they may be transcended. Religion is shaped by secularism when it takes a form compatible with the status quo; often this means that religion is confined to the heart, treated as a personal choice, entailing only those normative claims that match ambient values. The black secularist domesticates the revolutionary impulses of black theology—and is richly rewarded by the powers that be. Some black secularists tame the content of black theology while maintaining its radical style. Other black secularists turn away from revolutionary change, toward an exploration of the supposed complexity and diversity of our current racial and religious landscape in order to discern how a coalition might be assembled to affect incremental change. Still other black secularists turn away from religion altogether, leaving themselves with little leverage to separate themselves from the terms of the white world.

Secularism has attracted a wide variety of critics who have called attention to the ways that it is entangled with the disciplining impulses of modernity, with neoliberal ideology, and with Western imperialism. Yet these critics, particularly those on the academic left, are often deeply invested in their *critical* posture, diagnosing problems but at most gesturing in the direction of practices that evade the grasp of secularism—and usually these practices occur in some exotic locale, like Egypt, with little chance of affecting life in elite academic circles.[6] Malcolm's speech is so powerful because he locates himself as an organic intellectual, one among the masses, challenging the ideas of the elite, of the house Negroes. This is the particular contribution that black theology has to make to intellectual discussions of secularism. It names a perspective that is widely embraced, allowing us to see secularism as an aberration. But taking up black theology as a critical perspective also means grappling with religious ideas and practices *for us*, not just the shortcomings or potential of ideas and practices held by others. This may be uncomfortable, for the critic is always invested in her object of critique, and the academic critic of secularism often feels uncomfortable around ideas that are too Christian, particularly when they are taken as normative. But we must embrace the masses rather than preach to the masses (a role for the house Negro), and this means grappling with black religious ideas and practices, particularly those that are Christian.

Just as the religion of the house Negro was Malcolm's prime target for critique, today black secularism must be the intellectual's prime target for critique. Particularly at a political moment when the grassroots are energized, we can see all the more clearly that it is only white-funded black leadership that is holding back radical social transformation. The religion of the field Negro is religion orthogonal to the ways of the world, claiming sovereignty for blackness. What might that look like?

Black theology has been too modest. It has forgotten its original ambition. All theology, properly understood, is black theology. All social criticism, properly understood, is theological. Black theology is social criticism; social criticism is black theology.

The reason black theology has become so modest is secularism. Secularism confines theology to the status of one among many disciplines, and secularism makes theology's hold even on that diminished status tenuous. Secularism's conjoined twin, multiculturalism, confines black theology to one of many ways to pluralize theology. Black theology no longer understands its role as social criticism—yet today that role is more important than ever.

To revive black theology, the question of secularism must be named, and it must be addressed directly. Once secularism is rejected, black theology will return to its origins, will realize its ambition. Black theology will again be social criticism, and social criticism will be black theology.

Theology means speaking rightly and rigorously about God. It is impossible. If we could speak rightly and rigorously about God, God would not be God. God would be a product of humans, reducible to human terms, conjured by human minds. So theology takes its task to be speaking more rightly and more rigorously about God, acknowledging the distance between the human and the divine. This, however, is not the only response available to theology. The alternative I propose is twofold. First, what theology can succeed in saying, rightly and rigorously, is what God is not. Theology can expose idols as idols, showing how concepts, practices, feelings, and images that purport to be divine are really made by humans, advancing human interests in the name of the divine. Second, theology can hold up examples from those sites where God is most likely to be found, which is to say from those sites where the hold of idols is the weakest. These are sites where the violence and tragedy of the world demystify idols, where the world's hubristic aspirations to omniscience and omnibenevolence are greeted with scorn. Theology can hold up the wisdom of the weakest, the most marginal, and the most afflicted. This wisdom of the oppressed shows what is right, but it is not rigorous; the critique of idolatry is rigorous, but it does not show what is right. Together, theology comes closest to fulfilling its task.

This is not to say that theology should abandon tradition, or sacred texts, or systematic inquiry. I am describing the stance that should be taken toward the practice of theology. The aspiration to speak rightly and rigorously about God, or just to speak more rightly and more rigorously about God, too often leads to idolatry—whether it is in studying Leviticus, Augustine, or pneumatology. Sometimes this happens directly, in the claims that are made by theologians. More often it happens indirectly, in the self-confidence implicit in theology as a practice of elite academics. This is white theology: white theology is idolatry. The way to challenge white theology, the way for theology to fulfill its task, is for theology to take on the twofold mission of challenging idolatry (which is to say, challenging white theology) and holding up the wisdom of the most marginalized (which is to say, holding up black experience).

These racial categories seem too simplistic. Surely the world is more complicated than black and white. Surely religion is more complicated than black and white. How is labeling God with a color not paradigmatic of idolatry? The fundamental claim of black theology is that God is black. Blackness here must be understood in two senses at once. Blackness names the position of the weakest, the most marginal, and the most afflicted; blackness also names a specific group of people who are the weakest, the most marginal, and the most afflicted here and now, in the twenty-first-century United States of America. Neither sense of blackness has to do with skin color; in the most empirical sense, blacks are those subject to the racializing regime of contemporary America, the regime that marks one as black. Whiteness, similarly, refers to the position of the comfortable, the privileged, and the wealthy—whether it is the wealth of financial capital, social capital, or cultural capital. At the same time, whiteness refers to those treated as white here and now, in the current American racial regime. To say that God is black means that God is to be found among blacks, among those who are systematically denigrated. Those who are comfortable, privileged, or wealthy are those most likely to confuse their own interests with God's will; they are most likely to worship idols.

Rich people do not go to heaven, as the Bible so clearly says, and white people do not go to heaven—when whiteness is understood as comfort, privilege, and wealth. Whiteness can be renounced, and it must be renounced to do theology or to worship God. Renouncing whiteness means giving away the wealth (financial, social, and cultural capital) that comes with whiteness. This is not only a bank transaction. Whiteness is secured by a set of practices and networks, including clothing, style of speech, friends, relatives, neighbors, cultural references, suspicions, affections, and much else. These must be renounced. But are these not necessary for the black theologian to practice theology? Particularly today, with black elites superficially integrated into historically white institutions and cultures, does the black theologian also have to abandon whiteness? There are rich resources for theological work—for the critique of idolatry and the lifting up of marginalized communities—made available by elite institutional settings and academic networks, and these should not be undervalued. But those settings and networks also encourage the forgetting of theology's tasks. They encourage theology to imagine itself speaking rightly and rigorously about God: they encourage theology to be white theology, idolatry.

We need to change the whiteness of these settings and networks, but this is a seemingly paradoxical task. How can elite institutional settings no longer be white if whiteness is defined as comfort, privilege, and wealth? The answer: those who inhabit these spaces must not live their lives in ways that closely track with the practices and networks definitive of whiteness. There is a problem when all of the professors at the seminary live in the same suburb, shop at the same organic supermarket, send their children to the same private school, and play tennis at the same club. When black professors hired by the seminary move into that neighborhood, go to that store, send their children to that school, and go to that tennis club, little has improved—indeed, the situation has worsened. Blacks who aspire to whiteness offer comfort to whites, reinforcing the idolatry of whiteness. In reality, however, the situation is often more complicated. Blacks in elite spaces embrace some but not all of the practices and networks of whites in those spaces, creating discordance that potentially disrupts the complacencies of whiteness. The more blacks in such spaces, the more varieties of such discordance, and the hold of whiteness on theology is loosened. Theological institutions and networks should not be aspiring to proportionately represent blacks—12 percent, 15 percent. For theology to fulfill its task, for theology to be black theology, we should be talking about spaces where 60 percent or 80 percent of participants are black. Only with those sorts of numbers can the centripetal force of whiteness be curtailed. With those sorts of numbers, the grotesqueness of whiteness, of the tennis clubs, the suburbs, the kale, is obvious. Then, the varieties of black experience, which is to say the varieties of experience of the marginalized, which is to say the varieties of experience of the human, can flourish.

What about our increasingly diverse nation, and about global diversity? What about diversity within the black community? The aspiration to speak for everyone, to speak universally, is an aspiration of white theology. It is an aspiration of the powerful, of the prison guard: to make sure each is accounted for. The aspiration of black theology is to speak theologically motivated by the situation here, now. Theology (like all aspects of the world, and like life) is most certainly accountable to the authority of tradition. Tradition provides the substance of the norms and practices that are the waters in which our lives swim. Ignoring that water, we drown. But how we swim, where we swim, these are questions about the orientation of black theology, and that orientation must take into account concerns of the present and the local. Anti-black racism in the United States in the twenty-first century is pervasive and violent. Its violence involves blood but also the distortion of personality, involves micro-aggression and police harassment but also wealth inequality and limited economic opportunity. There are many social problems, many injustices, but none is so stark, so sharp, so pressing here and now as anti-black racism. In other places around the world, other urgent injustices should inform theology in analogous ways. The struggles of tribal communities in India, of Palestinians, of Sudanese refugees, and of many other groups are pressing, and they are not unconnected with each other and with anti-black racism in the United States. But these struggles must not be subsumed into a global account of injustice, for such an account ultimately only speaks to those concerned with global control—that is, to whites.

Unfortunately, we cannot just *do* black theology, understood as critiquing idolatry and holding up the wisdom of the oppressed. This is because black theology has been systematically distorted by black secularism. We must untangle black secularism from black theology before we can do black theology: *Religion of the Field Negro* attempts this prefatory work. Secularism is the exclusion or management of the theological. Banning prayer from public schools is a form of secularism; having a moment of silence at the beginning of each school day is also a form of secularism. Secularism acts in a particular domain, such as American political discourse, media, or public schools. Secularism changes what it is possible to say and do in these domains. In the last quarter of the twentieth century, American conservatives and evangelicals were up in arms about secularism. The religious (supposedly Judeo-Christian) ambiance of American culture had quickly transformed in the 1960s and 1970s to the point where mention of God or Jesus became a marker of those outside the mainstream. I am not interested in the question of secularism in the public square. Indeed, I suspect that anti-secularist reactionaries are themselves a product of secularism, and I suspect that the supposed era before secularism was not religious in the way that anti-secularist reactionaries suppose. I am concerned about secularism in the domain of theology or, more precisely, about the effect of secularism on the practice of theology. In this context, the theological origins of the concept of the secular should be remembered. The secular is the worldly in contrast to the divine. Secularism then suggests a supreme confidence in the worldly, a foreclosure of the divine. Secularism suggests an appreciation of the expansiveness and complexity and diversity of the world, but also a refusal to consider that there is any excess. The world is what there is, and we are in the world, solving problems we encounter by worldly means. We must study the situation, assess the options, and then make a decision, knowing that sometimes we will miscalculate, sometimes we will need a course correction. Too often, this is how theologians approach their work.

Secularism infects theology when theology envisions that it can speak rightly and rigorously about God. God becomes an element of the world that humans can aspire to figure out, just like all other elements of the world, like minerals and comets and brain tissue. At the same time, however, secularism takes away the raison d'être of theology because secularism forecloses the possibility that theology has anything unique to say about the world. Everything could be said just as well, probably better, by other disciplines, by other traditions of inquiry. What makes theology distinctive is its commitment to address what is irreducible to the terms of the world—that to which the world is ultimately accountable. This is why theology deserves its place of preeminence among the disciplines: it addresses an authority higher than the others, and so it attends to limits and blind spots ignored by the other disciplines. The other disciplines imagine that the world is ours, fully graspable with the right amount of effort and training. Theology reminds us that the world is God's, that our world (perceivable, knowable) never matches God's world, and it is God's world, which is to say the world itself, that matters. It is the latter world that pushes back against us, that frustrates us, that surprises us, and that fuels our desire—it is only theology that speaks to this.

The stories of secularism and racism are entwined. Histories could be written, and have been written, about how religion is thematized at the moment of the colonial encounter, at the moment when race takes on its modern significance. Religion and race come into the world at once, and theology is left behind. The worldly powers that fuel colonialism and empire use both whiteness and religion as tools of conquest and management. Theology at its best, critical and marginal, suffocates under the control of worldly powers. In recent years, when many act as if colonial and racializing legacies have been shed, religion and race become two identity categories, boxes to be checked on forms, categories of classification constructed by and for the powers that be. Once again, theology at its best, critical and marginal, suffocates.

Historical narratives always elide complexity. At any moment the powers that be attempt to control or manage religion and race, and there are ingenious religious and racial forces that contest the powers that be. It is this complexity, these entanglements, that must be unpacked in order to open the space for black theological reflection. In the specific case of black theology in the contemporary U.S. context, secularism has been particularly pernicious. In the late 1960s and early 1970s, whiteness could finally be named for a broad audience as that which distorts racialized lives and theological inquiry. Through probing the distortions of whiteness and exploring unfettered blackness, black theology developed creatively and critically. Time passed, the powers that be regrouped, and black secularism triumphed by splitting black theology into two groups. Secular religious studies scholars examined the history, sociology, and culture of black religion. Scholars of black religion within the theological academy took black experience to be one of many approaches to religious experience, and they took black experience itself to be multiple and fragmented. Both sides understood blackness in worldly and secular, not theological, terms. Both sides understood religion as essentially one component of worldly life, at most a particularly meaningful one. The original insights of black theology, that all theology should be black theology and that blackness refers to the most marginalized, were forgotten. Those insights need to be retrieved.

Even those original claims of black theologians were too modest, or at least they did not advertise their expansiveness. All theology must be black theology, but once secularism is rejected theology must not confine itself to its role as one discipline among others. All other disciplines, all other modes of inquiry, are accountable to theology. More precisely, all other disciplines are subject to theological critique. This is sometimes the role that critical theory, or more broadly social criticism, assigns to itself. The critic observes and declares the limits of a conversation, the assumptions that have never been interrogated, and the failures that go overlooked. In other words, the critic challenges those who aspire to fully understand the world, to capture the world in thought—which leads to action, which leads to violence, often at the expense of the most vulnerable. The critic challenges idolatry, the affective and rational investment in human-constructed systems that aspire to omniscience, and sometimes to omnipotence and omni-benevolence. The difference between the critic and the theologian is that the theologian does the work of the critic, challenging idolatry, but also something else. From the critic's perspective, this something else is an illicit belief in God. From the theologian's perspective, when theology is rightly understood, this something else is a commitment to hold up the wisdom of the marginalized. (From the theologian's perspective, this is another way to proclaim her belief in God.) The theologian views the critic as ultimately an elitist, one who never really renounces whiteness, its sustaining institutions and networks. The practice of criticism as it is understood in the academy is an elite practice, made possible by elite institutions, practiced by those in the 1 percent—if not of financial capital, then certainly of social and cultural capital. In contrast, the practice of theology is humbled by its extra belief in the authority of the poor. For the theologian, at her best, one foot is in the world of the elite and the other foot is in the world of the afflicted. Her scholarship does not compulsively proclaim the world's fallenness. Her scholarship always pairs criticism with stories of those on the margins whose wisdom is greater than the scholar's, those whose capacity to see through the illusions of power has not been dampened by the comforts of the elite.

I have not succeeded in this task, but I have tried to present a taste of what this vision for black theology, and so for theology as such, might look like. This vision is, by necessity, not systematic. I commend systematic theologians, and I think their work, at its best, can also be oriented toward the criticism of idolatry and toward the stories of the marginal. It is this orientation I am interested in, and it is how this orientation is forgotten that is the focus of my book. In the chapters that follow, I explore a variety of figures and themes from black religion and culture, probing the ways in which they challenge secularism and the ways in which secularism distorts. The critique of idolatry, understood as the criticism of ideology, has been rigorously developed outside of the confines of black theology and of theology altogether. In the chapters that follow, I use nontheological as well as theological sources, black as well as white sources, to sharpen the critical analysis. My attempt is not to apply "theory" to black religion, but to show how there are resources in critical theory that complement resources in black theology for addressing the problem of idolatry—that is, the problem of whiteness. The chapters are intended as essays: rather than enacting the same critical maneuver over and over in each chapter, on different subject matter, each chapter approaches its theme differently, demonstrating the variety of forms that theological criticism can take.

I seek a return to the early days of black theology, the days when black theology was unabashedly black and unabashedly theological. These early days have been obscured by black secularism, and black secularism is the antagonist throughout this text. Black theology is the reclusive protagonist, beckoned forth but never fully revealed. My claim is that grappling with black secularism is the prerequisite to black theology, to all theology, and I aim to offer examples of such grappling. What of the passion that so characterized the early days of black theology? What of the anger at white theology, at whiteness? Though I try to smile, I am angry. I feel little else. Oh, the stories I could tell. But we must be wary of the temptation to treat theology, and academic writing more generally, as more than it is. This is not the place for emotional catharsis on the part of writer or reader. My aspiration is not to tell you something about God or about me. My aspiration is to help us attend to those who do have something to tell us about God and to help us learn the rigor necessary to identify and demystify idolatry.

The first set of four chapters takes as its starting point thinkers who can serve as resources for black theology. James Cone is broadly recognized as the founding figure of black theology, but Chapter 1 argues that Cone's work after the early 1970s takes a subtle secularist turn. In his earliest, most powerful writings, Cone embraces paradox. Blackness is at once empirical reality and ontological symbol. Hope is at once this-worldly and otherworldly. The agent of historical change is at once the human and God.

These and many other paradoxes echo the central paradox of Cone's work: Jesus Christ is at once human and divine. This chapter argues that Cone's early work proposes for black theology an aesthetics of paradox that short-circuits both white supremacy and secularism. However, as the conversation about black theology expanded, and as Cone's work itself developed, paradox was abandoned in a misguided effort at inclusiveness. As black theologians saw parallels between anti-black oppression and other forms of oppression, and as they explored the intersections of race, gender, sexuality, migration, and other issues, black theology became tethered to worldly concerns. This chapter ponders whether it might be possible for black theology to be responsive to multiple and intersecting oppressions while embracing a decidedly theological idiom that takes paradox as its heart.

The black American writer James Baldwin famously broke with his youthful formation as a preacher, transferring his creative energies from the pulpit to the pen. Chapter 2 argues that Baldwin's literary endeavors can be read as black theological reflection—not in the sense that they employ theological images and tropes but in the deeper sense that they engage with theological ideas. Specifically, the chapter argues that Baldwin puts forward a black negative theology: he argues that black theology goes wrong when it tries to make positive claims about God; it goes right when it reflects on God's continuing influence despite our inability to name God accurately. In other words, Baldwin presents a way of doing black theology in a context of secularism, where religion is managed or excluded. The chapter further argues, however, that Baldwin himself falls prey to the dangers of secularism when he does not sufficiently attend to judgment, instead prescribing love to solve the theological problem he diagnoses.

The Cameroon-born political theorist Achille Mbembe has produced a body of work that deeply engages with Christianity: the role of Christianity in postcolonial and particularly African contexts, the role of Christianity in securing Europe's self-image, and the role of Christian ideas in providing a framework for postcolonial resistance. In Mbembe's most recent work, he has turned his critical apparatus from postcolonial contexts to blackness more generally, engaging with questions of race and religion across Africa and the diaspora. Chapter 3 argues that Mbembe's work offers promising resources for black theology, but it also has crippling limitations because of underlying secularist assumptions. Mbembe helpfully diagnoses postcolonial and black contexts as suffering from what is effectively theological heresy: a distorted relationship with ultimate authority brought about by colonialism and racialization. While Mbembe's diagnosis deeply engages with theology, his prescription is secularist, embracing plurality that black experience is said to model. The chapter juxtaposes Mbembe's reflections on colonial and racializing heresy with theologian John Milbank's reflections on secularist heresy to explore the limitations and possibilities of each.

Chapter 4 explores the way race and religion are articulated together in the work of leading critical theorists Jacques Derrida and Giorgio Agamben. It probes how these theorists stand on the border between the philosophy of religion and theology, and it argues that it is only because of secularist assumptions that this divide between the outsider's philosophy of religion and the insider's theology can be maintained. For Derrida, both religion and race function as loose threads that can be pulled in order to unravel a system of thought. For Agamben, the protagonist of modernity, *homo sacer*, is both racialized and sanctified. Yet Derrida and Agamben's accounts are skewed by a Eurocentrism and a failure to take religious ideas sufficiently seriously. The black feminist Sylvia Wynter offers an antidote, similarly linking race and religion but doing so in a way that attends to how racialization is produced theologically and to how racialization, patriarchy, and theology are tied together. Wynter's work implies that a philosophy of religion that refuses secularism is always black theology and that black theology must engage seriously with questions in the philosophy of religion.

Four questions form the themes of the next chapters. Tradition is a central theological category, and it has also been a central category in black studies as scholars recover, for example, the "black radical tradition." Yet tradition is particularly fraught in the context of black experience, since a constitutive feature of black experience is the involuntary severing of tradition. Paradigmatically, the Middle Passage detached blacks from families, culture, and language, leaving blacks orphaned in the New World. Colonialism and mass incarceration also have functioned to sever black men and women from their past. In such a context, to speak of black tradition is necessarily theological, and this chapter tracks how theological ideas and images have repeatedly been so employed. The prophetic and the messianic, in particular, are theological means of conjuring impossible tradition. But Chapter 5 also shows how the desire to imagine black tradition too often falls back on a patriarchal desire to create a right relationship with fathers and sons, a result of black secularism contaminating black theology.

The past two decades have seen a rapid growth in faith-based community organizing. Such organizing efforts often understand themselves as "broad-based," drawing support from a range of religious communities, racial groups, and neighborhoods. In doing so, these organizing efforts often elide the specificity of racial and religious difference. Chapter 6 draws on feminist critiques of community organizing traditions to develop a black theological critique—and the beginnings of an alternative approach to community organizing that draws on the longstanding organizing traditions already present in black communities. By bringing together secular and religious traditions of black organizing, and by coupling black organizing with black theological reflection, this chapter shows how black community organizing can move beyond pragmatic appeals that sideline racial and religious identity.

Recent theorizing in black studies, under the label "Afro-pessimism," argues that hope for ending racial injustice is misguided. Racism is deeply woven into the metaphysics, or onto-theology, of the West—an argument that is made both through readings of philosophical texts and through empirical observation, contrasting the conditions faced by blacks with other ethnic groups. This challenge has not been substantially addressed by black theologians, who often romanticize the hope implicit in, for example, slave spirituals. Chapter 7 points to theological responses to secularization as offering a model for black theological responses to racial injustice. According to Edward Schillebeeckx, secularization purged theology of false hopes while also orienting theologians to the future. This chapter explores what it might mean for Afro-pessimist insights to purge black theology of false hopes, and it asks what might remain of Christian hope after this purgation.

Before directly addressing its titular question, for what are whites to hope?, Chapter 8 examines how secularist conceptions of hope lead us astray. In analytic philosophy, hope is often understood as a desire that is not entirely justified with reasons. In cultural studies, hope has recently been looked upon suspiciously, as an affect, the circulation of which is intensified by neoliberal economics. In mid-twentieth-century German theology and theory, hope is viewed as other-worldly. In liberation theology, the object of hope is identification with the poor. This chapter argues that each of these views grows out of concealed secularist premises, and each of these views ends up perpetuating the status quo: white supremacy. After exploring the antinomies of hope, the chapter urges that whites are to embrace these antinomies. They are to hope for despair.

The final set of four chapters focuses on figures from twentieth-century culture whose work has relevance, expected or unexpected, for black theology. Chapter 9 focuses on the dramatic change effected by the South African anti-apartheid leader Steve Biko. The apartheid regime had used racial labeling to divide Indian, African, and mixed-race communities, preventing them from seeing their shared interests. Rather than reading Biko as a secular militant in the black power tradition, this chapter argues that Biko is best understood as rejecting a pragmatic, secularist understanding of politics. Through a seemingly simple practice of relabeling, grouping all nonwhites under the label "black," Biko was able to transform not only political language but also political practice and ultimately political possibilities. This transformation is best understood in theological terms, as revelation that solicits fidelity; understood thusly, whiteness is identified with heresy. The chapter concludes by comparing Biko's work of revelation with the reactionary, secularist racial labeling in a U.S. context, where words are tied increasingly tightly to worldly referents (from "Negro" to "black" to "African American").

While the Black Panther Party has often been presented as the secularist reaction to the politically ineffective religiosity of the civil rights movement, religious histories, symbols, and concepts are closely connected with the Panthers and particularly with their photogenic leader, Huey P. Newton. Reading the iconography of Newton along with Bobby Seale's hagiography, *Seize the Time*, and Newton's own *Revolutionary Suicide*, Chapter 10 suggests that the Panthers offer a black theological aesthetics that has political implications. Moving between an analysis of Newton and attempts at political reflection made by white critics, this chapter makes a case for black theology that takes political practice seriously, that takes political practice as a form of theological practice, in contrast to those who would simply apply abstract theological concepts to political problems.

All saints are, in a sense, postracial. By definition, saints transcend worldly concepts and categories, but in doing so they draw on the specificity of their worldly features. During the 2008 election campaign and in the early days of his presidency, Barack Obama was represented as saintly. Was this merely a metaphor, or is there something about the theological structure of sainthood that captures Obama's representation (and self-presentation)? By moving back and forth between analysis of Obama's image and a reflection on sainthood, Chapter 11 attempts to move conversations about black politics and about sainthood forward, helping us racially inflect our understanding of saints and helping us theologically deepen our understanding of the first black president.

Chapter 12, the final chapter, focuses on the British social theorist and Jewish convert to Christianity Gillian Rose. What lessons can we learn about the difficulties of theorizing blackness from Rose's reflections on her Jewishness and her gender? The chapter argues that Rose points to useful resources for challenging racializing logics but that Rose's blindness to the racialized soul limits the possibility of struggle growing out of racialized communities. I reflect on my own experiences as a scholar "too black to be white and too white to be black" (Rose considered herself "too Jewish to be Christian and too Christian to be Jewish") to explore the complications of black theological reflection when the boundaries of race blur at the same time the boundaries between the secular and the sacred blur.

The book concludes with a reflection on the meaning of black religious community in light of the critique of black secularism performed throughout the book. When paradox and tradition, sainthood and messianism, hope and love, and most of all blackness and theology are understood in the ways I develop in these pages, how are we to live together? Put another way, once again, what is the religion of the field Negro?

PART I

Cornerstones

CHAPTER 1

Cone

Black theology, it often seems, consists of movement in two directions, one political and one cultural. Black theology is the religion of black power, and black theology is the religion of the black community. The task of the black theologian is to explain how these two directions complement each other and to join them into a unified project. What sutures them, somehow, is theology. Secular reason alone is not up to the task. It is only when secular reason is supplemented by the language (or concepts, or beliefs) of faith, God, Christ, and Spirit that radical black politics and black culture no longer seem independent of, or even at odds with, each other. When God is aligned with the poor and oppressed and God's work is to free the poor and oppressed, God is to be found in the language and practices of the black community—the community systematically oppressed. God's work is to free this community from oppression—work that is necessarily political.

When black theology is presented in this way, a worry quickly presents itself. Black theology would offer a solution to a problem defined in secular terms. Radical politics and black culture in this picture are, at their root, understood in the same way in both secular and black theological discussions—the black theologian just adds something on top of the secular understanding. Black culture *not only* is X, *it also* is where God is at work in the world. Recent critics, both from the secular and theological academy, have pointed to the contingency of such a position: our "secular age" is relatively recent and brings deep, highly specific assumptions.[1] Theology may appear autonomous as a supplement to the secular, but in fact its autonomy is lost; the secular sets the terms for the theological. What would it mean for black theology to start from a commitment to the genuine autonomy of the theological?

It is my contention that a compelling response to this question is implicit in the early work of James Cone. My interest here is in making those implicit commitments to the autonomy of the theological explicit by emphasizing the role of *paradox* and *tradition* in Cone's work and in the project of black theology more generally. This pair of terms presents a means of affirming the primacy of the theological while at the same time articulating core commitments of black theology. Moreover, the language of paradox and tradition returns black theology to its radical roots. Not only does the theological come before the secular, but *black* theology emerges as the only orthodox theology; white (and ostensibly colorblind) theology emerges as crypto-secular heresy.

Critiques of Black Theology

Two critiques of the current state of black theology, from quite different directions, have underscored the aporias that result when a theological project starts from secular foundations. First, reformulations of liberation theology have argued that the purported focus on the poor and oppressed that once motivated liberation theology has been lost.[2] In some cases, this loss is due to an aspiration for middle-class status that overshadows a commitment to the struggles of the oppressed. In other cases, this loss is due to a celebration of specific communities or cultures—for example, Asian American, or African, or Latina, or queer—that overshadows the reason that these groups were originally of interest to liberation theologians—namely, their oppression or poverty. Yet oppression and poverty have not gone away, nor has the need for concrete projects to address them diminished. In the face of neoliberalism and the unchecked power of international financial institutions and multinational corporations, these critics contend that what is needed is to bring together all those reduced to dire poverty by these policies and institutions. For such a project cultural issues may be used pragmatically, for mobilization, but they are ultimately of secondary concern.

Advocates of this new approach to liberation theology offer a powerful challenge to black theology. When the emphasis of black theology becomes a celebration of black culture, when de jure racial oppression becomes de facto, and when a black middle class develops in whose interest it is to celebrate black culture while ignoring de facto racial oppression, black theology easily strays from its seminal commitment to the struggle of the poor and oppressed. This critique naturally leads to a condemnation of "black" as a name for the poor and oppressed, where the critic objects by pointing out that (a) there are poor and oppressed people who are not black, and (b) there are black people who are neither poor nor oppressed. I will argue that abandoning black theology is not the necessary result of this critique.

This first critique of the current state of black theology is immanent criticism rather than a theological critique, arguing that black theology does not live up to its own commitments to the poor and oppressed. The critic proceeds through secular reason, using empirical data to identify who qualifies as poor and oppressed, and in doing so appears to expose inconsistency in the black theologian's own position. In contrast, the second critique is thoroughly theological. These critics charge that black theology, in its current state, overlooks the deep connections between Christianity and racism. They assert that a careful genealogy of race reveals that race is a theological problem, arising because of Christian heresy.[3] White theology is not a recent problem; it names the theological heresy of supersessionism. White theology refuses to grapple with the theological significance of Jesus's Jewish flesh, instead imagining a radical break between Judaism and Christianity. The old law of the flesh overturned, white theology sees Jesus as inaugurating the age of the spirit. In the process race is invented as that by which Christians are not marked, quickly slipping into that by which Europeans are not marked. In other words, black theology must be reframed as a defense of theological orthodoxy that offers the only avenue for addressing the (ostensibly secular but actually theological) problem of racism in society.

This second group of critics laments the thin theology that has become characteristic of black theological reflection—too little talk about pneumatology, about the economy of the Trinity, about the Christian tradition.[4] In order to combat problematic theology, it is necessary to offer better theology: for example, to explain how white theology differs from the Christology found in Irenaeus, Gregory of Nyssa, and Maximus the Confessor. According to these critics, the early work of black theologians offered some promise when it emphasized the similarities between God's identification with the Jewish people and God's identification with blacks, restraining inclinations toward supersessionism. But early work in black theology also tended to rely on the theological concepts of white theologians like Karl Barth and Paul Tillich, who, like many mid-twentieth-century white Protestants, sometimes evince a commitment to supersessionist positions.

If the first critique of black theology takes theology to be implicit in its political point, the second critique takes politics to be implicit in its theological point. For the former, focusing on the most marginalized has the effect of advancing the Christian imperative to identify with the poor. For the latter, once the theological problem is resolved, the intellectual apparatus that authorizes racism will be crippled, with the consequence that racism itself will crumble. Each critique is compelling, but the two are at odds. Each builds on the flaw targeted by the other. The first critique builds on the sort of thin theology targeted by the second, while the second critique ignores the centrality of the poor and oppressed recalled by the first.

Rather than forcing an artificial resolution to such a tangle—and just pulling the knot tighter—perhaps the concerns raised by both sides can be alleviated when the terms of the debate are altered. To show how this might work, the foundational scholarship of James Cone is enormously useful. A story is often told about Cone's work, sometimes by Cone himself, that divides his writings into two stages. In the first stage, which includes *Black Theology and Black Power* (1969) and *Black Theology of Liberation* (1970), he was heavily influenced by white theologians, particularly Barth and Tillich, and white philosophers, particularly existentialists. After being criticized for simultaneously proclaiming his independence from white theology and relying on white theological categories, Cone turned to resources within the African American tradition to undergird his theological position.[5] He proceeded to write *The Spirituals and the Blues* (1972), and he relied on these black musical traditions in *God of the Oppressed* (1975). In contrast to this story about Cone's development, I argue that Cone's first works offer a novel account of Christian paradox. In a sense, my task is to translate the *secular* existential idiom of Cone's early work into a *theological* idiom of paradox, where the human encounter with paradox indicates participation in the ultimate paradox, that of Jesus Christ. With this translation, we are able to address questions such as, What does it mean when Cone writes, "The logic of liberation is always incomprehensible to slave masters"?[6] Might it mean something deeper than an accusation of willful ignorance or false consciousness? Might it suggest that there is a fundamental link between the incomprehensible, the black, and the theological? And might this incomprehensibility be linked with the essential character of black life, which Cone describes as filled with contradictions?[7]

Paradox and Tradition

Before turning to Cone's writings, I will sketch what I mean by paradox and tradition. These are both concepts irreducible to a vocabulary authorized by secularism. From the secularist's perspective, there can be no genuine paradox. Moments of perplexity or incongruity can be explained through secular reason, with the tools of the natural sciences, social sciences, and even humanities.[8] It might seem as though things don't fit together, but from the secularist's perspective ultimately they must—even chaos has a theory to explain it, even *anomie* has a sociological explanation. And from the secularist's perspective, tradition is obsolete. Just because something has been done before is no reason to do it again. Tradition is better described as the sum of a community and its history, stripping away the normative connotations. For the secularist, tradition is something to be rationally studied or romantically embraced; either option is taken by the autonomous agent.

Paradox and tradition might not be part of a secular vocabulary, but are they thickly theological? Are they uniquely Christian? Cornel West, following Kierkegaard and others, suggests that at least paradox is: "The paradox of the Christian tradition is that it precludes its own descriptions from grasping the truth; that is, the Christian notion of the fallenness of human creatures does not permit even Christian descriptions to be true. This is so because, for Christians, Jesus Christ is the Truth and the reality of Jesus Christ always already rests outside any particular Christian description."[9] This might sound like a trendy morsel of Eastern wisdom—*the Truth cannot be spoken*—except West goes on to assert that there is a very specific test for this ineffable truth. The test involves comparison to the person of Jesus Christ. Certainly, every description of Jesus gets Jesus wrong, but all descriptions are not equally wrong. The paradox doubles: not only does Christian discourse claim to speak truthfully and claim that all speech is untruthful; it also claims that there is an embodied criterion for truthfulness, but that embodied criterion itself can only be spoken of untruthfully. Unlike Beckett's dreary tragi-comedy—"Ever tried. Ever failed. No matter. Try again. Fail again. Fail better"—West presents this Christian tragi-comedy with the glass half full, paradox as joyfully difficult. From a secular perspective paradox brings frustration; from a Christian perspective, with an existential commitment to its embrace, paradox brings salvation.

By paradox, then, I simply mean moments of irresolution, without the possibility of resolution through secular means. Paradox without tradition is blind; tradition without paradox is empty. Theologians too often forget this, either wallowing in the fallenness of the world, in paradox, or triumphantly proclaiming the Christian story absent even a hint of genuine humility. A commitment to paradox means a commitment to trying as hard as possible to understand the ultimate paradox, Jesus Christ, knowing that one's efforts will always fall short. There is no quick and direct access, no shortcut. It is a difficult task, working through the accumulated tryings and failings of the centuries and of one's contemporaries, of visible churches' stammering as they seek to speak in one voice with the church invisible. In other words, a commitment to paradox means immersion in thick tradition. But immersion in thick tradition all too often leads paradox to be forgotten. It starts to seem as though one's descriptions are right, that one's feelings are true, that one is indeed participating in the Body of Christ. That is when paradox humbles. Paradox reminds that as soon as one feels comfortable with one's commitments—one's descriptions, one's feelings, one's participation—those commitments are misdirected. Christian commitment is ultimately to paradox, to the One who is Paradox, the God-Man, and to nothing else.

The Theology of James Cone

The challenge of writing theology, like the challenge of writing good fiction, is at once to tell a compelling story and to tell a story that is fundamentally equivocal. Doing one or the other is sometimes manageable; to do both is nearly impossible. The theologian's prayer is to fail better. It is the aspiration to do both that I find in Cone's theology. It is not that Cone locates one paradox (other than Christ) at the heart of his theological project. It is that in articulating the Christian *logos*, Cone weaves together multiple irreducible paradoxes. Sometimes Cone hesitates, does not fully embrace the moments of paradox. (Even more often, his readers and critics hesitate for him.) These hesitations can give his theology the appearance of excessive alignment with radical politics or African American culture—that is, the appearance of conceding its heart to the secular. Yet Cone's theological writings, even his early work, grow out of an immersion in African American religious life. In other words, Cone is immersed in the Christian tradition; such immersion always is located in a specific time and place. In his early works, Cone prevents that specific location from crippling his theological imagination through his use of paradox. The pillars that hold together Cone's descriptions of African American religion are each paradoxical, either underdefined or defined multiply with each definition in tension with each other. I will analyze these pillars, including blackness, liberation, freedom, and humanity, showing how each of them, in Cone's account, is ultimately paradoxical. We must not forget, however, that these concepts are each pillars of Cone's explication of the Christian tradition. Cone is explicating tradition equivocally: he is employing what might be called *an aesthetics of paradox*.

First among the paradoxes woven together by Cone is the paradox of blackness. Cone describes it as both "ontological symbol" and "visible reality."[10] Does this mean that sometimes Cone writes about blackness in the symbolic sense and other times he writes about it in the literal sense? Certainly not: throughout his writings, and most prominently in his early writings, the word "black" refers to *both* senses at once. This usage stymies the desire to dismiss Cone's terminology as merely metaphorical or as absurdly ethnocentric. At a deeper level, it stymies the desire for theological certainty, for everything to fit together comfortably. Theological certainty is achieved by abandoning theology, by endorsing secularism in the guise of theology. Cone is clear that blackness is an idea of God, not humans, and so it is not comprehensible in exclusively human terms: "Blackness or salvation (the two are synonymous) is the work of God, not a human work. It is not something we accomplish; it is a gift."[11] Further, "blackness and divinity are dialectically bound together as one reality."[12]

Cone writes autobiographically that his "turn to blackness was an even deeper conversion-experience than the turn to Jesus."[13] At times, Cone writes of this turn as a change from understanding himself as a "Negro"—that is, understanding himself in white terms—to understanding himself as "black," in autonomous (and Christian) terms. To be black is not simply to have a certain skin color, but it is also not detachable from a specific community. Indeed, to be black, to be converted to blackness, means a commitment to a specific racial community and to the struggles of that community. In a sense, Cone means by a turn to Jesus an embrace of community: seeing oneself as a participant in the tradition of Jesus-worshippers. To turn to blackness means to turn to an impossible position, to confidently claim an identity foreclosed by the world.[14] To turn to blackness is to turn to paradox. Cone's juxtaposition of his two conversions should not be read as coincidental: they are complementary. It is from within the tradition of Jesus-worshippers that Cone can claim his blackness; his blackness is precarious unless it is rooted in (or hovers above) the tradition of Jesus-worshippers.

The black church thus has a privileged position, politically and theologically. This is the black church invisible, not the black churches occasionally maligned by Cone and recently declared dead.[15] Black churches in the world are repositories of tradition, conveyers of the words and rhythms and performances of dark-skinned worshipers of Jesus Christ. But that does not make black churches *black*. Blackness is the paradoxical claim to an impossible position—and so necessarily an identification with struggle (occupying a space that does not yet exist can only take place by force). The black church is invisible because it conjoins the paradox of blackness with the Christian tradition. It is an impossible mixture, as tradition and paradox are incapable of binding with each other, yet the effect of this impossibility is to reduplicate the paradox, to elevate the black church to the position of ultimate paradox: the black church becomes the Body of Christ.

What else can be meant by Cone's statement, drawing on lessons learned from Malcolm X, that "colorless Christianity is a joke—only found in the imaginary world of white theology," or his statement that "no group has been more evil than whites"?[16] Obviously Cone is aware of the historical specificity of race language, not to mention the American cultural context that frames his remarks. The race language here brings Christ into the contemporary context, bridging the two-millennia divide. From our side of the divide, colorless Christianity is a distortion of Jesus into a figure of neutrality, not distinguishing between rich and poor, privileged and oppressed. Translated into our context, the poor and the oppressed are the black. But the gap cannot be forgotten. It is absolutely certain that Christianity is not neutral, but a different sort of certainty is needed when asserting that Jesus is on the side of specific poor and oppressed, or on the side of black people. These are fallible translations of the eternal and absolute Word into specific historical and cultural circumstances. Translation itself is a misleading term when moving from the register of the absolute to the register of the worldly and contingent. No concept in the latter can accurately represent the former. An image, or icon, perhaps is more promising. But the representational effectiveness of such an icon is proportional to the break it effects with the domain of representation. This is precisely the work of paradox. Two images are held at once, irreconcilable in worldly, secular terms: blackness as at once literal and symbolic.

Black theology is about liberation; it is a theology of liberation. But what is liberation, what is freedom? It is true, but too simplistic, to say that freedom remains undefined, or underdefined, in Cone's work. Freedom plays a central role, an ideal animating Cone's theology, but freedom remains purposefully empty. Writing in the midst of the U.S. civil rights movement, Cone seems to portray freedom as simply the lack of oppression achieved by boycotts, marches, and urban revolt.[17] In the midst of such a movement, the contrast between oppression and freedom seems obvious. But as the movement waned, and as Cone reflected on Martin Luther King's later work against the subtler forms of oppression found in the Northern United States, the meaning of freedom became more opaque.

Yet even in Cone's earliest writings, the apparently obvious meaning of freedom is less secure and comforting than eerily, and importantly, hollow. As he writes, "[D]eath is preferable to life, if the latter is devoid of freedom."[18] Freedom evokes a total commitment, but for what? Not for any reason: Cone dismisses rational discourse as sometimes useful but always subordinate to something greater. "Black Power . . . is by nature '*irrational*,'" he writes.[19] But this commitment to death is also not some outburst of madness: it is an "existential" commitment. Black theology makes use of both reason and passion, but it is essentially a commitment to a higher order, to "something that is placed above everything else," felt "in their guts" by those who "really knew oppression"—this is the commitment to freedom.[20] Freedom is prerational, prelinguistic: it does not require justification because it is "self-evident."[21]

Oppressors use the language of freedom in quite specific ways, attaching (often implicitly) specific content to it. When specific content is attached to freedom, it can be rationally discussed, plans can be worked out for its supposed gradual achievement, and methods can be declared legitimate or illegitimate. Concealed in these very rational discussions are deep, systemic injustices that will never be addressed so long as the discussion continues on the plane of practical reason—put another way, so long as the oppressor's definition of freedom is adopted. As Cone writes, white liberals want "change without risk, victory without blood"; the white liberal "is still white to the very core of his being."[22] Black theology involves a commitment to freedom without content, which is just another way of saying a commitment to freedom defined by the oppressed.

On the one hand, freedom is the goal, the outcome of liberation. On the other hand, freedom is achieved in the process of liberation, in the identification with the struggle against oppression. Cone writes, "No one can tell us what liberation is and how we ought to struggle for it, as if liberation can be found in words. Liberation is a process to be located and understood only in an oppressed community struggling for freedom."[23] Elsewhere he writes that freedom "is not a pious feeling in the heart. Freedom is a struggle wrought out of the blood and tears of our mothers and fathers."[24] There is no way to articulate freedom, no worldly content of the term, except in the experience of those working for freedom. "To be free in Christ is to be against the world."[25]

Equality is achieved through the fight for freedom—which is to say, through the pure struggle. The human being is in solidarity, in communion, with all other human beings when she fights for freedom.[26] But something more is also happening in the fight for freedom. The human is not only in communion with other humans, she is also participating in the divine drama. The sense of freedom here is both empty and absolute: "Through Christ the poor are offered freedom now to rebel against that which makes them other than human."[27] Freedom has no worldly meaning, but it has an otherworldly meaning: it is offered by Christ. To receive the gift of freedom means to participate in rebellion against oppression. In other words, the reception of God's gift of freedom is the work of achieving freedom for others: performing the work of God on earth. The image of God in the human is not a little picture but a mirror, reflecting the divine light of freedom onto the corners of the earth darkly burdened by oppression.[28] For this reason, Cone can write, "Black rebellion is God himself actively involved in the present-day affairs of men for the purpose of liberating a people. Through his work, black people now know that there is something more important than life itself. They can afford to be indifferent toward death, because life devoid of freedom is not worth living."[29] The black church is constituted by those who struggle for freedom: participation in struggle makes the individual a part of the Body of Christ. Participation in the struggle for freedom offers authority: it is the only worldly access to the absolute. (Cone asserts that our access to truth through scripture, tradition, and the visible churches is always imperfect.)[30] Everything opposed to struggle, Cone suggests, is "the work of the Antichrist."[31]

This paradoxical status of freedom echoes the ultimate paradox of freedom: Christ's achievement of freedom from the old law leading to servitude (or freedom) under the new law of love. "Christian freedom means being a slave for Christ in order to do his will."[32] Cone takes on the stark—worryingly supersessionist—opposition all too present in mid-century Protestant thought between old and new law in order to emphasize that Christ's liberating work results in a freedom that is itself commitment. Under the new regime the Christian does not wallow in her freedom. She joins in the work of liberation. Her participation in Christ means participation in the work of Christ, a constant battle against the forces of oppression. In this implicit reworking of the imagery of liberation, Cone calls into question the mid-century supersessionism on which he draws.[33] The God of both Old and New Testaments is a God of liberation, a God who sides constantly with the oppressed, with those in a slavery that is both material and spiritual. Cone identifies blacks living in the United States with the Israelites of the Old Testament, finding God on the side of the dominated in both instances. But this identification is made possible by the Christ event, allowing for participation in the work of liberation by all those who are oppressed, allowing for the Old Testament narrative to be read as speaking to a twentieth-century black American.

Is the freedom offered by Christ a worldly freedom or an eschatological freedom? Cone suggests that both answers are right and both answers are wrong: another knot of paradox. Eschatological freedom has been manipulated by oppressors, including white slave owners, in order to pacify the oppressed. They say, "Just wait until after you die, then you will be free." Through readings of slave spirituals, Cone points out how the referent of heaven was sometimes the North, or Africa: purely secular, worldly ideals. It is hope that joins the eschatological and the historical. On the one hand, "Hope in God's coming eschatological freedom is always derived from the suffering of people who are seeking to establish freedom on earth but have failed to achieve it."[34] In other words, the struggle for worldly freedom precipitates eschatological freedom. The taste of freedom on earth suggests what might be ahead, at the *eschaton*. On the other hand, eschatological freedom motivates the struggle for worldly freedom. By knowing that one is eschatologically free, one is able to act in this world as if one is already free despite living in a world in which freedom is denied. Neither worldly nor eschatological freedom is complete without the other, yet they cannot be identified, or even thought of as perfectly complementary. Paradox is woven in again. Hope is not exactly happy waiting for the *eschaton*, nor is it exactly mournful longing for that which would make life more comfortable. Cone writes that hope "is not patience but impatience, not calmness but protest."[35] As it impossibly holds together the historical and the eschatological, hope elicits participation in struggle—which is to say, participation in the work of God.

Cone emphasizes the commitment of black theology to analysis tied to action, but he also emphasizes the precarious nature of this analysis and action. Freedom means, in part, "the existential burden of making decisions about human liberation without being completely sure what Jesus did or would do. *This is the risk of faith*."[36] Action is dependent on analysis, but analysis is always imperfect. Unless paradox is embraced, we are left with paralysis. Debates about biblical interpretation and the contemporary situation will go on without end. But faith does not mean reasonable confidence; it means commitment beyond reason. As Cone emphasizes, this means faith is necessarily risky. Flawed analysis can produce misdirected actions. This is not the exception, but the norm. In the fallen world, faith is the aspiration to fail better.

This commitment entailed by the risk of faith is not generic piety. It is not virtuous living. It is not following moral principles or making the right decisions. Faith, in Cone's view, is a commitment to one group rather than another, to the oppressed and against the oppressors. Rather than fixating on the subtleties of a situation, the purpose of analysis is to make a cut between two groups, enabling commitment to one.[37] How crude a distinction, one might respond. But the point is that all analyses are flawed, that no amount of subtlety will succeed. The aspiration for success—the will to (worldly) truth—is a distraction, a tool of the oppressor. The paradoxical commitment of faith acknowledges finitude and recognizes the need for commitment not grounded either in the delusion of possessing worldly truth or the aspiration for worldly truth. Commitment is to the oppressed, no matter how elusive they are, no matter how often they are misidentified. The commitment of faith is to fail better at siding with the oppressed, not to fail better at describing the world.

From Cone's perspective, whites don't take risks. Not because of a choice they make to play it safe. Whites don't take risks because they don't see risks. The white vocabulary is sufficiently complete, smooth, slick, that opportunities for risk do not arise. The white world is saturated with descriptions and reasons that fit together just so. The joys of surprise and the sorrows of tragedy are eliminated, replaced with simulacra.[38] This make-believe world is composed of the image of the human purged of the image of God. It takes upkeep, bloody upkeep. All that does not fit in its spick-and-span interiors must be eliminated. "[S]in is whiteness—the desire of whites to play God in the realm of human affairs."[39] Moreover, "whites have only one purpose: the destruction of everything that is not white."[40] Cone describes the nature of whiteness as "satanic," and he writes, "Whiteness characterizes the activity of deranged individuals intrigued by their own image of themselves, and thus unable to see that they are what is wrong with the world."[41] Black theology is less the opposite than the obverse of white pseudo-theology (really, secularism). The heart of black theology is paradoxical, that which cannot be grasped, the image of God in the human and nothing more. It sees clearly what is amiss and endlessly grapples to make right what is forever broken. Black theology's task is "the destruction of whiteness, which is the source of human misery in the world."[42]

Once again, Cone weaves together the paradox of commitment with the other paradoxes he explores: *"Freedom is not a gift but a risk that must be taken."*[43] Commitment and freedom both dwell in the register of paradox. But this statement appears to oppose risk to gift, and the apparent claim that freedom is not a (divine) gift seems to run counter to Cone's discussions of freedom elsewhere in his work. Here we see the difficulty of translation from the register of paradox to the world. Freedom in its empty and absolute sense, in its supremely paradoxical sense, is certainly divine gift. But divine gift in the world becomes a risk. Pure gift in the fallen world is always contaminated. The gracious response to pure gift is risky commitment, commitment unsupported by worldly reasons, commitment that may very well misfire.

In that commitment lies yet another paradox. On the one hand, the commitment of faith is a call to identification with the poor and oppressed. On the other hand, it is a call to the liberation of the poor and oppressed. If the poor and oppressed are no longer poor and oppressed, the black theologian will be left identified with the comfortably bourgeois. Consternation about this possibility has motivated some of the recent critics of black and liberation theology. Liberation seems to be liberation into middle-class life, with the implicit effect of "liberating" the oppressed by turning them into oppressors. This objection can now be addressed when we are mindful of paradox. The objection arises when liberation is thought of in exclusively secular—nonparadoxical—terms. It supposes that liberation is making poor people richer, so what is needed is a more flexible account of who counts as a poor person (e.g., not every African American). But if liberation is thought *theologically*, not exclusively in secular terms, it means participation in the divine drama of liberation, of commitment not to the oppressed as judged by any empirical measure, but to those who play the role of the oppressed in the drama, as imperfectly discerned by us fallen humans. Blackness is privileged not because of empirical data about African Americans, but because of the paradox that blackness names, at once included and excluded from the secular world, at once oppressed and invisible.

Another moment of paradox concerns the role that humanity—and the human—play in Cone's work. For Cone, humanity and freedom are closely linked; in a way they are different expressions of the same paradox. "To be human is to be free, and to be free is to be human. . . . This is the paradox of human existence. *Freedom is the opposite of oppression, but only the oppressed are truly free.*"[44] Black theology exalts the human, and, strangely enough, the black person turns out to be quintessentially human. Cone writes, "Jesus was that reality who empowered black people to know that they were not the worthless human beings that white people said they were."[45] To be human but to be worthless: this is the paradox of black humanity. Humanity is valued, and blacks are human, so black humanity should be valued—but it is not. Logic fails. The truths of the world shudder in light of the reality of Jesus Christ, an absolute revealed through worldly paradox.

In one sense, the near oxymoron of black humanity is shaped by oppression. It is the oppressors, whites, who set what it means to be black—and what it does not mean. There are no worldly terms in which to be black besides the white terms. Christianity, when it is not naturalized into a secular vocabulary, provides other terms or, better, an alternative account. For it is not just another set of terms, a vocabulary for black humanity where there was not one before. A new vocabulary would be parasitic on the vocabulary of white humanity. What black theology suggests is something much more radical. An account of black humanity is an account of humanity as such, and humanity itself has been distorted by racism. Humanity is invisible in the world today, and it is only by making visible black humanity that any humanity becomes visible. What does it mean to make visible black humanity? It means to recognize the paradox constitutive of the human, the image of the ultimate paradox that makes a human being human. It is to acknowledge that *who* we are is never exhausted by *what* we are, and yet each is necessary for the other.[46] The white world attempts to provide an exhaustive description, but it is dependent on a blatant omission (of blacks). Every such attempt fails. Black humanity names that failure, names the impossibility that distinguishes humans, and individuates each human.

There is another approach to the paradox of humanity, one that echoes Cone's discussion of the paradox of freedom. Cone writes, "To be human is to find something worth dying for. When the black man rebels at the risk of death, he forces white society to look at him, to recognize him, to take his being into account, to admit that he *is*."[47] In other words, from the location of one excluded from humanity, the starkest means of demonstrating one's existence as human is to demonstrate the capacity to become nonhuman: to die. Here we have humanity without content. The only characteristic of such humanity is that it is not nonhumanity. While the white person who risks death does so for a reason, for a cause, in terms explicable according to white (secular) discourse, there is no vocabulary to describe the black person risking death, no reason or cause to which one can point. And yet one does have to point, because risking death cannot be ignored. The only thing to which one can point is humanity itself—black humanity, the paradox of humanity.

Yet another knot of paradox is woven into Cone's writings when he addresses the problem of evil. He does not offer a solution. Indeed, he asserts that no rational or philosophical solution is possible. Yes, worldly life involves suffering, but faith in God means commitment without reason, commitment despite evidence to the contrary, commitment in the face of suffering. From the perspective of black theology as encapsulated in the music of the spirituals, the singer "does not really question the justice and goodness of God. He takes for granted God's righteousness and vindication of the poor and weak. Indeed, it is the point of departure for his faith. The slave has another concern, centered on the *faithfulness* of the community of believers in a world full of trouble."[48] In other words, the commitment to God, which brings with it a commitment to all those who suffer, is in a different register than worldly concerns, including those of the suffering. In the register of faith, the register of the absolute, the register of paradox, all that matters is commitment.[49]

Cone's autobiographical writings underscore a lived paradox. In his hometown of Bearden, Arkansas, there was little physical violence or heavy-handed racial oppression, but there was pervasive, silent segregation.[50] On the surface, all seemed to live together happily. But Cone, his brother, and their parents refused a superficial understanding of the situation. The peace of the community was based on the characterization of blacks as inferior, but the Cone parents and children refused to accept this characterization. They also refused to wallow in anger at the injustice of the situation. Instead, each in his or her own way acknowledged the contradictions of the situation, acknowledged the paradox of superficial pleasantry and institutionalized racism.

Whites in Bearden preached all-embracing love, but they implicitly excluded blacks from that love. Is this not also a paradox, a paradox of white theology alongside the paradox of black theology? The difference is that the former is unacknowledged; it rests on false consciousness. It is commitment to delusion, not commitment to paradox. It is commitment to abstract ideas rather than to lived reality. It is commitment to secular reason rather than commitment to theological inquiry.

It was through tradition that those in Bearden were able to commit themselves to a life of paradox. Paradox was indeed lived: in sermons and prayers and shouting and dancing and song, each pointing to the paradoxical figure of Jesus Christ. These performances do not arise ex nihilo: they are transmitted from person to person, from generation to generation—bodily knowledge that eludes the confines of the archive.[51] Yet the black church life Cone observed was plagued by anti-intellectualism and ignorance, leading to an uncritical faith. Against these limitations of church life, Cone points to the way that paradox was also lived on Saturday nights, in the blues. Cone constructs a dialectical tension between the spirituals and the blues, between Saturday night and Sunday morning, portraying each as performing an aspect of black experience.[52] Although the activities of Saturday night were ostensibly secular, in Cone's portrayal the secular versus sacred division breaks down. Put another way, the secular, as it participates in paradox, is subsumed by the theological. Sunday morning would not be properly Christian without the performances of despair of the Saturday bluespeople—even if concurrent membership in both groups was impossible.[53]

Cone finds this difficult synthesis embodied in his own father, a sometime bluesperson, a sometime churchgoer. Implicitly, in this portrait of Cone the father by Cone the son, paradox is embodied: Cone's father was dissatisfied with each answer provided to resolve the contradictions of black existence, to black existence as problem. To be either a churchgoer or a bluesperson would be to make the problem too easy, to suppose that a set of answers, from God or the bottle, might prove satisfactory. To alternate between the two, in frustration, is to continue to grapple with the problem as paradox—and when its intriguing and frustrating force abates, to grapple even more.

In Cone's portrait of his father, the image of God as paradox shines through. In Cone the father we can see a way to begin responding to the two criticisms of black theology introduced at the start of this chapter. Against those who charge black theology with losing sight of the poor and oppressed: the blackness of Cone's father is defined not by his skin color (never mentioned) but by his simultaneous inclusion and exclusion from the community of Bearden, Arkansas. Poverty, oppression, and, most of all, blackness name this impossible position. Against those who charge black theology with overlooking the richness of theological tradition: for Cone's father the traditions of his people, including what they did in church, mattered, but what mattered most was his paradoxical location. He was at once committed and estranged.

Recovery of the Theological in Black Theology

One of the reasons that black theology seems so vulnerable to the criticism that it is insufficiently political and insufficiently theological is a shift that occurred in the decades after Cone's earliest writings. Discussions of black theology in the past four decades have become increasingly oriented by contextualism. This is often presented as a natural movement. Black theology criticized the false assumption of universality presented by previous theologians, yet there remained in black theology of the 1960s and 1970s assumptions of universality that went unquestioned. The first generation of black male theologians, writing with masculine words and styles, purported to speak for both men and women. But what of the perspective brought to black theology by women? Or by West Indians? Or by blacks in other parts of the world? Or by homosexuals? It seems natural that black theology should open the door to myriad theological enterprises growing out of the myriad cultural contexts in which Christians find themselves.

This chapter has sketched the outlines of a path not taken in black theology, a path that puts paradox rather than cultural context at the heart of black theology. Cone himself has moved toward an embrace of contextualism, writing in the 1986 preface of his book *Black Theology of Liberation* (originally published in 1970), "Theology is *contextual* language—that is, defined by the human situation that gives birth to it." Cone describes the importance of context as the "central thesis" of his 1975 *God of the Oppressed*.[54] As early as Cone's 1972 *The Spirituals and the Blues*, the first work in which Cone self-consciously privileged African American sources in both the content of his theology and its method, the authority gained from the struggle against oppression slips into the authority gained from personal experience.[55] By 1997, Cone writes that "black experience" has priority over the Bible. Cone suggests that this assertion makes him particularly aware of "the problematic character of absolutizing any theological claim," and he concludes that the necessary course of action is to listen to many voices from many contexts articulating many experiences.[56] My suggestion is that Cone's early work already took into account a deep humility—but in his early work it was a *theological* humility, while in Cone's later work, as voices from many regions and religions are taken into account, the humility loses its specifically theological nature. "Contextualism" is another name for "secularism."

The aspiration of contextualism is to acknowledge everyone's perspective: each person reads scripture and tradition from her or his own social setting; each person worships in the style of her or his own community. Theology has no neutral starting place, but implicit in this claim as framed by contextualists is the suggestion that every starting place is an equal one, that God's love is diffracted through each community and shines on all. A contextualist might object that there is an important proviso in her position: these are *oppressed* communities—African American, Caribbean, Hispanic, female, queer, migrant, and so on. Yet, as scholarship in the humanities has persuasively shown, every community creates exclusions.[57] The idea of pure oppression is illusory, as is the idea of pure domination. To choose particular communities to privilege with the title of oppressed involves political calculation. It is messy, worldly work. But that messiness is concealed, and worldly choices are implicitly issued divine sanction: *these* are the oppressed, *these* contexts matter. At the end of the day, the contextualist finds herself in a position uncomfortably similar to that of the white theologian proclaiming God to be colorblind. Certain worldly interests are advanced under the guise of neutrality. In contrast, when black theology is built around paradox and tradition, when the paradox of blackness reduplicates the paradox of Christ, humility is built into the identification of any particular community as the privileged oppressed. What remains central is the commitment to liberation; the specifics of the practice of liberation (who? how?) are secondary.

What does this mean for the fruits born of contextual theological inquiry? Does not the embrace of paradox lead to neglect, for example, of the critique of patriarchy? I do not think so. This is the task for another book. My point here is simply to suggest that untapped potential remains in the embrace of *blackness* as a privileged term for the theological enterprise, and I would assert that there are resources within *black* theology for the critique of patriarchy. An embrace of the paradox at the heart of black theology is necessarily opposed to the simplistic and hubristic assertion of male privilege, for black theology understood in this way is necessarily, and most centrally, a thoroughgoing critique of all idolatry.[58] This seems a more compelling approach than one beginning with the experience of, say, a gendered community, for a community has its characteristic virtues and vocations that are too easily criticized and transformed when the community thoroughly identifies itself with its status as oppressed. Paradox necessarily, perhaps uncomfortably, values tradition—indeed, needs tradition—and it is within the warm embrace of tradition that virtues and vocations are embedded. Yet the ultimate commitment to paradox is a reminder of the contingency of those virtues and vocations, of the possible imperative not to reform them but to transform them.

Cone notes that even when the theologian is humbled, when the theologian realizes that her vocabulary is a human vocabulary always inadequate to talk about ultimate reality, there remains a criterion by which to judge theology. It is not the suitability or elegance of the theologian's concepts that provide this criterion. It is, like Marx's eleventh thesis, not how well theology describes the world that matters but how well theology changes the world.[59] This change does not take place in the vocabulary of the day, not in a secular vocabulary. The task before us is to effect a "revaluation of all values," to formulate "a *new* law and a *new* morality" that will transform humanity.[60] It is a radical transformation not recognizable in secular terms. As Cone remarks, citing Kierkegaard, "there are no objective scientific criteria" to tell when and where God is at work in the world, and yet, for the faithful, there is absolute certainty and absolute commitment.[61]

CHAPTER 2

Baldwin

Religious language, ideas, and images pervade the essays, plays, stories, and novels of James Baldwin. A product of Black Pentecostalism and a teenage preaching prodigy, Baldwin describes his writing style as influenced by the King James Bible and the storefront church.[1] Verses from the Bible and snippets of gospel music pervade Baldwin's texts. Yet religion also appears in Baldwin's work as something he has overcome, a distasteful encounter with authoritarianism that he passed through to reach his present secular, democratic enlightenment. If Christianity is in Baldwin's past, the religious language that appears in Baldwin's texts could be read as rhetorical flourish, leveraging the persuasive power of a Christian idiom without any commitment to Christian beliefs.

Some have suggested that Baldwin occupies a religious office, that of the prophet. Standing at the margins of a community, the prophet makes explicit that community's values, and the prophet condemns the community for its present deviations from those values.[2] Now that the world has secularized, the prophet no longer must invoke God's name in her condemnations. Furthermore, instead of holding out the promise of otherworldly rewards, the secularized prophet would hold out the promise of this-worldly happiness once we accept human finitude. On this reading, Baldwin is the quintessential democratic prophet, explicating democratic values and enumerating the ways nations ostensibly committed to democracy fall short—where an acceptance of human finitude is a core commitment of democratic politics.[3]

Neither a focus on Baldwin's religious language nor on Baldwin's prophetic posturing considers the possibility that a specifically Christian set of ideas might frame Baldwin's political vision. Scholarship on political theology has shown the fruitfulness of examining subtle connections between theological and political ideas, how they can mirror each other and how they can shift together. Recovering these connections can help us understand a writer's political vision more clearly. It can reveal weaknesses in that political vision by illuminating incoherence or by showing how the theological premises on which a political argument once implicitly relied no longer have traction.

I will argue that James Baldwin transformed, rather than rejected, his father's Christianity. The components of that Christianity—ideas about innocence, salvation, sin, truth, and much else—are reworked by Baldwin, and in their new form they are inextricably linked with Baldwin's political vision. Race is essential to this theological transformation, for Baldwin charges most Christians with misunderstanding race and so misunderstanding their religion; the condition of blackness produces a natural (although often suppressed) attunement to truth. As he writes, "Black is a tremendous spiritual condition" (E471).[4] In Baldwin's transformed theology, whiteness represents idolatry, represents worldly interests elevating themselves to the place of the transcendent, defining the true, the good, and the beautiful. The theology that Baldwin offers in its place is negative, part of the long tradition of Christian negative theology for which the only true thing that can be said about God is what God is not. In this tradition, the work of theology is the critique of idolatry. Baldwin does not offer a black theology to oppose white theology; he offers a thoroughgoing critique of the religion of whiteness, and he posits a name for what remains when that critique is successful: love. Baldwin partially participates in the tradition of black theology, but he falls away from that tradition when he ultimately idolizes a vague, postracial concept of love.

Fathers and Gods

Baldwin's negative political theology begins with his father, who serves as the paradigmatic symbol of authority and of idolatry. Fathers play central roles in Baldwin's fiction and essays, from his first books (a working title for his first novel was *In My Father's House*; his first essay collection is *Notes of a Native Son*) to his last. Throughout, fathers are identified with gods—false gods. They seem to have absolute power, but in fact that power is compromised and precarious. Fatherhood itself is unsettled, with apparent fathers revealed not to be fathers at all, creating a world of bastards (unlike Wright's, Baldwin's "native son" carries irony). Baldwin describes himself as a "bastard of the West" (E7), and he names black Americans "nameless and unnamable bastards" living in "the great Western house" (E468). Yet the need for a father persists; Baldwin is haunted by the question—posed by his first minister and by Elijah Muhammad, as well as by the even more idolatrous gods of the street—"whose little boy are you?" To which he responds, in retrospect, "I unquestionably wanted to be somebody's little boy" (E303). We long for a father, or for a god; for an authority in absolute control. Acknowledging this longing and rejecting any object that would sate it is at the center of Baldwin's political-theological vision.

The eponymous essay of *Notes of a Native Son* is the story of two days in which Baldwin's father, a preacher, dies, Baldwin's sister is born, Baldwin himself comes of age (it is his nineteenth birthday), and the world descends into chaos, into race riots. It is the story of the collapse of absolute authority and its aftermath, personally and politically. Chaos and violence could result, or new life could result. With proper reflection—and, ultimately, with the activity of writing itself—we are able to opt for the latter. We are able to critically appropriate the legacy of the father, of the god, accepting how that legacy shapes us but also acknowledging its pathologies.

Baldwin introduces his father, the preacher, as almost mythical, godlike. No one knew his age. He was handsome and proud and "very black." He looked "like pictures I had seen of African tribal chieftains: he really should have been naked, with war-paint on and barbaric mementos, standing among spears" (E64). His power, it would seem, came from time immemorial, and it was sanctioned by the heavens; indeed, its provenance was the heavens. He "lived, like a prophet, in such unimaginably close communion with the Lord that his long silences which were punctuated by moans and hallelujahs and snatches of old songs while he sat at the living room window never seemed odd to us" (E66).

The seemingly absolute power of this god-father, of this father-sovereign, was, Baldwin recalls, undermined as soon as he encountered the white world. In the essay, Baldwin recalls how one of his white teachers took an interest in him and went to his home to ask permission from the young Baldwin's parents to take him to a play. "It was clear, during the brief interview in our living room, that my father was agreeing very much against his will and that he would have refused permission if he had dared. The fact that he did not dare caused me to despise him" (E68). The will of the father was not absolute, and the young Baldwin now knew it. It was always already undermined by another will, the will of the white world that surrounded them, putting fatherhood under erasure for black Americans. If the father's role is traditionally to teach the child social norms, to impose rules so that the child can learn the rules of a society, the black father necessarily fails at this task. As Baldwin puts it in a later essay, the black child "must be 'good' not only in order to please his parents and not only to avoid being punished by them; behind their authority stands another, nameless and impersonal, infinitely harder to please, and bottomlessly cruel" (E302). Here we start seeing how blackness is a "tremendous spiritual condition," for Baldwin wants to claim that this precariousness of authority—divine, paternal, or political—is a part of the human condition writ large; black Americans just have the opportunity, as it were, to encounter it much earlier, and more frequently, than whites.

The result of trying to be a father in a land that makes fatherhood impossible is madness; Baldwin's father went mad, and it eventually killed him. The world also went mad: race riots left New York in disarray. "As we drove him to the graveyard, the spoils of injustice, anarchy, discontent, and hatred were all around us" (E63). The young James Baldwin went mad, too, but only for a moment. When confronted, at the "American Diner," with a waitress who refused him service because of his race, Baldwin felt hatred become madness in him, hatred that he imagines his father also felt, hatred that animated his father's life. But then, Baldwin grew up. Unlike his father, he was able to acknowledge his own hatred and to see how it could detrimentally affect his life. He saw how his father's Christianity was motivated by this hatred, how its apocalypticism and worldly denial were a product of American race relations—and how they would not remedy racial injustice.

At the end of "Notes of a Native Son," as Baldwin recalls his father's funeral, recalls the officiant speaking Christian words that so falsely described the man he knew, he reflects on a biblical passage his father would preach: "But as for me and my house, we will serve the Lord." Baldwin decided to embrace this sentiment, and in doing so he affirmed his faithfulness to both a divine and a human father. Instead of rejecting any figure of fatherhood, Baldwin would—impossibly—affirm it, affirm a figure of authority that could never come into existence in the world as it is. In doing so, Baldwin professed a faith that entailed not blind belief but the difficult work of identifying and disavowing idolatry. For Baldwin, faith in a god-father ought to mean "acceptance, totally without rancor, of life as it is, and men as they are": which leads, Baldwin continues, to rejecting every distortion of life, indeed, fighting every such injustice (E84). The god-father is not rejected; he just comes to motivate criticism rather than adherence, to motivate the struggle against purported god-fathers, encapsulated by the regime of white supremacy—the "Great White Father" (E410).

Baldwin's semi-autobiographical first novel, *Go Tell It on the Mountain*, is also a story of impossible fatherhood. It begins with an alienated son, destined to follow his father into the pulpit, turning fourteen and seeing himself as a sinner. His mother affirms the omniscience of his father: "Your father knows best. You listen to your father, I guarantee you you won't end up in no jail." Then, in the next words out of her mouth, it is God who provides assurances: "there ain't no safety except you walk humble before the Lord" (N23). One of the sons ponders, "I know the Lord ain't as hard as Daddy." The novel culminates in the protagonist's conversion, a conversion that effectively replaces the human father with a less stringent divine father. At the very end of the novel, the protagonist and his father have a quiet confrontation. "He turned to face his father—he found himself smiling, but his father did not smile" (N215). The father recognized his authority undercut by another; indeed it was undercut twice: After the conversion, on the way home, the father is reminded by his sister that he is not actually a biological father at all, but rather a stepfather. Just as in *Notes of a Native Son*, seemingly absolute authority is exposed as less than absolute. In this case, the relationship between authority and biology is also destabilized (to be a father is not necessarily to be genetically related to a son; Baldwin's own "father" was a stepfather, though this is not mentioned in *Notes*). Yet at the same time that the narrator of *Go Tell It on the Mountain* is refusing his father's authority, he necessarily remains within its orbit: his father, after all, is a preacher, and the protagonist, because of his apparent paternity, was destined to follow his father into the church.

Baldwin's 1974 novel *If Beale Street Could Talk*, published some twenty years after his first novel, continues to press the question of the impossibility of black fatherhood in America—that is to say, the question of the impossibility of black authority. The novel opens with a woman on her way to tell her unjustly imprisoned lover, Fonny, that she is pregnant. It ends with the birth of this baby coinciding with the suicide of Fonny's father. The book's epigraph, "Mary, Mary, / What you going to name / That pretty little baby?," from a hymn, presses the religious significance of fatherhood. The female protagonist, whose lover was her childhood friend and who persists in a childish innocence about the world, is in a sense mysteriously inseminated (her lover, after all, is in prison, though he was not when she conceived). Where Jesus's paternity was other-worldly, the father of this new, unnamed baby is also taken away by the world—to "the Tombs," the Manhattan Detention Center. The protagonist remarks to the reader that "when I first had to go and see him in the Tombs, and walked up those steps and into those halls, it was just like walking into church" (B26). Fonny, imprisoned, can only be an absent father to his Mary-like lover; Fonny's father, in the ghetto, a prison without bars, can never do enough for his son. Despite working long hours and stealing from his employer, there are always more lawyer's fees and a high bail. "I don't know if I was ever any kind of father to him—any kind of *real* father—and now he's in jail and it ain't his fault and I don't even know how I'm going to get him out. I'm sure one hell of a man" (B126). Enraged by the impossibility of his position, the father ultimately kills himself. Baldwin dramatizes this crisis of authority by depicting Fonny's father's divine aspirations. Fonny's mother is an assertively pious woman; Fonny overhears his parents making love: "And she'd say, Oh, Frank, let me bring you to the Lord. And he'd say, Shit, woman, I'm going to bring the Lord to *you*. *I'm* the Lord" (B16).

The fathers depicted in Baldwin's works are authoritarian and aspire to omnipotence, omniscience, and omnipresence. Those aspirations are rejected, but the fathers are not. Fatherhood is inescapable, and the attempt to escape brings doom. Baldwin calls on us to acknowledge the impossibility of the black father's position, and we must take that paradox of authority-under-erasure as an invitation to purge ourselves of the false authorities that grip us. The same is true—and not merely by analogy—for Baldwin's God. Discussions of political theology, following Carl Schmitt, often focus on the relationship between political sovereign and God's sovereignty, accepting the need for some concept of sovereignty as a given. Perhaps we can read Baldwin as questioning the sovereignty of God and father—and so, the purported sovereignty of political entities, of states or rulers. Then, Baldwin would be posing the question, *how can we think sovereignty without authoritarianism?*

Idolatry and Theology

When Baldwin discusses religious ideas—that is, when he does more than employ religious language for rhetorical force—he contrasts two types of theology or, more properly, idolatry and theology. Idolatry is the religion of his father, of Richard Wright, and of Elijah Muhammad, to name a few.

Theology is Baldwin's own constructive proposal for how religion ought to fit together. Commitment to idolatry leads to (and is fed by) confusion, anger, hatred, and fallacy; correct theology results in communion and salvation. Baldwin has much more to say about idolatry than theology. This is because the primary content of theology, for him, is the critique of idolatry, and Baldwin is always critiquing idolatry.

In Baldwin's account, idolatry, first and foremost, is motivated by the desire for safety, which in turn is motivated by fear of death. "Perhaps the whole root of our trouble, the human trouble, is that we will sacrifice all the beauty of our lives, will imprison ourselves in totems, taboos, crosses, blood sacrifices, steeples, mosques, races, armies, flags, nations, in order to deny the fact of death, which is the only fact we have" (E339). Because we fear death, we turn to symbols, rituals, and institutions that promise us safety—but at a high cost. The "principles governing the rites and customs" of churches, black and white, are "Blindness, Loneliness, and Terror, the first principles necessarily and actively cultivated in order to deny the two others" (E305). Christianity most often functions as idolatry, offering ways to worship but ultimately concealing truth, ultimately enforcing blindness about ourselves and our worlds. The result is that we feel alone, that we fear, and so we seek safety—back in church.

The desire for safety may be the desire to know that one is saved in the afterlife, or it may be the desire to live in a neighborhood free of crime, or it may be the refusal to acknowledge one's own complicity in sin. Closely related to the desire for safety, but often concealed, is the desire for innocence. Baldwin worries that the desire for innocence necessarily simplifies the world, overlooks the way that we are not in control of ourselves, overlooks the way that sinful histories continue to shape us, and overlooks the culpability we have for the actions of those with whom we relate, even when their actions are not clearly caused by our own. We make distinctions and create categories that insulate us, keeping us safe, protecting our innocence, and we cling to them with religious fervor. We make out of our history a myth, refusing critical engagement in favor of stories about the past that comfort us in the present. Idolatry is supremely dangerous: "The dream of safety can reach culmination or climax only in the nightmare orgasm of genocide" (ET102). Safety ultimately means complete elimination of that on which one's fears are projected, or complete pseudo-communion in rape. It motivates hate crimes that, even when committed by an individual alone, represent idolatrous "communion." Such hate crimes are acts of pseudo-religious sacrifice of the innocent: "the orgasm of the mob is drenched in the blood of the lamb" (E840).[5]

The quintessential form of idolatry, for Baldwin, is the belief in a white god. Sometimes this white god has a religious name, but not always. Belief in a white god entails belief in a black devil, in blackness as evil. As Baldwin puts it, "the black man has functioned in the white man's world as a fixed star, as an immovable pillar" (E294). Whites are safe when sin is projected onto blacks, allowing whites to ignore their own misdeeds and the complications of their own lives—and to ignore the fact that the fantasy of blackness was created by whites. Baldwin sympathetically cites Bobby Seale's notion that "one of the things that most afflict white people is their disastrous concept of God; they have never accepted the dark gods, and their fear of the dark gods, who live in them at least as surely as the white God does, causes them to distrust life" (E437). Life, for Baldwin, is what idolatry conceals. It is complex, impossible to systematize, and always morally ambiguous.

Idolatrous faith in the white god also affects blacks. Some blacks believe it: They believe that whites are inherently superior. This is the problem, Baldwin asserts, with Wright's Bigger Thomas. "Bigger's tragedy is . . . that he has accepted a theology that denies him life, that he admits the possibility of his being sub-human and feels constrained, therefore, to battle for his humanity according to those brutal criteria bequeathed him at his birth" (E18). This is also the problem with Baldwin's own father. (Baldwin, it should be noted, describes Wright as "alas! My father" [E253].) Despite angrily rejecting whites' belief in God (he describes them as heathen), he accepts their theology. As Baldwin writes in the letter to his nephew that begins *The Fire Next Time*, his father "was defeated long before he died because, at the bottom of his heart, he really believed what white people said about him. This is one of the reasons that he became so holy" (E291). Baldwin's father believed, in effect, that by becoming a better idolater he could be saved; this is why he was defeated.

Others blacks, such as Elijah Muhammad, construct their own gods in opposition to the white god, but in so doing reproduce the structure of idolatry—the desire for safety, innocence—that comes with the white god. Baldwin feels as if Muhammad is asking him, "Whose little boy are you?," the essential appeal for safety and innocence: for a father-protector, for a god-sovereign. And he feels as if Muhammad is volunteering his services as substitute-father. Baldwin appreciates the anger that motivates Muhammad, the urgency with which he speaks, and the need to affirm the worth of black life. But Baldwin cannot accept that race is fundamental to theology, only to idolatry. Further, he cannot accept the mystification of the past that he felt the Nation of Islam promoted. Baldwin cannot accept a substitute father. He must honor his own father—his Christian father—by developing a more compelling theological vision, a political theological vision. Essential to this vision is the notion that idolatry, ultimately, is cowardice: it is faithlessness.

"Complexity is our only safety," Baldwin writes (C165). Baldwin's own statement of the theology he has developed, found in a late essay, begins by repudiating fear and the desire for its elimination as a religious motivation. "Salvation is not precipitated by the terror of being consumed in hell: this terror itself places one in hell. Salvation is preceded by the recognition of sin, by conviction, by repentance" (C164). Idolatry, religion motivated by fear, results in damnation; souls are saved when they have faith and turn away from sin—coolly, as it were, motivated not by immediate emotion but by clear perception. Baldwin does not offer a crisp statement of what he means by sin, but he specifies that it is "not limited to carnal activity" and such bodily acts are not "the most crucial or reverberating of our sins" (C164). Once salvation is approached in this way, we near supreme communion, "union with all that is or has been or will ever be" (C164). This vision of union is also specific and personal. It involves making whole our broken selves and our broken relationships with others. Salvation is approached but never achieved. It is a process that happens in time rather than a one-off event. Baldwin maintains that the need for faithfulness and disavowal of sin (both themselves processes, and interconnected ones) is pressing: as he famously writes, "The time is always now" (E214). This temporality of redemption helps to decipher the apocalyptic conclusion of *The Fire Next Time*. If faithfulness and disavowal of sin are not happening now, salvation is impossible: we are condemned to damnation.

This is not simply an expansive use of religious rhetoric, adding oomph to a moral or political argument. Baldwin describes salvation as a relationship with God ("accepting and reciprocating the love of God," C164), although of course the theological and the political are inextricable here. I am arguing that we should understand God in Baldwin's theology negatively, as the name for what remains when idolatry is rejected, rather than metaphorically. Some would see Baldwin as affirming, in the tradition of American Transcendentalists, transcendence without the transcendent, a sense of the divine without God. Such a reading misses the specifically Christian commitments that Baldwin maintains. Unlike the Christian caricature of Judaism, as a religion in which salvation is achieved by strictly following rules, in Baldwin's theology salvation has already been achieved for us. We just need to accept it, accept it by rejecting false belief. Baldwin develops a specifically Christian name for this acceptance: love. In a sense, the idolatries that Baldwin rejects are precisely those that Christ rejects: the beliefs of those who claim to condemn in the name of God, who cultivate fear for their own benefit, and who refuse to critically examine themselves and their worlds. Specific worldly practices are not needed, on Baldwin's account; all that is needed is faith, lived in daily life, manifesting as love.

Secrets of the Heart

Baldwin writes, "[T]he value of the human being is all that I hold sacred" (C205). But, given the deeply Christian outlook that informs his theological (and political) writings, Baldwin is not best understood as a humanist. He is not simply rejecting the projection of human desires onto a godfather and instead affirming the divinity of the human, her inherent worth and dignity. Baldwin does, indeed, value the human being greatly, but he values the human being insofar as the human being contains the image of God—remembering that, for Baldwin, the image of God is what remains after the rejection of idolatry, which is to say, that which exceeds and eludes human concepts. The "human riddle," writes Baldwin, is that a "mighty, unnameable, transfiguring force . . . lives in the soul of man" (C56). This soul, in which Baldwin clearly and emphatically believes, is a mystery, and that mystery humbles us and reminds us that the world is saturated with mysteries that no ideology can ever explain. The attempt to explain them, to the soul or to the world, inevitably does violence, both metaphorically and literally. Yet the attempt to understand the soul and the world is crucial: this is Baldwin's main article of faith. It is a task of understanding that will always fall short. Our job is to try again and to fail better. This is the opposite of the humanist's claim to respect the human being for certain reasons, because of certain attributes. Baldwin calls for reverence, not respect, and this reverence is due precisely because the human has a soul that is indescribable—that is incomprehensible by reason. Accepting such ineffability is difficult work; it is the work of faith. But the indescribable nature of the soul is the only proposition that, for Baldwin, deserves the label of truth.

Particularly in Baldwin's early writings, what might be called, somewhat misleadingly, the *question of identity* is the driving force. It is not quite right to call this the question of identity because the answer to the question, of who Baldwin is, of who the protagonist is, is an essential opacity accompanied by an affirmation of the continuing urgency of the question. This is the flip side of Baldwin's account of fatherhood (and God): the object in question has overwhelming importance and requires rigorous attention but will never yield clarity, except that one must clearly reject those who peddle in clarity. Of his adolescent experience as a pious Christian, Baldwin writes, "I rushed home from school, to the church, to the altar, to be alone there, to commune with Jesus, my dearest Friend, who would never fail me, who knew all the secrets of my heart. Perhaps He did, but I didn't, and the bargain we struck, actually, down there at the foot of the cross, was that He would never let me find out" (E307). The young Baldwin, puzzled by his changing body and desires, sought clarity in God, who knew what the boy could not discern about himself. In this religious phase, this idolatrous phase, Baldwin delegated the task of self-examination to God (it had once been delegated to his father). This is the structure of idolatry that Baldwin would later disclaim, the thought *deep down I have a secret that God knows*, rather than *knowing that deep down I am opaque is how I can know God*. The former thought is what leads to pathologies, sexual and political; it supports blindness, the desire for safety. The latter thought motivates self-examination, and it gives meaning to life—Baldwin affirms the Socratic maxim that the unexamined life is not worth living (E391).

The opacity of the human being makes the human being sacred—that is, marks the image of God in the human. Recognizing that essential characteristic (or rather noncharacteristic) of humans is what allows for communion: we recognize that "all men are brothers" (C205). Baldwin writes that Americans are "in desperate search for something which will help them reestablish their connection with themselves, and with one another" (C6). In a world of heterogeneity, community can only be achieved by recognizing and probing the sacred opacity of each human and so reverencing each human (this is, for Baldwin, salvation). The result is neither heterogeneity nor homogeneity, but complex connection. The world conspires to conceal essential humanity, to categorize people by race, and, in other ways, to assert that color marks humanity all the way down. In accepting this, we are refusing our own humanity. As Baldwin remarks, "It is a terrible, an inexorable, law that one cannot deny the humanity of another without diminishing one's own: in the face of one's victim, one sees oneself" (E179). A victim is not attacked because of who she is but because of what she is, because of the way her humanity is categorized. An attacker deceives herself into believing that questions of "who" can be reduced to questions of "what," a belief applied to the victim and so becoming definitive of the attacker.

All humans, even the most stubborn and prideful, contain a sacred remainder, and they sense it. Such a remainder manifests as charisma. As Baldwin writes of his father, "there was something else in him, buried in him, which lent him his tremendous power and, even, a rather crushing charm. It had something to do with his blackness, I think—he was very black—with his blackness and his beauty, and with the fact that he knew that he was black but did not know that he was beautiful" (E64). Baldwin's father was black, that is what he was; but he was also more, he also had a sacred remainder—a remainder that was good, and true, and beautiful—but it was a remainder of which Baldwin's father was unaware. He was not totally unaware; that was the source of his charisma, of his power. Baldwin sees in the white world only the faintest hints of a sacred remainder, of a "who" beyond a "what." The secrets of the heart can continually be contained, the categories structuring the world seeming to fit well. But this is a refusal. When the terms "you think describe and define you inevitably collide with the facts of life," we are posed with "a very narrow choice." We can do as Baldwin's father did and have a mighty but tragic power, or we can say "*Yes, Lord.* Which is to say yes to life" (C73, Baldwin's emphasis). We can welcome God by welcoming God's image in our hearts. Blacks are confronted with this choice more pressingly than whites, and this is a grand opportunity. Baldwin concludes blacks must "grow up under the necessity of questioning everything—everything, from the question of one's identity to the literal, brutal question of how to save one's life in order to begin to live it" (E431). In this way, blacks have privileged access to the sacred, living that "tremendous spiritual condition."

Most people do not have an opportunity to reflect on the ways that the world misrepresents them. Most people depend on the wisdom of the world, on the concepts and categories of the world, to go about their lives. (Most blacks realize there is misrepresentation at work but do not have time to reflect; most whites do not realize there is misrepresentation.) Writers are the exception. Such reflection is the writer's vocation, according to Baldwin. It is, in a not particularly metaphorical sense, a religious vocation, a calling to pursue the good, the true, and the beautiful. The only "real" conversation Baldwin ever had with his father, he recalls, is when his father asked him, "You'd rather write than preach, wouldn't you?," to which Baldwin simply responded, "Yes" (E80). The religion of the father is preaching, the law; the religion of the son is writing, grace. Preaching is the practice of idolatry; writing is practical theology. Writers, he writes, are "the only people who know the truth about us" (C42). He adds, "Art is here to prove, and to help one bear, the fact that all safety is an illusion. In this sense, all artists are divorced from and even necessarily opposed to any system whatever" (C42). Baldwin is not here proclaiming allegiance to art for art's sake. He is making a theological assertion, a negative theological assertion: the pursuit of the beautiful (aligned with the true and the good) means the rejection of all worldly attempts to describe the beautiful, the true, or the good—the rejection of "any system whatever." The alienation of the artist—"for reasons he cannot explain to himself or to others, he does not belong anywhere" (C42)—is not alienation at all, but faithful commitment to the ineffability of the human soul, to probing the secrets of the heart. In so doing, the writer reminds those who are swept up in the inertia of ordinary life about that "mighty, unnamable, transfiguring force" that resides within them, and within every human being—and so the writer serves to the reader words as communion wafers, making of humanity a sacred unity and bringing redemption. At least this ought to be the writer's aspiration, writes Baldwin.

The writer, as a member of the spiritual elite, embodies freedom, and the writer is an evangelist for this freedom. For Baldwin, freedom, genuine freedom, is not freedom from constraint, nor is it freedom as constraint, freedom achieved by following a set of religious rules. Rather, Baldwin understands freedom in a highly Christian sense: "Ye shall know the truth, and the truth shall set you free" (John 8:32; E432). Freedom comes when we are not constrained by worldly concepts and categories, when idolatries are discarded and we are left in what remains, which is truth. Americans, Baldwin charges, make freedom synonymous with comfort, that supreme idol. In his view, in contrast, "to be free . . . you have to look into yourself and know *who you are*" (C70, Baldwin's emphasis). Baldwin describes realizing that he, like his father, was not free, that he was in bondage to his hatred of whites. Whiteness, after all, is a worldly category and the ultimate idol. The result of Baldwin's bondage: "I thus gave the world an altogether murderous power over me . . . in such a self-destroying limbo I could never hope to write" (E8). Acknowledging and accepting that feeling of hatred, rather than repressing it, made him free: free of the world's power over him, not to "be himself" in some anodyne sense, but to participate in the beautiful, the true, and the good: to write.

No Salvation without Love

Baldwin's early work poses a question and makes questioning the answer. Later, Baldwin offers a new answer, an even more Christian answer. *Who am I? I am a lover.* When idolatry is refused, when we realize our essential identity, the proper response to that opacity is not simply reverence; it is love. Like writing, love is difficult. "Love is a battle, love is a war; love is a growing up" (E220); love is "quest and daring and growth" (E341).

This work, though, offers a rich reward. Baldwin writes, "[O]nly that work which is love and that love which is work will allow one to come anywhere near obeying the dictum laid down by the great Ray Charles, and—tell the truth" (E426). Baldwin's early writings focus on the opacity of the self, while his later work focuses on the opacity of others, of those we love (including ourselves). When we experience love, we realize that we cannot control our lover, not with our bodies or our desires or our concepts. For the same reason, we cannot merge with our lover, despite our desires. Love happens as we explore the opacity of the other, as we desire to know her (as we desire to know ourselves), knowing that we will never know her, knowing that we can at best fail better. In that process of failing better, fueled by desire, comes pleasure—not from attaining or capturing an object but from accepting distance, accepting it as sacred. "When two people love each other, when they really love each other, everything that happens between them has something of a sacramental air" (B143).

Put another way, if writing is a practice for the spiritual elite, Baldwin turns later to love as a practice for the masses. Baldwin recalls that his first love affair, in France, taught him the significance of love as a practice accessible to all. Love, he found, "was breathing and belching beside me, and it was the key to life. Not merely the key to *my* life, but to life itself" (E365). In other words, love offers access to that world beneath ideology, beneath concepts that always misrepresent. Love does not offer this access through fantasy or through the imagination, but through the direct contact it entails with the unsentimental realities of life: "breathing and belching." Through love, according to Baldwin, "the masks that we fear we cannot live without and know we cannot live within" are removed (E341). In other words, love functions to expose and critique idolatry. But love also names Baldwin's eschaton, the state in which all idolatry has been removed, the state of perfect communion. This is not, in fact, a state, but a process in which we participate when we love. In other words, we do not love (or write) so that we can eventually achieve a state of perfect harmony, of communion. The work of loving (or writing) is itself participation in that communion. In political terms, we do not struggle so that one day we can live in peace. We struggle because the process of struggling itself is desirable—indeed, is salvific. "There is absolutely no salvation without love" (C164–65).

Love, for Baldwin, means seeing rightly (a formulation that strikingly resonates with the reflections of Simone Weil and Iris Murdoch).[6] When we love an object, we see it in truth, its imperfections as well as its virtues. We are compelled to be honest about both. Baldwin describes himself as a lover of America and so a critic of America. If his affection for America resulted only in praise, it would not be love at all but fantasy. Love allows its object freedom to be what it is and so assures that the lover maintains her own freedom, to live truthfully. Baldwin asserts that blacks are privileged lovers of America because the stakes of seeing America rightly are so high: black life depends on it. Is it then the case that seeing rightly requires love in the same way that love requires seeing rightly? Baldwin would seem to respond in the affirmative, for the process of seeing rightly, of carefully observing and reacting, recalibrating, observing some more, the process of what Simone Weil calls attention, *just is love*. It brings with it affective investment. It is not a process directed at most objects in our worlds, just those we care about—whether because of our desire or by necessity. (Similarly, the writer only writes well about things she cares about.) For most objects in our worlds, we accept the wisdom of the world; we regurgitate the things most people say about them. This is why Baldwin's vision remains preeschatological. This side of the eschaton, it is only in small corners of our lives that we can aspire to see rightly, truthfully—to love.

Idolatrous love is motivated by fear; it distorts and it controls. It is, in fact, not love at all. Baldwin describes his youthful preaching in this way: "I hoped to love them [his audience] more than I would ever love any lover and, so, escape the terrors of this life" (C160). Eventually, he realized the destitution of such love, how it made him "a liar." "I did not want my love to become manipulation. I did not want my fear of my own desires to transform itself into power—into power, precisely, over those who feared and were therefore at the mercy of their own desires" (C160). Such love produces sexual pathologies: consider Baldwin's story, "Going to Meet the Man," in which a white policeman is only able to make love to his wife when remembering the arrest and lynching of black men. Whites, in Baldwin's view, systematically deceive themselves in all areas of their lives. Because of their privileged position and their desire for safety, their fantasies are not tested against the realities of life, so their love is systematically deformed. White love often requires the presence of blacks, on whom unacknowledged fear and desire is projected. But this is a service that blacks can, and should, according to Baldwin, refuse. The only hope whites have of salvation lies in blacks who might genuinely love them: "we, with love, shall force our brothers to see themselves as they are, to cease fleeing from reality" (E294). Blacks have privileged access to truth, and to the truth about white Americans; it is truth, practiced in love, that brings salvation.

Genuine love, because it is love of who rather than what a beloved is, disregards race: "one must accept one's nakedness" (E366). The nakedness involved in love, whether of baby or lover or aging parent or nation, brings with it vulnerability, exposure, risk: the opposite of safety. This points toward the political implications of Baldwin's account of love. Love is an ethical practice, a practice that teaches us to live well and to live well together. Love prepares us for democratic politics: when our souls are accustomed to uncertainty and risk and to the distortions of worldly wisdom, we are well equipped for the precariousness of democratic political processes, processes that demand commitment and imply contingency at once. Moreover, it is the least of these—in the case of Baldwin's America, blacks—who are best equipped for democratic politics. Whites, because of the unexamined fears and desires accompanying their loves, including their love for America, enter democratic deliberation with anti-democratic tendencies.

In Baldwin's political theology, must authorities love? Baldwin concludes that his father, despite much harsh treatment and apparent cruelty, did, in fact, love his children, albeit "in his outrageously demanding and protective way" (E64). His father's love was misshaped by hatred and fear, distended but not destroyed. Fatherhood brings love because it brings attentiveness, close observation from birth through life. Love, Baldwin asserts, is "constant" even if "we may not always think so" (E339). This seems quite different from the love Baldwin described in France, the love that first awakened him to love. But for Baldwin there is only one type of love, for truth is unequivocal. Love may be more or less intense, may be more or less revelatory, but it is still love, whether it is of a sexual partner or a father or a son. Indeed, love blends into sensuality, which Baldwin describes, in rather religious terms, as presence, "from the effort of loving to the breaking of bread" (E311). Indeed, the closeness of the protagonist and his brother in *Tell Me How Long the Train's Been Gone*—they hold each other in bed and masturbate together—points to the way Baldwin blurs the lines between intimacy, love, and sensuality. Ratcheting up the intensity of love is desirable because it thrusts the lover toward truth. Hence Baldwin promises his nephew, Big James, to love him "hard, at once, and forever, to strengthen you against the loveless world" (E292). Given the pervasive distortions of the world, given the prevalence of idolatry, it is necessary for fatherly figures to love as much as possible. Love, says Baldwin, provides a home, but home does not mean safety and security. It means being comfortable with risk, with the precariousness of life.

Love or Lust?

Political theology has traditionally focused on political and theological concepts of sovereignty; Baldwin's negative political theology, naming as idolatry each attempt to establish a sovereign authority—sovereign God, sovereign father, sovereign self, and political sovereign—offers a refreshing alternative approach. Politically troubling, however, is Baldwin's second move: christening what remains after (or, better, through) the critique of idolatry love. This is politically troubling because love stands astride the division between ethics and politics. Martin Luther King Jr., for example, famously suggested a deep connection between love and social justice, yet love is also a virtue, one of the three theological virtues, together with faith and hope. If all Baldwin were claiming for love was its ethical relevance, that it shapes the soul in a way that makes citizens ready for democratic deliberation, say, this seems reasonably defensible. But Baldwin claims something more. For him, love happens between individuals, sexually, between family members, between friends, between enemies, between citizens and nations, and between authorities and their subjects. He suggests that there is genuine love and distorted love, the latter animated by fear and unacknowledged desire. But beyond this distinction, Baldwin offers no help in picking out what we might call, following Augustine, "rightly ordered love."[7] There can be no right ordering, on Baldwin's account of love, because love precisely names that which is without norms, that which remains when worldly concepts recede.

Baldwin's novels in general, and especially *Another Country*, explore the varieties of love and desire and the way that race in America shapes desire. But Baldwin has a tendency not to discriminate when giving accounts of desire: each desire he represents is part of the work of love, each desire an imperfect part subsumed into the perfect whole. Even in *Go Tell It on the Mountain*, he remains curiously equivocal regarding the protagonist's sensuality, particularly his attraction to the older Elisha. Sensuality is present in the narrative, but it marks a narrative dead-end. Put another way, sensuality marks a region of stability—unequivocally praiseworthy—in an otherwise fundamentally equivocal text. It moves above the complexity of the world, and so sensuality seems as if it is not subject to worldly norms. At most, this sensuality serves as evidence of our opacity to ourselves, evidence of the self's sacred remainder. Read in light of Baldwin's later prose, where this opacity is named "love," *Go Tell It on the Mountain* becomes a struggle between idolatrous loves, of father and God, and genuine love, the sensual/sexual love of John and Elisha, a love emanating directly from the boys' opaque selves, a love performing the end of idolatry.

I worry that the political potency of love, which comes about when love is connected with justice, is lost when love is placed in a realm free of norms. Recalling his relationship with his father, paradigmatic for his relationship with authority, Baldwin decides that "serving the Lord," the god-father, means putting new content in old form. "All of my father's texts and songs, which I had decided were meaningless, were arranged before me at his death like empty bottles, waiting to hold the meaning which life would give them for me" (E83). Such images point to the distance at which Baldwin holds norms. His father provides empty bottles that can be filled with anything; it is only the bottles that are given. Paternal love might involve struggle, but it is the struggle to make sense of what is given; whatever results from that struggle (essentially with oneself) will be judged morally praiseworthy. Every art project receives an A+ so long as it is not captive to the father's rules. But what can it mean to work with the father's texts and songs but not the father's rules, not his judgment?

It was with the rise to national prominence of Martin Luther King Jr. that Baldwin began extolling love, but for King love and power were always deeply entwined. As he famously put it, "Power without love is reckless and abusive, and love without power is sentimental and anemic. Power at its best is love implementing the demands of justice, and justice at its best is power correcting everything that stands against love."[8] In contrast, it seems that for Baldwin power is necessarily disjuncted from love. The imperative to love may demand the use of power, to oppose idolatry, but this use of power is instrumental. Certainly, for Baldwin love is not an end state but a process, a struggle. But this struggle, which happens through worldly things—words and bodies—is directed toward a communion of souls free of worldly things. Put theologically, the worry is about the human desire to bring about the eschaton in a world of sin and the violence inflicted on creation as a result. For Baldwin, we can approach redemption when worldly distinctions are eliminated between familial and sexual love, between love and sensuality, between love of nation and love of self. Bodies and pleasures mingle without form as souls commune. But in the Christian tradition the image of God in humans is not an indiscernible secret of the heart soliciting love. It is manifested in words and bodies; it is these that are to be loved. These are to be loved for the way in which they image God, for their beauty, goodness, and truth. All words and bodies participate in beauty, goodness, and truth to some extent, but that extent varies. It is in this way that love, power, and justice combine: loving rightly does not require accepting and so bracketing all worldly distinctions to commune with the soul; it requires judging worldly distinctions, the good and the bad, the beautiful and the ugly, and embracing the good and the beautiful while using power to correct the bad and the ugly. Baldwin has much to say about lust: about its motivations in fear and false consciousness, specifically, in fantasies of racial difference. But instead of seeing lust as disordered love in need of correction, he places it in a different category than love. For Baldwin, love is blind to race. This distinction between love and lust is the official position presented in Baldwin's essays; in novels such as *Giovanni's Room* and *Another Country*, Baldwin seems to be teaching the reader lessons in how love can be disordered, lessons in the continuity between love and lust. With the line between love and lust blurred, and with both mixed with sensuality, Baldwin slips from his old role as a critic of idolatry to his new role idolizing love.

Baldwin generally avoids discussing political institutions (are we to love the president? the presidency?). This could lead us to read Baldwin as, strictly, a theorist of social movements, movements that can, more plausibly than political institutions, be animated by love. But Baldwin does consider, in both his fiction and nonfiction, one political institution: the judiciary. The legal system brings to the fore the issue with which Baldwin's political theology is least well equipped to deal: judgment and condemnation. Judgment, of course, is the essence of courts; ideally, judgment animated by justice. Baldwin's negative political theology reserves judgment and condemnation only for idolatry, not for individuals. To condemn an individual, for Baldwin, implies a commitment to idolatry. Baldwin describes condemnation as "fueled by terror and self-hatred": "Salvation repudiates condemnation, since we all have the right, for many reasons, to condemn one another. Condemnation is easier than wonder" (C165). Law enforcement is, expectedly, viewed by Baldwin as theology gone wrong: as idolatry.

> Both the white fundamentalist minister and the deputy are Christians—*hard-core* Christians, one might say. Both believe that they are responsible, the one for divine law and the other for natural order. Both believe that they are able to define and privileged to impose law and order; and both, historically and actually, know that law and order are meant to keep me in my place. (C161–62, Baldwin's emphasis)

The legal system, like Christianity of the worst sort, condemns, and the burden of condemnation most often falls on the backs of blacks. Yet what Baldwin's alternative would be, in the political rather than religious realm, remains unclear. His reconfiguration of theology does not so easily transform into a reconfiguration of politics. What is a court system that would reverence the souls of the accused?

Baldwin writes, "I do not claim that everyone in prison here is innocent, but I do claim that the law, as it operates, is guilty, and that the prisoners, therefore, are all unjustly imprisoned" (E444). It is not clear what implications Baldwin intends from statements such as these. However, it is clear, from his reflections elsewhere, that he is not simply concerned with particularly high incarceration rates in the United States or particularly harsh prison conditions (though he is concerned with them). Baldwin is concerned with the institution of the prison itself and the prisoner. But it is hard to say whether he is saying that prisons should be abolished (together with courts?) or if he is reminding us that any human institution that purports to judge guilt and innocence will fail in that task. This latter claim seems to be, in effect, a reminder that there is sin in the world and that we live on the near side of the eschaton, rather than a statement about politics. If politics means figuring out how to live together in a fallen world, it does not seem to be a topic that interests Baldwin much at all. In his account, making judgments, for individuals, is inescapable, but when judgment is institutionalized it becomes farcical. "Each of us knows, though we do not like this knowledge, that a courtroom is a visceral Roman circus. No one involved in this contest is, or can be, impartial . . . the ability to suspend judgment is, in each of us, suspect" (ET1).

The injustice of the criminal justice system is a theme that pervades Baldwin's writings, from his early autobiographical essay about his arrest in Paris through his reflections on the persecution of the Black Panthers juxtaposed with the persecution of his much more anonymous black friend Tony in *No Name in the Street* to his late account of the Atlanta child murders, and the trial that resulted, in *The Evidence of Things Not Seen*. *If Beale Street Could Talk* is a novel that entirely revolves around unjust policing and imprisonment. Police harassment follows Fonny and lands him in jail for rape. He navigates a byzantine legal system with the "help" of a morally ambiguous lawyer. Fonny reflects on his captivity, realizing that he is not in jail because of his acts, and the other prisoners are not, either. "These captive men are the hidden price for a hidden lie: the righteous must be able to locate the damned" (B192). In contrast to the world of unjust and irrational condemnation in *Beale Street*, Baldwin creates an alternative world of love: Tish's love for Fonny. It is love that reveals truth. Tish is our trusted narrator, giving us an honest account of her experiences, an honest picture of the misunderstood Fonny (who only wants to create, to sculpt). The world is dishonest, its norms and concepts misleading, to the extent that Tish and Fonny can live honestly only when they use names that have no relation to their own (Clementine and Alonzo). *Beale Street* is such a hopeless novel because the two worlds, of love and of justice, have nothing to do with each other.

This worry about Baldwin's account of love may be addressed by recalling his account of writing, for love and writing do the same work of revealing truth. They are both, for Baldwin, spiritual practices. Writing has the effect of conveying truth, but the writer does not simply write truth. "I do not like people who are *earnest* about anything," he writes (E9, Baldwin's emphasis). To write truth—to write *earnestly*—would be to suppose that words had the ability to represent reality perfectly, but they do not. Words do quite the opposite, in Baldwin's view, functioning as idols, keeping us safe from the complexity of ourselves and our worlds. The writing that Baldwin considers exemplary manipulates and persuades in the service of truth. The "protest novel," in contrast, manipulates and persuades in the service of politics. Baldwin does not position his own writing as apolitical, but as doing politics better, more thoroughly, more rigorously. To do the work of persuasion that is necessary for writing, the writer must be "thoroughly disciplined," must be fully versed in social norms (and the norms of literary traditions) (C8). The writer looks out onto a mix of the good and the bad, the true and the false, the beautiful and the ugly, and the writer produces work that draws an audience toward the good, the true, and the beautiful. The writer does not simply condemn the false and wallow in truth. The writer does not condemn—that would be too earnest—but her writing has the effect of condemnation, the effect of judgment.

Yet Baldwin's account of love seems to be missing this sense of judgment found in his account of writing. Baldwin does not explain how loving could have the effect of condemnation or judgment. The result is that Baldwin's political theology, his constructive account of love, is apolitical. It is his negative political theology, his dogged critique of idolatry—of ideology—that is of lasting import.

CHAPTER 3

Mbembe

Before his work was translated into English and he was recognized as one of the leading critical theorists of our time, a reviewer wrote that Achille Mbembe's work "is more likely to appeal to theologians" than to his fellow political scientists.[1] The reviewer went on to associate Mbembe's intellectual project with those of Jean-Marc Éla and Eboussi Boulaga, two African theologians who subtly explored the relationship between theology and culture. While European and American Christianity has since largely forgotten the insights of Éla and Boulaga, Mbembe's stock has risen dramatically—but in the secular academy, not in theology. Mbembe was, indeed, trained as a historian and a political scientist, albeit in a French Africanist tradition particularly attuned to questions of culture. But religious questions have been central to his work, and Mbembe insists that he has been deeply shaped by Christian theology and that his research poses questions of Christian theology.

Joseph-Achille Mbembe was born in Cameroon in 1957. His early education was Catholic. He reflects, "The Bible and to a certain extent Christianity have exercised the ... most crucial influence on my intellectual itinerary." What were important to the young Mbembe were not the specific beliefs of Christianity but something much broader. Christianity provided "the structuring mental landscapes against which the formative years of my life as a scholar unfolded."[2] After schooling in Cameroon, Mbembe moved to France to pursue further studies. There, he immersed himself in the world of French theory, engaging with the ideas of Foucault, Derrida, Bataille, Castoriadis, Lacan, Deleuze, and others.[3] Despite this early immersion in heady philosophy, Mbembe was essentially a social scientist. In his first three books, *Les jeunes et l'ordre politique en Afrique noire* (1985), *Afriques indociles: Christianisme, pouvoir et État en société postcoloniale* (1988), and *La Naissance du maquis dans le Sud-Cameroun (1920–1960)* (1996), and in articles published in *Politique Africaine* and elsewhere, Mbembe examined the complications of African society, drawing on politics, history, and sociology. His second book, *Afriques indociles*, focused specifically on the interaction between religion and the state in postcolonial African contexts. In this work, Mbembe was not content to look exclusively at the domain of formal politics. He found religion and politics in a wide variety of cultural sites, far from the halls of a parliament or a cathedral. The religiosity of the ordinary African need not be dismissed as false consciousness, nor need it be reduced to the purely pragmatic. In Mbembe's view, popular religiosity can be a site of agency, and it can be a site at which power relations are navigated or contested.

In this early work, it is already clear that Mbembe is pushing away from the conventions of the social scientist as he attends to the complexities of ordinary life. He does not turn to the subaltern as authorities, nor does he turn to ethnography (his writings have an at times frustrating level of abstraction). Rather, Mbembe embraces the theoretical currents of French intellectual life. He understands power to be circulating through all levels of a society, not just emanating downward from the state. He understands these many veins through which power flows to be unified by the domain of the symbolic, where fantasy reigns. And he understands this symbolic domain to shape the lives of ordinary individuals imperfectly, always with a remainder that allows for negotiation and contest. Mbembe himself is never this explicit: he swims in the (seemingly disparate) waters of Foucault, Lacan, and Derrida without dwelling on the mechanics.

Mbembe's publications in the third millennium have turned explicitly to theorizing, but their subject is not theory. In *De la postcolonie* (2000), *Sortir de la grande nuit* (2010), and *Critique de la raison nègre* (2013), as well as in articles for the U.S.-based journal *Public Culture*, theory forms the backdrop but not the occasion for analysis. The topic of the first of these three books, which Mbembe envisions as a cycle, is postcoloniality, the topic of the second is Africa, and the topic of the third is blackness.[4] This should be read as a sign of Mbembe's own intellectual development: the central problem with which he was concerned changed from colonialism to the racialization accompanying colonialism, with blackness naming the starkest form of racialization. Each of these three books is composed of a series of essays on culture, with examples largely drawn from Africa, though the Caribbean and the United States play an important role in the third text. Each of these three books is an attempt to reveal the contours of the symbolic: the organized, even rigid structure of feelings, thoughts, and fantasies that are the a priori for experience in a given context. Such a structure exists independent of any particular individual, and it is not to be found perfectly reflected in, for example, the writings of the leading statesmen. It is a structure that is unavoidable: it shapes how the domain in question is viewed by outsiders and determines what possible ways of living are accessible for those situated in the domain itself. From the outside, the former colony, Africa, or blackness is viewed in certain ways: violent, hyper-sexual, uncontrollable, unintellectual, and so on. While it may be tempting to dismiss these views as mere stereotypes, easily shaken off with more education or personal experience, Mbembe suggests that they point to something much deeper. Those living in the former colony, in Africa, or blacks in the diaspora have their experience shaped by these fantasies of the exotic other even as lived experience is obviously not reducible to these fantasies. Attending to the domain of the symbolic unleashes impressive explanatory power. Apparent pathologies of African society (for example) can now be understood as standing on top of this surface of the symbolic—and Mbembe repeatedly reminds us that the contours of the symbolic were crafted in slavery, colonialism, and apartheid. In other words, postcolonial, African, or black experience today cannot be understood apart from white, European, colonial oppression. But the implication of Mbembe's theoretical point is also that there is no place for the postcolonial, the African, or the black to stand outside of that legacy of oppression, outside of the symbolic. If there is to be struggle, it is struggle within the terms set by that legacy. This need not be stifling or depressing. While the symbolic gives the conditions of possibility, helping to constitute who we are, there is always a remainder. Mbembe's essays each explore a different site of tension between the seemingly overwhelming power of the symbolic and the realities of lived experience—realities inexpressible apart from the symbolic but also never fully captured by the symbolic.

Mbembe's main theoretical achievement is not to combine the ideas of Foucault, Lacan, and Derrida and then apply them to an African context—

that is too specific and pragmatic. Rather, Mbembe's achievement is to synthesize these ideas and apply them to sites that are perceived as utterly abject, as utterly dissimilar from the refined, bourgeois contexts in which these theoretical tools were developed. In doing so, Mbembe challenges any latent assumptions we may hold about whites or Europeans living in a world of symbols while blacks or Africans live in a world of animal desires. The deep structure of our world is the same everywhere, Mbembe effectively argues, because we share in a common humanity. This humanity is not defined by a capacity to reason, or even by a capacity to emote. This humanity marks the limits of the symbolic, the place where the structuring principles of our world do not quite work—and have the potential to short-circuit. In a refined European salon it is easy to forget that power runs through the symbolic, power that maintains the status of elites and holds down the marginalized. For those in a context of apparent abjection, where the externality of the symbolic is often so grotesquely obvious (for example, as personified by the dictator), the imperative to creatively contest the symbolic becomes all the stronger—which is also an imperative to realize our humanity. In short, Mbembe is arguing that we can all learn how to be better humans by paying attention to the experiences of postcolonials, Africans, or blacks. At its best, Mbembe's theorizing offers a stark contrast to the melancholy typical of French theory. Instead of lamenting the iron grip of ideology, or the episteme, or the symbolic, Mbembe shows how those not insulated from the violence accompanying these are energetically, creatively engaged in contesting that violence. Or, put differently, rather than looking at Africa imagined as lack, as non-being, from comfortable European and American seminar rooms, Mbembe actually sees the inhumanity in those very seminar rooms while he sees humanity at its most vibrant, being overflowing in fullness, in Africa, among blacks.

In the last few years, Mbembe has increasingly engaged with conversations in political theology. Theoretically, he has added the work of Carl Schmitt and Giorgio Agamben to his frequent points of reference. More significantly, Mbembe now takes a question of political theology to be central to his own work: "My project is really to look into ways in which we can render politically fruitful the critique of religion while taking very seriously religion itself as critique—especially a critique of the political."[5] In dialogue with scholars such as Talal Asad and Saba Mahmood, who interrogate the supposed identification of secularity and critique, Mbembe is inviting us to think about subtle connections between religion and politics.[6] Religion here is not just religious belief but religious practice and religious aesthetics, as well. Yet it is crucially important that the turn to practice or aesthetics is not a turn away from critique, in his view. When critique is understood to mean explicating the symbolic, or ideology, and exposing the extent to which it preserves the interests of the powerful, religion in all its dimensions can have a robust critical function. When religion and culture are understood as inextricable, this is simply to state a point familiar to the cultural studies scholar: the domain of culture is a site where the ideas of elites, imperfectly implemented and embodied, are contested by marginalized communities.

Yet Mbembe is making a stronger point. His argument is not just that religion has critical potential because culture has critical potential and religion is one element of culture. He writes, "My reflection is clearly located within the Judeo-Christian tradition—a tradition which, by the way, is no longer simply Western."[7] Tradition is quite different from culture. Tradition involves structures of authority, shared practices and values, norms, a history, contest over its own meaning. As Mbembe makes clear in his autobiographical reflections, Christianity shaped the way in which he sees the world; Mbembe was formed in the Christian tradition. In a sense, Christianity offers Mbembe a way of seeing the world that comes before the symbolic; put another way, the symbolic sits on top of, and perhaps obscures, tradition. By reclaiming childhood memories, turning to a time before the violent imposition of the racist, colonial order on the young boy, the hold of the symbolic does not seem so tight.

How does Mbembe understand the Judeo-Christian tradition with which he identifies? The death and resurrection of God-in-humanity is central. Equally important, and not unrelated, is Christianity as a name for living poetically, imaginatively, beyond the bounds set formally or informally (in the symbolic) by the powers that be. "For me, the oneiric power of Christianity derives from the enchanting idea that closure can be overcome; that the question of our genealogy can never be settled once for all."[8] Instead of taking Christianity as an element of the symbolic, Mbembe uses Christianity to name points of resistance to the symbolic. In a sense, this is all there is to the Judeo-Christian tradition for him: the collection of limitations, potential short-circuits, of the symbolic, which is to say the collection of human beings realizing their humanity—turning the death-in-life imposed by the symbolic into new life through creative, poetic assertions of their inwardness. In this view, Christianity cannot name certain statements of belief (such statements could only be articulated in the symbolic), nor can it name membership in certain worldly collectivities (again, such collectivities are always already inscribed in the symbolic). Rather, Christianity names a collection of singularities, each a human who is more than the world sees in her, whose life consists in more than regurgitating the wisdom of the world. To embrace such an identity is to embrace Christianity, Mbembe would likely argue, and such an embrace is unusual. Most people are afraid of themselves, preferring the familiar comfort of embracing the identity the world gives to them. This is a sin.

There is much familiar to those conversant with French theory's turn to religion in Mbembe's understanding of Christianity. The focus on religion naming a community of singularities resonates with ideas developed by Georges Bataille, Maurice Blanchot, Alain Badiou, Jean-Luc Nancy, and others. But Mbembe moves the conversation a step further; this is a step that takes him toward black theology. "Most of my critique and writing of Africa," Mbembe asserts, "has been up to now an endless commentary on the drama of crucifixion and the hope for resurrection."[9] Postcolonial contexts, then Africa, and now, in Mbembe's most recent work, blackness are privileged theological sites. They are sites where there is the strongest possibility of encountering and fully appreciating the death of God (of God-in-the-human), and so they are sites where it is easiest to be faithful to this God. The privilege of these contexts has nothing to do with the quantity of suffering encountered. Indeed, focusing on that suffering can distract. It can solicit humanitarian concern from the privileged, giving the privileged a false confidence in their own religiosity as they text donations to their favorite charity. This is not love of neighbor; indeed, in Mbembe's view, it is just the opposite. The comfortable white European or American texting donations to her favorite charity as prompted by a television commercial fully embraces, and so reinforces, the symbolic: the image of Africans (or Indians, or blacks) as essentially sufferers. Cast in that role, the object of charity is denied humanity. But the most serious effect is not on the African, the Indian, or the black. Rather, it is on the subject of charity herself, the one who gives. Her humanity is also refused, for to embrace the symbolic is to deny our own humanity; it is to accept what is given by the powers that be rather than to exercise our characteristically human (and so divine) powers of creativity, practical wisdom, and imagination. Those capacities are required when the normative order, the symbolic, is necessarily uncomfortable, when its violence is unmitigated—in the postcolonial, African, and black experience. In these contexts, it is starkly clear that following the ways of the world will lead to death. Sitting back and following the mandates of the state, the police officer, the teacher, even the parent will result not in comfort but in brutality; it is suicidal. In such contexts, the choice is clear: embrace the symbolic and die or embrace the human and gain the chance to live. Possibility but not certainty: this is the place for faith and hope fueled by the belief that resurrection is possible. To embrace the human means, in Mbembe's idiom, to embrace the divine, to embrace the Judeo-Christian tradition. It is to acknowledge the limits of the ways of the world, to recognize the impotence of the powers that be, and to enlist that characteristically human ability to combine reason, emotion, imagination, and practical wisdom to find new ways of living. This is what life is like every day for the postcolonial, the African, the black.

In this way, Mbembe clearly is situated in, and adds theoretical sophistication to, the discourse of black theology. For him, God is black in the same sense that God is black for James Cone. Christ identifies with "the least of these," and in our contemporary context that means the postcolonial, Africans, or blacks. The further point that Cone makes, a point that often goes unappreciated but is equally if not more important, is that blacks have privileged access to the divine and specifically to religious ethics: the epistemic privilege of the oppressed. It is not that blacks are God's chosen people; it is that blacks are uniquely capable of faith, hope, and love because the experience of oppression attunes blacks to the divine. Worldly norms ring hollow when those (whites) enforcing them are so obviously duplicitous, so obviously morally corrupt. There must be some higher normative order not reducible to worldly terms. The work of discerning and explicating that higher normative order is the work of black theology, an academic discourse that continues the practical and intellectual work performed by black Christianity during centuries of enslavement and injustice. This is clearly also an impulse embraced by Mbembe, even if he does not fill out a positive account of that higher normative order to the same extent that black theologians in seminaries and divinity schools do. But that positive content would seem to have limited significance. It is an expression of a fundamental dynamic—the death and resurrection of God as human—that takes different forms at different places and times, just as oppression takes different forms at different places and times. Africa may now be the privileged site for theological reflection, but this has not always been the case, and it will not always be the case. Similarly, the particular way that reflection comes into language will change. In short, it is not necessary to see Mbembe as merely an honorary member of the guild of black theologians because his words or inflections differ from those of a Regius professor of divinity.

Mbembe makes a theoretical idiom, drawn especially from Foucault, Lacan, and Derrida, accessible to and productive for black theology. There is another, even more significant way he advances the discourse of black theology, as well. Just as John Milbank and his colleagues tell a powerful and often compelling story about European Christianity's distortion at the hands of secularization, Mbembe tells a powerful and even more compelling story about the distortion of Christianity through colonialism and, in his more recent version of the narrative, through racialization.[10] Milbank's story operates at the level of both ideas and practices. The aspiration to participate in the divine once reigned theologically and organized life in late antique and medieval Europe. Participation here suggests an all-encompassing aesthetics: individuals, states, organizations, and objects exist in relationship to each other, with their own boundaries but also as part of others, constitutive of others, and constituted by others. The desire to fix boundaries around self, state, group, or object was sin; the desire to acknowledge and embrace participation was divine. The individual could not be understood apart from his family, his guild, his neighborhood, his town, his diocese. Moral excellence meant excellence in relationship to these multiple communities; it could never be evaluated independent of these contexts. There was hierarchy, but there was also accountability. The father may have told the son what to do, but if the father's demands were excessive, were beyond the familiar norms of a community, there were other relatives, neighbors, priests, and friends who would urge the father to reconsider; the same was true, *mutatis mutandis*, for the employer, the municipal government, the bishop, and so on. This was life in Europe until the late thirteenth century, so the story goes. Then a combination of intellectual, economic, and social developments transformed how the European world saw itself. Borders around individuals, states, objects, and groups became harder and more well-defined. Complex social space came to be understood hierarchically, with God on top, issuing commands, political leaders similarly standing above those they commanded, employers standing above the workers they ordered about, fathers standing above wives and children they ordered about, and so on. To believe, to command, to act, these now emanated from inside the closed borders of the self, from the will, accountable to nothing beyond the self, save the laws or commands of those higher up the social hierarchy. Freedom came to mean freedom from constraint rather than freedom to creatively participate in (navigate, negotiate, reimagine) a world saturated with norms and relations.

This new worldly order, emerging intellectually with Duns Scotus and the dominance of nominalism, was essentially a secular order. It paved the way for the familiar features of modernity: sovereign self and sovereign state, a capitalist economy, the discourse of human rights, unleashing of instrumental reason, the separation of autonomous domains with religion over there, politics of there, science over there, economics over there, my self here. No longer did theology reign. Previously, theology did not stand above everything else in the world; rather, theology named the principle of participation, the way all people, objects, and entities related to each other—when those relations were harmonious, beautiful, they were divine. To envision theology as a separate domain above others would be to embrace the worldview of secularism, a worldview equally expressed in the conception of the autonomous subject, the sovereign ruler, the privileging of exchange value over use value, and much else. This dramatic story of the world's fall via secularization and the implicit call to retrieve an earlier, purer, more theologically orthodox way of seeing and living in the world has been rightly criticized for its nostalgia and its Eurocentrism (the two clearly being tightly linked). Yet the rhetorical and explanatory force of this story is undeniable. It does seem like there are many things wrong with the world, that this story names many of them and shows how they are linked, plausibly gives this linkage the name "secularism," and then—the biggest leap, where the most readers are reluctant to follow—names old-fashioned Christianity as the antidote to this set of linked problems, the antidote to secularism. Secularism, like this old-fashioned Christianity, goes deeper than the symbolic or ideology; it names the conditions of possibility for any symbolic or any ideology in our secular age. The conventional (Marxist, psychoanalytic, discourse analytic) toolkit of critical theory is not enough because it shares in the premises of secularism. Only Christianity offers the leverage needed to challenge the frustrations and injustices of the world—and only Christianity offers a constructive picture of what a world organized radically differently, organized theologically, might look like. Or so advocates of this position hold.

Mbembe agrees that Christianity offers access to something deeper than the symbolic, deeper than ideology. He also agrees that the world is seriously amiss in many ways and that these problems have a common root. For Mbembe, this root, importantly, is not exactly in the domain of the symbolic. What is most important for him, for his account of African or black life, is the relationship between the symbolic and lived experience. Whereas in contexts of privilege (whiteness, Europe) the friction of the symbolic on lived experience is only rarely evident—for example, in neuroses that occasion visits to the psychoanalyst—this friction is evident continually and felt as violence in African and black contexts. The reason for this difference does, in part, concern the content of the symbolic. That content is deeply shaded by the overdetermination of the postcolony, Africa, or blackness as abject, devoid of humanity. What happens when the symbolic, that which constitutes a subject, excludes the possibility of subjectivity? Mbembe answers in a word: death.[11] More specifically, it is living-death, human life as animal life, included and excluded from humanity at once, continually exposed to the possibility of death. These are themes developed by Giorgio Agamben in reflections on Nazi concentration camps, a structure Agamben finds repeated in the camps of Guantanamo Bay, a structure that, at a lower but increasing intensity, Agamben believes is coming to characterize all contemporary life—the world is becoming a camp.[12] Mbembe persuasively argues that Auschwitz was not so exceptional when situated in a global perspective: the condition of Auschwitz was the colonial condition and continues to be the condition of the postcolony, of Africa, of blackness. (As Mbembe notes, this was a point powerfully made by Aimé Césaire shortly after the Second World War.) But Mbembe does not go all the way with Agamben, for doing so is to take the road to political and ethical impotence, a cul-de-sac that does not continue toward resurrection. Rather, Mbembe sees in this death-in-life an opportunity for life-beyond-death, for the emergence of authentic humanity, humanity irreducible to worldly representations of the human. For this to be the case, the postcolony, Africa, and blackness (and Auschwitz) cannot be domains outside of the symbolic. Life in the camp, for Mbembe, is governed by a particular configuration of the symbolic, shaded by the devaluation of human life, but still functioning as the symbolic always functions, still constitutive of the subject. In other words, what is at issue is a systematic deformation of the symbolic, not the existence of the symbolic as such. There is no doubt about the causes of this systematic deformation of the symbolic: colonialism and racialization. And, in Mbembe's view, there is no doubt about the solution: faith in the possibility of resurrection, which is to say an embrace of Christianity as he understands it.

Secularism, Milbank and his colleagues effectively charge, is also a systematic deformation of the symbolic. On their account, the problem with secularism is not the specific beliefs, affects, or values present in a secularist context. The problem is with how those beliefs, affects, and values are configured: as those of autonomous, atomized individuals (or, for the postmodern secularist with the false consciousness of rebellion, the free flows of affects and ideas from body to body without regard to boundary or hierarchy). In each place and time infected by secularism, the symbolic is distorted in these ways even as it still functions as the symbolic always does, constituting individuals and making it possible to perceive, communicate, and live in the world. The theological alternative is not an embrace of the beliefs, affects, or values of a quaint medieval village. The symbolic supervenes on the theological (or the pseudo-theology of secularism: heresy).

Those villagers are still charged with navigating a world constituted by the symbolic; that process of navigation is what makes them human and not angels. (Milbank and his colleagues have the unfortunate tendency to at times mistake the Fall for the move from theology to secularism rather than seeing it for what it is: the relationship of humans to the symbolic.)[13] In our secular age, we also are charged with navigating a world constituted by the symbolic, but this task is immeasurably more difficult when that symbolic is systematically distorted, as it is by secularism. Because individuals are not really autonomous atoms, because we really are constituted in relation to our family, friends, neighbors, communities, and much else, the symbolic of our era greatly misrepresents lived experience, resulting in violence and horrors (war, economic inequality, abortion, euthanasia), the opposite of peace. The symbolic always misrepresents, but when the symbolic is systematically distorted these occasions of misrepresentation proliferate, and their violence becomes more severe. This is Milbank's point, but it is also Mbembe's point. If it is evidence of violence and horrors that makes this point compelling, that calls for a return to the theological, Mbembe's evidence is rather stronger than Milbank's. The intermittent discomfort or existential angst of the European bourgeoisie is mild compared with the everyday violence faced by those living in the postcolony, in Africa, or in the black diaspora.

Mbembe's work offers many examples of what a deeply distorted symbolic looks like and how it does violence. To speak in images, if Milbank's account of distortion suggests a change from overlapping circles with fuzzy boundaries to carefully measured and hierarchically arranged lines, Mbembe's account suggests a shift from a similar starting point to an image of an arbitrary tyrant standing far above an array of hierarchically arranged dots. At the heart of colonialism and slavery, according to Mbembe's account, is arbitrary rule by one who is qualitatively different from the subject population. This combination of distance and arbitrary rule is the model for all social relations. Those enforcing the will of the ruler use their own power arbitrarily and aim to keep a distance, or the impression of distance, from those over whom they wield power. Ostentatious displays of wealth and status become common. So, too, does hypermasculinity, an identification with the phallus marking a qualitative difference and the capacity for arbitrary decision (rape). The role of time in the symbolic is shaped by the potential for arbitrary command from above. Instead of a sense of future possibility arising from potentialities in the present and the complexities of the present arising from layers of history, the present is highly unstable. The future is only accessible by taking risks in the present. The past is romanticized as solid ground now inaccessible in the flux of the present. The present does not only seem unstable; it is unstable because arbitrary rule remains the principle through which power operates even decades or more after the end of colonialism and slavery. Those experiences distorted the symbolic, and those distortions have never left. They remain because the symbolic relevant to Africa or blacks is not independent of the symbolic relevant to Europe or whites; they are co-constitutive. Even if the formal institutions of slavery or colonialism are gone, the role of the (now post-) colony or the black in the symbolic remains. When Africans or blacks are taken to be less than human, the only way by which Europeans can relate to Africa, by which whites can relate to blacks, is through arbitrary (even if indirect) rule. The comfortable European texting a donation to a charity after seeing starving African children on her television is maintaining the logic that authorizes genocide, sexual abuse, homophobic violence, and corruption in Africa.

Where Milbank and his colleagues point quite precisely to moments before theology was replaced by secularism as our underlying social logic, Mbembe usually resists pointing to moments before colonialism and racialization. It is hard to make such a gesture without romanticizing a "traditional" past, a move that he diagnoses as itself a symptom of colonialism and racialization. Mbembe does gesture toward precolonial social configurations in Africa, and he points to his own childhood before he fully entered into the colonial symbolic, but in general he is more concerned about possibilities for the future than he is with retrieving the past. "Writing the world from Africa, this is how I understand the project of theory and criticism—to bring back to life that which is asleep, that which has been put to sleep; to bring back to life that which is threatened by the forces of the night."[14] Through engagements with varied popular media, literature, intellectual work, and cultural practices, Mbembe points to openings, sites of possibility. Such sites are qualitatively different from sites of uncertainty. The latter are inscribed in the symbolic, an aspect of the words, feelings, and thoughts that are available to us as we engage with the world. What Mbembe lauds are possibilities unimaginable in the terms of the symbolic. (He self-consciously associates his development of this theme with the thought of Derrida, Benjamin, and Bloch.) To access such possibilities, he points to places where the friction of the symbolic as it is lived is exposed. The critic's task, in Mbembe's view—could this also be the task of the theologian?—is to survey the cultural terrain for such openings and compile them, making them available for a broader audience and so magnifying their potentiality. This occurs in two ways. First, by pointing to such sites of friction, the temptation is lessened to naturalize the symbolic, to believe that the symbolic perfectly maps the world. The weaker this temptation, the greater the possibility for thinking about a radically different future. Second, by juxtaposing multiple, disparate sites of friction, there is an opportunity for resonance between these sites. Newly aware that they are not alone, those at any given site are motivated to pursue it, to commit themselves further to challenging the symbolic even when that comes at a high cost. In other words, the critic's task is to catalyze the challenge to the symbolic posed by a community of singularities, a community of individuals realizing their humanity, the divine in the human—a community of singularities that theologians name *church*.

At times, Mbembe begins to fill out what this radically different world might look like. The problem with his suggestions (a problem also faced by Milbank and his colleagues) is that the distinction between the registers of the empirical, the symbolic, and the theological begins to blur when describing this future. That the essential characteristic of this future is its indescribability in terms of the present leads to such confusion. Mbembe often writes of a future that embraces multiplicity, a future for which African and black experience can be a model, given that living in multiplicity is already familiar to Africans and blacks.[15] This future will embrace the human, but the human will not be reduced to an atomized individual subject to the commands and desires of the powers that be. Rather, we will recognize that the human is multiple and irreducible, with plural and porous borders, poetically living and relating to the world and other humans. Abstractions such as nation, ethnicity, gender, and sexuality will no longer provoke violence as the complications of lived experience replace the crude borders of the world that is. This is an appealing, perhaps poetic version of the future, but it is unclear precisely how it is to be understood. Is it an eschatological vision meant to animate but not describe real possibilities for life in the present world? Or does Mbembe mean for us to take this future of multiplicities literally, as a form of society that we should attempt to advance (with policies, political interventions, social movements) in the present? Mbembe chooses both options at different times in his writings, but the two options are incompatible.

Certainly, it is always tempting to describe the indescribable—witness the prolix writings of negative theologians. If there is a serious commitment to indescribability, it is essential to mark a shift in register to the metaphorical when descriptions begin or, even better, to perform in description that failure of description, for even the metaphorical is in the domain of the symbolic.[16] Before the eschaton, to realize our humanity can only mean to do so in relation to the symbolic. The great insight of Milbank and Mbembe is that it is possible to talk about the symbolic being systematically distorted; the great threat of their writing is to encourage the presumption that the symbolic can be eliminated or that the symbolic can be structured in such a way as to perfectly correspond to reality (which is really another way of saying that it is eliminated). What goes undertheorized in the writings of both is what life is like in a world where the symbolic is undistorted. In such cases, to realize humanity still means creating, imagining, and navigating life in a way that necessary exceeds and so calls into question the terms set out by the symbolic. As long as we are human, we will have to live in a world of arbitrary signs; our humanity will be realized at the moments when we refuse to cede the pattern of our life to those arbitrary signs. The world of multiplicities envisioned by Mbembe is a world beyond the law, beyond norms, beyond arbitrary signs—a world beyond the symbolic. We are faced with a paradox. If the postcolonial, the African, or the black is in a privileged theological position, a position to have faith, to love, and to hope rightly (or rather less wrongly), does not that privilege vanish as soon as the position of these who are most marginalized improves?[17] Once the symbolic is no longer distorted by the legacy of colonialism and slavery, by arbitrary rule, will this not be a theological loss, a move away from God?

The best response to this worry would be to suggest that, just as there can be systematic defects of the symbolic, there can be particularly good configurations of the symbolic, configurations that make it easier for us to realize our humanity. This seems to be what Milbank and his colleagues try (with limited success) to invoke with images of the European Middle Ages: not a system of signs that gets the world right but rather a system of signs that is, indeed, arbitrary and is, indeed, violent, but that is configured in such a way as to make possible creative, imaginative, and wise realizations of the human. There is authority and there are norms, but there are multiple authorities issuing varied, sometimes conflicting, and always contestable norms, allowing and even encouraging humans to navigate such a world creatively—and ultimately in a way that approaches the good, the true, and the beautiful. The problem with Mbembe's hints at a future vision of multiplicity is that there is no space for normativity or for authority. Apparently in response to the arbitrary rule of the colony, Mbembe abandons rule altogether. Such a vision cannot be a productive inflection of the symbolic; it can only be taken as an abandonment of the symbolic. When authority, norms, and the arbitrariness of signs are abandoned, we cannot but believe that what we see is what we get: the way we represent the world corresponds to the world itself. Unfortunately, claims to the Real often bring with them dreadful violence—a violence not dissimilar to the violence of arbitrary rule that Mbembe so detests.[18] This is a lost opportunity. Mbembe offers a convincing diagnosis—colonialism and racialization systematically distort the symbolic—and promises a prescription, but that prescription results in just another version of the crippling disease.

Perhaps the problem is that Mbembe is insufficiently theological, that he acknowledges but does not grapple seriously with the Judeo-Christian tradition in which he was formed, particularly the Christian tradition. Mbembe writes that the African theologians Boulaga and Éla are, indeed, important to his thinking, but they are only "almost as fruitful" as the Jewish thinkers Franz Rosenzweig, Walter Benjamin, Ernst Bloch, and Jacques Derrida.[19] (Let us set aside the question of just how traditional the Judaism of these four figures may be.) The Christianity that Mbembe retrieves is a poetics without form, an aesthetics without normativity—contradictions that can only be resolved by reducing his religious evocations to rhetoric.[20] Put another way, Mbembe's is the Christianity permissible in a secular age, a Christianity of gestures, feelings, and allusions, not a Christianity of tradition authoritative for life, not a Christianity that might conflict with regnant worldly norms—not a Christianity that could challenge colonialism or racism (or capitalism). What Mbembe seems to miss, crucially, is the extent to which race and religion are constructed and managed together. (There is a burgeoning scholarly literature on this point.)[21] If Mbembe wants to cure the continuing, metastasizing cancers of racism and colonialism, a thorough analysis of the historical, sociological, and metaphysical constructions of the colonial and racialized subject is not enough. An examination of the surprising and creative ways that religion is mobilized in colonial and racialized contexts to exercise political power is not enough. Study of the exclusion or management of religion and race, yoked, is needed, together with a study of the rich resources of theological and racial worlds before this management took its current form. A focus on slippages in the present that point toward openings for the future forecloses the possibility of normativity and of restoring the broken relationship of past to present and present to future. What is needed is a genuine embrace of tradition, and it remains an open question—ignored by Mbembe—what that might look like in a postcolonial or racialized context.

Reviewers have claimed that Mbembe has an "undisguised disdain for empirical facts" and that his theoretical eclecticism is often more chaotic than compelling.[22] Mbembe has responded that his "style of writing [is] aimed at speaking directly to the senses."[23] He does indeed cast a wide net (in Africa) for his examples and a wide net (in France) for his theory, all synthesized in polished prose that begins to enchant. Writing with style is certainly not a vice, and empirical evidence need not be fetishized, but the perceived problems with Mbembe's writing echo the limitations of his theory; or, put differently, they remind us of the reasons he remains a secular—secularist—theorist and not a theologian. The flows of affect and sensation embraced by Mbembe and performed in his theoretical bricolage preclude the normative and foreclose engagement with tradition.[24] That theoretical bricolage is motivated not by diverse problems but, it seems, by a desire to evoke the feeling of authority. This is the problem when tradition is set aside: authority is derived from posturing, and there are no resources to contest this authority except further posturing. In such a performance, Mbembe (who now splits his time between Johannesburg and North Carolina) asserts:

> I am a citizen of nowhere in particular. But nor do I define my condition as that of an exile or a nomad. Belonging to nowhere in particular, I have become my own home, a portable house I take with me wherever I happen to find a roof. . . . This state of permanent motion and fugitiveness has become an important dimension of the way I think.[25]

This is the sad state of the intellectual who refuses the authority of tradition. There may seem to be creative self-formation at work, but ultimately there is an atomized individual accountable to nothing, fleeing from everything, solipsistically posturing. Here the object of Mbembe's insights—the postcolonial, African, or *Nègre*—and the theorist himself become indistinguishable, except that the former at least knew himself to be wretched.

CHAPTER 4

Derrida, Agamben, Wynter

The concept of religion is now being historicized and contextualized. The concept of race was historicized and contextualized a generation ago. Recent scholarship has argued that the genealogies of religion and race are linked, that they emerged at the same historical moments in the same places due to some of the same forces. If this is the case, then the philosophy of religion is always the philosophy of religion and race. Ignoring discussions of race in the philosophy of religion distorts the philosophy of religion as much as ignoring, say, religious practice in favor of a focus on religious belief.

What is the philosophy of religion? It is often defined by a set of questions: Does God exist? What is evil? Is faith in God justified? Can we be good without God? But the philosophy of religion could also be understood as a tradition of inquiry defined by certain conversations, institutions, values, and authoritative texts. While much of a tradition of inquiry does involve grappling with certain questions, the two perspectives on the philosophy of religion, defined by questions or by tradition, are important to keep distinct. Exploring the entangled genealogies of religion and race may add qualifying clauses to those questions that make up the first definition of the philosophy of religion, transforming philosophy into intellectual history. Instead of asking, what is evil?, it may now be necessary to ask, what is evil for white European Christians? Or, what is evil for African American women who are spiritual but not religious? The philosophy of religion would then cease to be an exchange of arguments and instead track the arguments of others, in a particular place, at a particular time.

If the philosophy of religion is considered in the second way, as a tradition of inquiry, the entangled genealogies of religion and race push that tradition forward; philosophy is not reduced to intellectual history. As a tradition of inquiry, the philosophy of religion is already understood to be a predominantly white, European and American enterprise. Its authoritative texts were written by white men—Plato, Voltaire, Hume, Nietzsche, Plantinga; it flourishes in predominantly white institutions; and it is informed by concerns of its predominantly white practitioners. The qualification—*for white men*—is built into the definition of the tradition. So is Christianity, or something like it: the tradition of inquiry is implicitly informed by specifically Christian concerns, even when Plato is being read in a secular classroom. That is the lesson taught by genealogies of the category of religion.

Whiteness and Christianity do not only make the philosophy of religion provincial. They also imply that the enterprise itself is implicated in naturalizing whiteness and Christianity, and these concepts are implicated in naturalizing the enterprise of the philosophy of religion. In light of the imperial legacy of Christianity and the racist legacy of whiteness, the philosophy of religion appears deeply political. As a tradition of inquiry, the values, institutions, authorities, and conversations that constitute this tradition have the potential to perpetuate white supremacy and to sanctify imperial hegemony. Indeed, this is the default effect of participation in the tradition. Very careful, strategic maneuvering within the tradition is necessary to have any other effect. To get such strategic maneuvering right, confronting either the legacy of white supremacy or the legacy of Christian imperialism is not enough. They must be deliberately confronted together.

Before such a confrontation—really a redemption of the philosophy of religion—is possible, it is necessary to fully and clearly understand how religion and race are entangled. In this chapter, I will examine how they are entangled historically, then conceptually. Next, I will consider two figures prominent in recent philosophy of religion, Jacques Derrida and Giorgio Agamben, attending to how religion and race are entwined in their work. Then, I will consider some worries about Derrida and Agamben's projects based on recent cultural and economic changes. Finally, I will take Sylvia

Wynter as offering an example of an approach to the philosophy of religion that takes race seriously but also takes account of late capitalism. Her work, I suggest, points to new directions this tradition of inquiry may take in the future. Implicit throughout this chapter is the argument that the philosophy of religion cannot be understood separately from black theology; indeed, that it must be approached from the perspective of black theology.

"Race" and "Religion"

Recent efforts to denaturalize the concept of religion have suggested that this concept emerges only with the confrontation of an "other." It is usually implied that this "other" is another culture, but this "other" could also be understood as another race. While an earlier generation of scholars of religion, led by Wilfred Cantwell Smith, located the concept's emergence in rifts between Catholics and Protestants in Europe, a more recent generation of scholars has pointed to evidence suggesting that it was the surprise of encountering those with dramatically different views of God that gave rise to the concept.[1] There is no consensus, however, among these more recent scholars about which particular foreign encounter consolidated the concept. Three candidates have been proposed: the encounter between Judaism and Christianity in late antiquity; sixteenth-century encounters with indigenous communities in the Americas; and nineteenth-century colonial encounters.

While projecting either race or ethnicity onto the ancient world brings with it risks, it also brings with it rewards, adding important dimensions to how we understand these categories.[2] According to Daniel Boyarin, Jewishness in the ancient world was an ethnic identity.[3] You could be a Greek or you could be a Jew, not both. Judaism only became a religion after Christianity had established itself. Christianity created "religion" as a concept where there was no religion before. The components of religion existed, of course, but they only congealed into the category "religion" with Christianity. Previously, religious beliefs and practices were simply characteristics of an ethnic group, along with laws and land. Christianity extracted religious beliefs and practices from this broader mix of beliefs and practices, placing them in the category "religion," which existed independent of ethnic identity. One could have both an ethnic identity and a religious identity—a Greek Christian or a Jewish Christian, for example. Then, in the third century, Jews also adopted the category of "religion" for their own identity, following the Christian example and identifying specific religious beliefs and practices that constituted Judaism separate from Jewish ethnic identity. Boyarin and other scholars have tracked the discourses of heresy that helped to consolidate these religious identities over and above ethnic identities as the conceptual space for "Jewish Christians" slipped away. In this genealogy of the concept of religion, religion supersedes race, offering a new way to identify what may be considered the most important aspect of human identity. The "Jewish Christian" example illustrates the contest over whether race and religion operate in the same domain or separate domains—in other words, whether religion is really separable from race. It is a contingent fact of history that this separation succeeded and that no "Jewish Christians" remain.

Boyarin's discovery of the origins of religion in late antiquity is unusual; more often, the moment of origin is located at an encounter with a previously unknown community.[4] Before this encounter, such accounts hold, there was a continuum of difference between us: those a little different from us, those a bit more different from us, and those quite a bit different from us. Europeans crossing the Atlantic introduced radical discontinuity. The Native Americans they encountered were extraordinarily different in many ways. Making sense of this difference required the invention of new tools for understanding self and other, and it resulted in two: race and religion. Both concepts were invented on both sides of the encounter, by Europeans and by Native Americans, at the same time. Jared Hickman makes this point compellingly, finding it allegorized in the encounter between Robinson Crusoe and Friday in Daniel Defoe's novel. When Crusoe was home, he never had to defend his religious beliefs and practices or even to conceive of them as a religion. On an island, confronted with drastic difference represented by the indigenous Friday, Crusoe realizes that what he has is a religion and that he must be able to articulate it as such. Taking himself to have a religion, Crusoe can share his beliefs and practices, argue about them, and refine them. As Hickman concludes, "Crusoe's previously unself-conscious Christianity thus becomes a self-conscious philosophy of religion in which Christianity is, to some extent, a subordinate point of reference."[5] Now that religion exists, Crusoe can see Christianity as one token of this type—and so engage in second-order inquiry, in the philosophy of religion. At the same time, Crusoe understands his racial distinctiveness: race and the philosophy of religion arrive together. Hickman also shows how the same transformation is happening at the same time on the indigenous side of the encounter, with Native American communities transforming their mythologies to include different peoples with distinctive, disconnected ancestors.

Other scholars locate the invention of religion not in the European encounter with radical difference but in the European conquest and management of radical difference—that is, in colonialism.[6] Before colonialism, in the soon-to-be-colonized context, religious practices and beliefs ran together in a cultural stew, mixing with all of a community's practices and beliefs. Creating a category of religion and removing a ladleful of cultural stew to be placed under this heading had several advantages for colonial administrators. Religion could become an apolitical, so unthreatening, category. Religious experts could be selected so as to leverage the persuasive force of religious idioms for the interests of the colonizers. Fractures could be named and managed, within a community that had been relatively unified, by naming sects. Christian missionaries could present a clear alternative to what was now classed as native religion. That native religion could be molded into the safe, manageable form of Protestantism (or Catholicism) even if it would never achieve Christian greatness—adjudicated by a discourse of comparative theology or philosophy of religion.[7] All aspects of this process of religion-making essentially depend on another element of colonial logic: a racial distinction between the colonizer and the colonized.

The concept of religion may come about through encounters with racial others, but the concept of race also leaned heavily on religion to be seen as plausible and, in some cases, as sacred. The concept of race, like the concept of religion, has a specific history and gained legitimacy for specific reasons. In the most famous case, of North America, it has been thoroughly demonstrated that the transformation of "black" from a color to a subordinate class of people was aided by Christian ideas. For example, the biblical story of Noah's curse of Canaan was interpreted in racial terms. Ham, who was Noah's son and Canaan's father, peered at the drunk Noah's naked body. In response, Noah decreed that Canaan would be a "servant of servants."[8] Ham was seen as black, the ancestor of present-day blacks, so blacks were justly condemned to servitude, according to American defenders of slavery.[9] This is but one of many examples in which religious texts, images, and authorities were invoked to naturalize racial categories: the Atlantic historian Colin Kidd goes so far as to describe race as *"primarily* a theological problem."[10]

Race and religion are connected historically, but they are also connected conceptually.[11] In other words, independent of their origins and development, the concepts of religion and race that we have now, that circulate in the contemporary social imagination, have deep affinities with each other. This is not obvious. Race would seem to name groups of people based on external characteristics, such as skin color, while religion would seem to refer to an internal disposition—to the heart rather than to the skin. Recent scholarship has challenged both of these approaches, with the result that race and religion no longer seem so distinct. If race was once thought a feature of biology, then a harmful fiction to be eliminated, now race is seen as a social construction with very real effects. Those effects include not only stigma and marginalization but also shared values, senses of belonging, and distinctive practices. In other words, rather than approaching race as a claim about individuals that may be proven or disproven, it is more helpful to examine what race does in the world. People act as if there is race and that is what matters, not whether they are right or wrong. Similarly, if religion was once thought to be a feature of the heart or soul—its attunement to the divine, for instance—or a certain set of beliefs, now the practical, material, and communal dimensions of religion are seen as crucial, as well.

When race and religion are cut loose from their anchors in biology and God, respectively, they begin to look quite similar. Both involve sets of practices, values, and beliefs shared by a community that help define a community in opposition to other communities. Both can overdetermine how minority groups are viewed, perpetuating the domination of those wielding power. Blacks and Muslims, in the contemporary Western context, are obvious examples, and examples that illustrate the fuzzy boundaries between these two categories when we consider darker-skinned French Muslims and darker-skinned Muslims in Israel. Both religion and race are also lived realities, to some extent imposed on the individual and to some extent resisted or creatively appropriated by the individual who is understood to be of a certain race or of a certain religion. There are clearly significant differences between religion and race that remain—religion involves formalized authorities and institutions more often than race, for example—but the similarities of form remain striking.

Furthermore, the similarities go beyond isomorphism. Race and religion both shape a world: how we see ourselves, others, and everything around us. They are not just one more aspect of our complex identities; they can each be seen as the definitive aspect of our subjectivity. This is obvious in the case of religion, as there are robust second-order discourses, *theologies*, that allow us to describe ourselves and our worlds in religious terms. That this is also the case for race has only recently become clear, at least in the scholarly literature. It is easiest to see in minority communities. Continually derogatory treatment clearly distorts an individual's self-image and perceptive capacity. This derogatory treatment varies depending on the specific racial dynamics at play. Racial communities manage to survive sustained derogation through a variety of techniques that allow for resilience in the face of seemingly unbearable circumstances. These techniques involve modes of understanding of self and world that counter the distortions inflicted by the racial majority. But it is not only racial minorities that are deeply shaped by race. Majority races—paradigmatically, whites—also suffer from distorted senses of self and perceptions of the world because of race. As Martin Luther King Jr. put it, "hate distorts the personality of the hater"; James Baldwin adds, "[T]he white man is himself in sore need of new standards, which will release him from his confusion and place him once again in fruitful communion with the depths of his own being."[12] Continually treating a class of humans as less than human inevitably disfigures the humanity of the racist herself. Racists in this sense are determined not so much by specific acts but rather by the racist (e.g., white) culture they participate in, a culture that includes not only the subordination of other races but also its own practices, values, and institutions. Race and religion can both be viewed as constitutive of our subjectivity, a conclusion that suggests but does not explain a strong relationship between the two.

In sum, recent scholarship has shown not only that religion and race are concepts that gained currency at specific points in time due to various contingent factors, but also that the genealogies of these two concepts are intertwined. This is a stronger claim than that religion and race are co-constituted, which would suggest only a close relationship at various points in time.[13] To study one without the other or, more specifically, to participate in a tradition of reflection on one but not the other therefore naturalizes both. Even beneath the concepts, in the sets of practices that constitute both, there are deep resonances that confirm the need to study both together. In the sections to follow, I will track how two prominent figures in the philosophy of religion succeed in treating similarly religion and race, but I will also suggest that they do not fully grapple with the shared genealogies of these concepts.

Jacques Derrida

In his later years, Jacques Derrida was fond of calling attention to his identity as an Algerian Jew, a label that blends the racial and the religious.[14] In the French context of his youth, to be Algerian was to be the quintessential racial other and to be Jewish was to be the quintessential religious other. Derrida explicitly racializes his Algerianness, describing himself as "a little black and very Arab Jew."[15] Indeed, this description comes as Derrida recounts his expulsion from school under the Vichy regime in 1942. He does not just happen to be a racial minority; he experiences the pinnacle of racial violence in Europe, the Nazi persecution of the Jews. Derrida's claim to black, Arab, and Jewish identity comes within his "Circumfession," a text offering a Jewish inflection on Augustine's *Confessions*. Derrida's text takes a religious form, and it also discusses religious topics. This book is the first place where Derrida extensively discusses his own identity, and Derrida comes out, as it were, as a racial and a religious minority at the same time, in the same place. He does so in a text composed as a challenge: Derrida was to write something that could not be fit into a systematic exposition of his own thought. Derrida's oeuvre was expansive; to meet the challenge, Derrida turned to himself, to his own life. Race and religion are presented as aspects of that life; as such, they also do not fit with the systematized Derrida. Indeed, they are not just components of that life. Derrida's choice of Augustine as his model puts race and religion at the center of the text and of his life. Augustine was not only religious but also non-European, in fact also Algerian.

One of Derrida's primary philosophical claims is that the attempt to distinguish form and content is always futile, a special case of his central philosophical claim—that every attempt to make rigorous distinctions or systems falls short, leaving an excess that threatens to undermine the distinction or system entirely. In "Circumfession" there is yet another level of recursion. The purpose of the text is to (systematically) demonstrate that Derrida's philosophical point holds for his own philosophy: that any attempt to systematize it falls short. In this light, Derrida is claiming that race and religion have a particularly privileged function in marking that which exceeds system. Derrida provides many names for this destabilizing force; among the most famous are "supplement" and "différance." When this role is named by words we use in ordinary language, Derrida is careful to mark the two distinct senses in which they might be used, the ordinary sense and the destabilizing sense: justice beyond justice, the gift beyond the gift, and so on. Such terms refer to something within a system (i.e., ordinary language) but also point beyond it. This, then, is how we should understand Derrida's references to race and religion, in "Circumfession" and elsewhere. By religion, he does not only mean a religious community, tradition, or belief, but also that which cannot fit into the well-ordered, essentially secular world—that which marks the precariousness of the secular world and threatens to scramble its well-ordered categories. By race, Derrida does not only mean skin color or marginalized community, but also that which cannot fit into the well-ordered, essentially white world, marking the precariousness of whiteness and the possibility of a non-white future. While both race and religion threaten "the system," as it might loosely be called, each term highlights a different aspect of "the system": its whiteness or its secularism. Understood in this way, with race and religion playing the same role in Derrida's critical project, we are implicitly invited to reflect on the ways in which whiteness and secularism are entwined and the ways race and religion are entwined.

Before Derrida turned to religion, and before he reflected on his own "black" identity, he already hinted at the entanglement of race and religion. In his 1971 article "White Mythology: Metaphor in the Text of Philosophy," philosophy is the system that imagines itself to be well-ordered and rational while mythology is the loose thread on which Derrida pulls to unravel the system.[16] "What is metaphysics? A white mythology which assembles and reflects Western culture: the white man takes his own mythology (that is, Indo-European mythology), his *logos*—that is, the *mythos* of his idiom, for the universal form of that which it is still his inescapable desire to call Reason."[17] At the end of the day, all philosophy is mythology: narrative, flexible, unsystematic, fictional, and reflecting the interests of those who circulate it—specifically, whites. But this is not just any story; it is *mythology*, a fundamentally religious story—concealed as its opposite, as entirely secular and rational, as *philosophy*. In this way, it is not just that race and religion (as two of Derrida's loose threads) can disturb the system, but that race and religion can secure the system, making what is a historically and geographically specific way of understanding the world seem natural, timeless, and universal. Colorblind philosophy is actually white mythology. Derrida famously embraces this sort of equivocal significance of his key concepts, pointing to the model of the *pharmakon*, the Greek term both for a poison and for a cure.[18]

Given this equivocation, so fundamental to Derrida's critical project, it is tempting to suggest that Derrida actually has nothing at all substantial to say about race and religion as lived experiences or social practices; he is, rather, concerned with them as concepts, part of the constellation of concepts that make up the ruling ideas of our day. The political implication of his project, in this reading, would be a challenge to the powers that be through a challenge to the purported stability of their ideas—their ideas that are sold to us as inevitable but that Derrida shows are deeply precarious. Yet Derrida also intervenes on concrete social issues involving racism in a way that takes sides; he does not confine himself to the indirect political work of destabilizing ideas. He advocated for the anti-apartheid struggle, mobilizing fellow intellectuals in support of Nelson Mandela through conferences and publications. In an essay on Mandela, Derrida explores how Mandela was loyal to the law and how he demonstrated that whites themselves, despite their claims to lawfulness, were the ones unfaithful to the law.[19] Here, as in "Force of Law," Derrida's essay that most directly focused on the topic of law, what is commended is a higher law, a law beyond the law of the land, and Derrida holds up moments when we catch a glimpse of such a law—including when Mandela exposes the limits of the law at his own trial.[20] In a sense, Derrida embraces a natural law theory, a commitment to a law whose provenance is beyond the secular world, whose provenance might even be called "divine."[21] He advances a religious idea in order to overthrow the racist regime. Yet even in a concrete political context defined by racism, it seems as though Derrida, using religion, wants to be rid of the idea of race, wants the postracial, rather than to advance an account of racial justice. In the conceptual realm, emphasizing the play of concepts like religion and race might have a powerful intellectual effect, but it remains unclear whether the postracial, postsecular society Derrida would seem to commend is a just society, as he seems to assume.

This tension between Derrida's aspirations for philosophical work concerning religion and race and concrete social realities was even more acute in Derrida's youth. Edward Baring has recently pointed out that Derrida's embrace of an Algerian Jewish identity came quite late in his life.[22] As a young man, Derrida aligned himself with the French colonists in Algeria, the Pieds-Noir. While he did embrace liberal politics, he was certainly not a radical, and he became defensive when Leftist intellectuals attacked the colonists. Like other colonists, Derrida's education during his Algerian childhood was entirely French, following the French curriculum and taught by Paris-education instructors. He transitioned seamlessly to the center of the French intellectual world, to the École Normale Supériere and the Sorbonne, and he remained there for his entire career, even while he was loudly advertising his purported marginality. In other words, in practice, Derrida was very much aligned with white, European Catholic or post-Catholic culture and politics, and he was appreciative of the Algerian resistance just as he was appreciative of Mandela—because they challenged the purported closure of a system, not because they brought about structural transformation that would result in racial justice.

Giorgio Agamben

Race and religion are front and center in Agamben's writings, but he rarely dwells on the connection between them.[23] Indeed, one way of reading

Agamben's most influential work, *Homo Sacer*, is as tracking a certain social logic that has existed in the West for more than two millennia, a social logic on which race and religion supervene.[24] What is foundational for Agamben is this logic; concepts like race and religion are content that fill in a preexisting form. While Agamben offers myriad historical examples, he is not concerned with historical causation. His historical examples, for the most part not given chronologically, simply exemplify the underlying social logic and bring into view further features of this social logic. Indeed, Agamben does not straightforwardly describe the social logic; it comes into view one glimpse at a time, each glimpse from a different angle, offered by a different historical example. For Agamben, race and religion are features of specific historical circumstances, so they enter into his writing here and there, in some of the historical vignettes he provides but not in others. At the end of the day, however, race and religion are essentially connected for Agamben because both race and religion play the same role in the social logic of the West.[25] They have no *philosophical* significance outside of this social logic, even though race and religion may have *historical* significance. Agamben is not concerned about God or evil or the good life; he is concerned about how claims about these religious concepts consistently show up in the same configuration at quite different moments in the history of the West and how racist concepts show up in exactly the same configuration.

What is the social logic that Agamben argues is so fundamental? Where Derrida valorizes concepts that are both included in a system and undermine a system, with the system remaining highly abstract, Agamben explores what this would mean in terms of society. What would it mean for a part of society, or an individual member of a society, to be both inside and outside at once? The social logic that Agamben identifies holds that for any society to function it must have certain elements in this special position, elements that are at once inside and outside. In a sense, *Homo Sacer* is a catalog of such elements with suggestive remarks about how they are necessary for the very existence of the societies where they are found. One such element, which is neither explicitly religious nor explicitly racialized, is the sovereign: "The paradox of sovereignty consists in the fact the sovereign is, at the same time, outside and inside the juridical order."[26] In other words, the sovereign is a member of a society, subject to the laws of that society, but the sovereign also stands above that society, capable of suspending those very laws (recall Carl Schmitt's infamous definition of the sovereign as he who decides on the exception). Agamben cleverly shows how the sovereign has a mirror image in the person or people subject to the sovereign's extralegal will. Whether they are offered clemency or arbitrarily detained, these figures are also inside and outside the law at once. Indeed, as touched, in a sense, by sovereignty, these figures themselves acquire an aura of sovereign power—and the sovereign himself always brings with him some of the abjection of his mirror image. This dynamic, Agamben shows, is often associated with the language of religion. Sacred man, *homo sacer*, labels this equivocal figure, abject and in a way sovereign.

Among the various approaches Agamben takes to describing the social logic of which *homo sacer* serves as the paradigm is an extended discussion of taboo in the history of religions. Marshaling the theories of William Robertson Smith, Sigmund Freud, Marcel Mauss, Émile Durkheim, and others, Agamben notes a "mix of veneration and horror" at certain people or objects—those that are essential to a community but also rejected by that community.[27] In other historical vignettes, Agamben describes how *homo sacer* can be killed but not sacrificed: sacrifice would imply that such figures are members of the society they have been excluded from, but that very exclusion entails their membership in the sense that the society still can make decrees concerning them, even if those decrees authorize their death. Such individuals are treated not as political subjects but as "bare life," stripped of social relations and exposed to death. Concerning the flip side of the logic of exception, Agamben develops Ernst Kantorowicz's reflections on the strangely dual figure of the sovereign. Like Christ's simultaneously divine and human nature, the medieval king is thought to have both a human body, subject to illness and death, and a political or mystical body that stands above the limitations of the human body. In this way, the sovereign is also inside and outside the law, both part of and above human society. This is made possible by the "mystical" body, by the Christian theological imagination, although such religious elements are contingent rather than necessary features of the logic in question.

While Agamben's many examples come from varied historical moments, and while he does not make any claims about historical causation, Agamben does make one crucial periodizing gesture. While the social logic that Agamben describes persists with the advent of modernity, modernity brings changes in social conditions that have important effects. Sovereign power is no longer exercised on individuals only in unusual circumstances. In the modern world, all life is politicized in two senses, both of which involve race. In the first sense, sovereign power extends beyond political life to bare life. Following Michel Foucault, Agamben observes how modern nations are concerned with the health of their population, with birth control and euthanasia, with census figures, and with issues that previously would have been considered outside of the political sphere. Among these issues, notably, is race: nations become concerned with classifying and organizing the races of their populations. Yet the social logic that Agamben considers foundational persists, and this is the second way in which life is politicized in modernity. There are still those who are both inside and outside political society, but now their number has grown and their condition has worsened. They are found, most notably, in concentration camps but also, more recently, in Guantanamo Bay.[28] Those in the camp are defined by a political regime but stripped of their political rights, reduced to bare life. An important but ultimately contingent feature of those interned in camps is their race: Jews or Arabs, for example, or, in today's U.S. immigration detention camps, Latinos. The ultimate worry of *Homo Sacer* is that the exceptional space of the camp will become the model for all state management of life: we will all become Jews, we will all be racialized. Put another way, the social logic that once produced the sacred now, in modernity, produces race, and this has potentially dire consequences.

There is another thread that runs through Agamben's work linking race and religion. One of the features of the premodern sovereign and his inverse is the blurred line between human and animal. The bandit, excluded from political community and exposed to death, was once considered a wolf-man, Agamben asserts. Inversely, Agamben points to myths that associate the werewolf and the sovereign, featuring kings transforming into wolves and back into kings—again, blurring the line between the animal and the human. This is a theme to which Agamben devotes *The Open: Man and Animal*, where he argues that the division between the human and the animal is essential:

> It is more urgent to work on these divisions, to ask in what way—within man—has man been separated from non-man, and the animal from the human, than it is to take positions on the great issues, on so-called human rights and values. And perhaps even the most luminous sphere of our relations with the divine depends, in some way, on that darker one which separates us from the animal.[29]

Agamben shows how the distinction he is interested in has been a perpetual concern of Jewish and Christian thought, and the concern takes on a malicious, secular form today with the camp, that space which blurs the boundary between animal and human. This boundary between the human and the animal is, in an important sense, about race: defining the human race and deciding who is excluded. Racialization, after all, is about exclusion from (what is imagined to be) the human race. Agamben urges us to think explicitly about this question of race and to make use of religious traditions in doing so—otherwise, with secular questions drawing on secular resources, we all become Jews. In sum, for Agamben, the philosophy of religion and the philosophy of race are both gateways to something deeper, to the questions that really matter—to the question of the social and, perhaps, to justice.

Secularism, Multiculturalism, and the Philosophy of Religion

Derrida and Agamben both reject the timelessness and universality of the concept of religion. They both demonstrate how religion and race are deeply entwined. And they both offer models for how philosophy that is concerned with religion can investigate religion and race together, cognizant of their entwined genealogy. Yet the issues addressed by these two authors are quickly being superseded by a new set of concerns motivated by rapidly changing social and especially economic conditions. One need not believe that religion is part of a superstructure that rests on an economic base to recognize that the dramatic shifts in production and consumption in recent years have affected culture, including race and religion. Specifically, the individual is no longer a consumer only in the grocery store; the consumer mentality privileging individual choice based on personal desire extends to romantic relationships, schools, hometown, job, and identity, including racial and religious identity. While this consumer mentality is certainly at odds with the realities of many who lack the financial or cultural capital to acquire what they desire, it is widely disseminated through media, government and cultural institutions, and social networks. The result is that race and religion, as identities to be chosen, must compete in the marketplace of identities and activities—yoga classes, charity runs, Facebook games, Caribbean cruises—and so are themselves directly or indirectly shaped into the form of their competitors.[30]

Closely related to the pressures of the identity marketplace is the now regnant ideology of diversity. According to this set of ideas, we are all different, and that is beautiful. It is to be celebrated. Culture was imagined as monolithic for too long, repressing valuable (in both moral and economic senses) differences; today we can be ourselves. This is not difference unlimited: there are discrete differences from which we are to choose, different tokens of the same type, different responses to the same question on the government questionnaire—male/female/transgender; white/black/Asian/Latino; Christian/Jew/Muslim/Buddhist/Hindu/atheist; and so on. This cultural embrace of diversity creates another set of pressures on religious and racial groups to conform to an ostensibly neutral model so as to fit comfortably next to a box on a government questionnaire.[31] Of course, no such neutrality exists: such standpoints simply mask the interests of the dominant group—whites, men, Protestants—allowing them to subtly exert pressure on minority or marginalized groups that stray too far from comfortable beliefs or practices. Or, from a more Marxist perspective, it is a neoliberal economic system that uses the language of diversity to manage unruly subjects, subjects who take their identities so seriously that it prevents them from laboring or consuming properly.

In this social and economic landscape, secularism and multiculturalism are the ideologies that come to manage religion and race. They implicitly offer a set of standards by which to judge which religious or racial expressions are proper and which are improper, all under the label of ostensible neutrality. In so doing they shape religion and race, with the result that any study of religion and race today will go wrong if it presumes to access its objects directly. Studies of religion and race must thoroughly account for the ways that their objects are not autonomous but are deeply and thoroughly shaped by these ideological pressures. Moreover, these same pressures shape the perspective of the academy at the present. So, for example, contemporary historiography and ethnography are naturally disposed to find religions and races in the far corners of the world and the far reaches of history that look curiously similar to the religion and race licit under our present regime of secularism and multiculturalism.

The philosophy of religion has so far had little to say about secularism and multiculturalism. In fact, there are ways in which Derrida and Agamben, as exemplars of recent scholarship in philosophy of religion, fit perfectly with the secularist and multiculturalist ideological program. Derrida embraces difference and delights in undermining monolithic systems. Certainly Derrida would resist any fixed set of differences—for example, on a government questionnaire—but the critical practice that Derrida performs and commends functions not at the level of social life but at the level of ideology. Secularism says: show us how your tradition complicates—adds spice to—the historically dominant Christian assumptions. Multiculturalism says: show us how your Latino or indigenous or Filipino identity complicates historically dominant white culture. But those intellectual questions result, when implemented by institutions, in questionnaires with boxes to check.

Moreover, for both Derrida and Agamben, religion and race have only contingent roles to play in their philosophical projects. They are two differences among many. Derrida is also deeply interested in gender, sexuality, nationality, immigration, ghosts, and much else as threads that can be pulled to undermine the system; Agamben explicates many other details of the historical and cultural snapshots he presents in order to develop the underlying social logic in which he is centrally interested. For both Derrida and Agamben, then, religion and race are two among many categories of difference. They are features of the world that point to what is really significant. Religion and race do not offer ways of seeing the world, and they do not name traditions.

What would it look like to approach the philosophy of religion in a manner that is cognizant of the entwined genealogies of religion and race but that is also cognizant of the way that religion and race are carefully managed in the present? Such an approach would explore the aspects of religion that are the most difficult to translate into a secularist idiom and the aspects of race that are most difficult to translate into a multiculturalist idiom.[32] Such an approach would also explore the dialectical struggle between an unmanageable knot of religion and race and the attempts to individuate and manage these categories. The philosophy of religion would be a deeply political project because it would recover something especially threatening to today's hegemonic ideology and expose the workings of that ideology. In a sense, the philosophy of religion would do in the world of social practices what Derrida attempts to do in the world of ideas: locate a knot of practices that is never smoothed over by ideology and ask what it might mean for this knot to thwart the system. The philosophy of religion has a distinctive role as second-order reflection on the always vexed process of translation between religious-racial ideas contaminated by secularism-multiculturalism and a nonreligious community of inquiry also contaminated by secularism-multiculturalism. Theology as a discipline has itself been subject to internalized secularism and to multiculturalism.[33] At its best, the philosophy of religion can help theology recognize and overcome these problems while itself being informed by the currents of religious and racial thought and expression that have long resisted secularism and multiculturalism. In other words, the philosophy of religion must listen and learn from black theology.

Sylvia Wynter

To explore what this style of philosophy of religion responsive to the challenges of secularism and multiculturalism might resemble, I turn in conclusion to the example of Jamaican writer and feminist theorist Sylvia Wynter. While not trained as a philosopher, Wynter has become a central figure in black feminist philosophy. She writes extensively about religion, but she has not as yet been embraced by the religious studies or theological academy, and she remains marginal, at most, to conversations in the philosophy of religion. Wynter is part of a group of black studies scholars who unapologetically embrace the uniqueness of black experience and the unique evil of anti-black racism. From her perspective, blacks do not just happen to be suffering violence at various points in time. Rather, anti-blackness is central to the metaphysics of the West, and anti-blackness will not go away until that metaphysics is overturned. Ameliorative social programs and even reparations are not enough. Wynter carefully examines how anti-blackness became so fundamental to the West, and in her investigations she shows how anti-blackness and religion have a deep, shared history.

Wynter describes the colonial encounter as coinciding with a shift in how Western man (the masculine gender is particularly significant for her) viewed himself. Once, in the feudal world, society was ordered hierarchically. God guaranteed this order. Then, with the rise of the nation state and its intellectual champions, God's role was to guarantee the rationality of each citizen (rational nature displacing noble blood), and in so doing God secured the position of humans as distinct from the natural world. When Columbus landed in 1492, he was acting according to this logic in claiming the newly found land for Spain and the newly found goods to repay his financial backers.[34] Most significantly, with the colonial encounter, "The construct of *Nigger* as well as that of the non-European *native* now came to serve as the inversion of the divinely instituted realm of the supernatural and therefore as the extrasocietal source."[35] Instead of humanity and the social order being defined by a God above, they came to be defined by subhumans below, by blacks and indigenous people whose nonhumanity secured the humanity of Europeans and whose exclusion from the social structure secured that structure. Wynter goes on to argue that this shift also involved the replacement of religious language with scientific language. Instead of theologically defined divine superiority there now was biologically defined black and indigenous inferiority. Wynter tracks the consequences of this linked process of secularization and racialization, including its psychic effects. In Christian Europe, subjects defined themselves against non-Christians, and that included their pre-baptismal selves. Each individual was split against herself, saved but still the same person who was once damned. This earlier self represents "the embodiment of 'fallen natural humanity' enslaved to Original Sin"; with the colonial encounter, it is now the black or indigenous who fills this role.[36] The result, postsecularization and postcolonialism, is that black and indigenous people who aspire to respectability must despise their blackness or indigeneity.

The thread that runs through this transformation, as Wynter describes it, is the figure of Man. Today, Man does not refer to humanity but rather to the Western bourgeoisie; this identification is part of a racial and theological history of exclusion. Wynter charges scholars who wish to be genuinely critical with the task of envisioning what comes after Man. In one formulation, she suggests that the category of the human has been contaminated by its association with the category of Man, given the latter's racial-theological origins, and she opens the question of how an uncontaminated category of the human might be recovered. Wynter acknowledges that this cannot happen by simply adding minority voices to the conversation that would purport to show more dimensions of our humanity. It is the "order of discourse" itself that must be overturned, because the current (anti-black, anti-indigenous) discourse can accommodate and even be strengthened by incorporating minority voices.[37] Wynter labels the critical practice she commends "disenchanting discourse," a challenge to explicitly or implicitly religious concepts that also functions as a confrontation with racism. Such disenchantment should proceed from multiple directions, for the exclusions created by the category of Man are many. The multiple lines of protest that flourished in the 1960s started this critical task, but they did not end it; ultimately 1960s critique was incorporated into the order of discourse itself, further enchanting it and further strengthening its hold.[38]

It might seem as though Wynter uses religion and race instrumentally, like Derrida and Agamben, as two differences among many that point toward a deeper philosophical problem. But for Wynter there is no philosophical problem deeper than the construction of Man as the hero of our order of discourse—that is, of our way of seeing the world. This construction grows out of a religious, specifically Christian, way of seeing the world in terms of the damned and the saved, and this construction takes on new meaning with the colonial encounter, as blacks and indigenous people play the role of the damned. For Wynter, the philosophy of religion must investigate religious and racial concepts together because of their shared genealogy and because it is the powers that be today, not the truth, that would separate them. Wynter's work demonstrates the value of engaging with the philosophy of religion as a tradition because of the continuing power of this tradition. But her work also suggests the importance of investigating religion and race together in new, unexpected, extracanonical sites that might provide novel ways of envisioning the human beyond Man. For example, she points to the fundamental Aztec theological commitment to a "flow of life" both on earth and in the heavens. According to Aztec belief, the world was created through gods' self-sacrifice, resulting in a sacred debt for humans. This debt could be repaid by the Aztecs' performance of sacrifice, including human sacrifice, which would then restore the flow of life. Wynter notes:

> Columbus's behaviors were not unlike the ritual acts of sacrifice of the Aztecs. Their behaviors, too, were impelled by an ethico-behavioral system based on securing what seemed to them to be the imperative goal of "ensuring the good of the Commonwealth," and to do this by maintaining, as their founding supraordinate goal prescribed that they should do, "the flow of life." Columbus's equally Janus-faced behaviors were to be no less prescribed by the emergent religio-secular political and mercantile goal of the state, which Columbus would come to see as the vehicle both for the spread of the faith and for the advancement of his own status. So the Aztecs' "flow of life" imperative would become for Columbus and the Spaniards (to the Aztecs' horror and astonishment) the imperative of maintaining a "flow of gold."[39]

Through such analyses, a pluralized philosophy of religion can complicate and destabilize the narrative of the colonizer, of the European, of the white—and of the Christian. Before they were Man, the Aztecs were human and Columbus was human, grappling with the religious ideas of their communities and their own self-interests. This is what the philosophy of religion at its best can discern, but this can only be discerned once the conceptual and physical violence of religion and race, twinned, is fully appreciated. At its best, then, the philosophy of religion extends the project of black theology, offering resources for the critique of intellectual projects that complement the cultural criticism entailed by black theology.

PART II
Questions

CHAPTER 5

What Is Black Tradition?

Barack Obama was going to write a book about the politics of race. His election as the first black president of the *Harvard Law Review* had brought him media attention and a book contract. He imagined that his book would cover public policy issues: affirmative action, civil rights laws, and so on.[1] But when Obama started trying to write, he reports, he was overtaken by recollections and tales, particularly of his father. "Compared to this flood of memories," he writes, "all my well-ordered theories seemed insubstantial and premature."[2] His story of race politics became "a story of race and inheritance," as the book's subtitle proclaims. It became a story of his (successful) search for an inheritance, which corresponded with his (successful) search for his father. The book opens with his father's gaping absence: a phone call announcing his father's death. The book ends with his father's presence, with the void filled: his relatives' detailed description of who his father really was (and who his father's father was) and so what Obama's inheritance is.

In between, Obama's narrative is driven by his unsuccessful attempts to find substitute fathers.[3] His mother, his Indonesian stepfather, his white grandfather, the black nationalists he meets in college, Harold Washington, and Obama himself all fall short. All are revealed to be inadequate fathers. When he does write a policy book, *The Audacity of Hope*, Obama frames each policy stance he endorses as the mature middle, available to him precisely because he has found his own true father.[4] His opponents on both sides of the political spectrum have daddy issues. They either are longing for the imagined order and discipline imposed by strict fathers or they are rebelling against that strictness. Obama himself, who relates properly to his father, who relates properly to his inheritance, is able to see clearly and truly—that the truth is always halfway between two extremes.

I want to investigate that conjunction named by Obama, "race and inheritance," and how it creates the horizon for black politics. More specifically, I want to investigate the antinomies of blackness and transmission, then to ponder theological and aesthetic responses to those antinomies. Obama's narrative is compelling because in it transmission seems so natural—parent to child, father to son, past to present to future.[5] It leans on conventional wisdom: where we came from and who our people are make us who we are, and ignoring or repressing this can only lead to disaster. In the United States, transmission is an anxious narrative. The precariously short history of America means that stories of American inheritance must be told all the more forcefully, and the force of their telling is only strengthened when their content contends with and so pacifies that history (most famously, *Gatsby*). Obama, of course, intends to make himself the protagonist in a great American story, and the ability to resolve the ambiguities of his inheritance does precisely the work that the nation needs done. But this nation, this America, is white America. Whereas transmission is so obvious and apparently natural in the European context that it requires little work, for America transmission needs work because whiteness is so unnatural. Showing that transmission from father to son can successfully occur in America—transmission of blood and values and memories and hopes—means affirming the precarious legitimacy of whiteness.

For black America transmission is both impossible and essential. This is the prime antinomy of transmission. Black fathers are absent—a statement that should not be read, as it too commonly is, as pejorative. Black fathers are absent because the role of black father in America is impossible to inhabit. Black fathers have been *absented*, through the disruptions of slavery, the undermining of paternal authority accompanying segregation, and the physical confinement and harassment of so many black fathers in our current era of mass incarceration—ruptures in transmission all. Because black fathers have historically been absented, their status, ontologically if you will, is that of being absent—better, under erasure. If the role of the father in American social imagination is to impose norms on the child that prepare the child for the norms of social life writ large, then the black father will necessarily fail in a world that does not recognize blacks as capable of exercising authority. The world (or nation) is this way because of history, regardless of whether that history happened to this particular black father. Obama's saccharine story of substitute fathers has them each incompletely fulfilling the role of father; the black American story of fatherhood is one in which substitute fathers are often violently imposed by the white power structure or by the state. Perhaps we can say: black fathers are absented today so that the state can assume the role of Great White Father (the role that Obama himself assumed upon his election). A black counternarrative of transmission, of failed transmission, would tell of the varied violence of norms imposed by substitute fathers, each confirming with all the more certainty the impossibility of black fatherhood—the impossibility of transmission.

To resist the paralysis caused by this impossibility of transmission, to resist wallowing in abjection, it is necessary to reimagine transmission in black America. It is necessary to answer the question, What is black tradition?, in a new way. This does not mean telling a black version of the American transmission story, as Obama does. Such mimicry leads to deep pathology, ultimately to the negation of the value of black life. Rejecting the American transmission story means rejecting its investment in naturalizing, in proving blood ties, father to son. Whiteness and the heteronormative are entwined in the American transmission narrative, and a black counternarrative promises to short-circuit both. Stories of the presence of the African past in America, from the mythical histories written by nineteenth-century blacks to the Garveyites to the Nation of Islam to the biomythography of Audre Lorde, affirm the transmission of the past into the present and the duty to transmit it to the future, all without mimicking the American investment in finding fathers and forefathers. Such narratives respond to an essential need to locate oneself, to locate a contemporary community—to refuse the refusal of black history without telling a white history of blacks. But such narratives also tempt us to forget the ontological impossibility of transmission, of black fatherhood, indeed, of blackness.

Some would resist this temptation by telling a story of transmission that begins with a dark past, a past that transmits only a message of negation. This is melancholia: an adamantine attachment to past loss, paradigmatically, in the Middle Passage. (Saidiya Hartman's title says it all: *Lose Your Mother*.) In such stories, the content of the past is purely negative, so the presence of the past can only be in disturbances, in hauntings (*Beloved*).

Such a narrative is Obama's, inverted. Instead of a happy resolution, the father found, there is perennial irresolution, the mother forever absent. Does the latter narrative succeed (at refusing the allure of whiteness, at invigorating black souls in the present) where the former fails? I worry, with Stephen Best, that melancholic transmission is still transmission, and something deep about transmission itself may be the problem.[6] Narratives of melancholic transmission presuppose and reinforce the need for the past in the present or the superlative power of the past for the present. Might the apparent neutrality of such need, such power, also conceal specifically American, read white, concerns?

So far, I have been considering transmission in what we might call social rather than political terms. Politically, emphasis on transmission seems to run counter to liberalism; indeed, it evokes the conservatism of old. Such conservatism values tradition—in Chesterton's famous formulation, it gives votes to the dead. Liberalism, with its emphasis on freedom and equality, has no place for the past: it is freedom and equality for us, here, now. Indeed, the social versus political distinction is essential from the perspective of liberalism, for it allows transmission to be understood as a social and *not* a political issue. American (white) liberalism cleverly deals with transmission by asserting that the content of what is transmitted is identical with the content of liberalism. In this way, transmission poses no threat to liberalism (as it does in Europe) because any appeal to the past, to the forefathers, will, understood rightly, simply affirm the liberal principles of the present, principles that have their own independent basis. The appeal of transmission to black Americans has been, in part, its ability to undermine this account of American liberalism, for the content of the American past from the black perspective so obviously is not the same as the content of liberalism. Freedom and equality have not always been affirmed. Moreover, transmission presents blacks, politically, an opportunity to resist. If melancholic transmission makes the past haunt the present socially, it could direct the energy of frightened response into political protest, turning the haunted into the haunting, black specters telling the world of America's failures. At the same time, within the black community, transmission reaffirms the power of existing black political institutions and social institutions with political impact (universities, clubs, churches, professional associations). These institutions tend to be far from radical. This is the conservative face of transmission, the votes given to the dead.

If the antinomies of transmission are unpalatable and irresolvable, for black Americans, the obvious alternative would seem to be brotherhood (classically, fraternity). Instead of the vexing impossibility of black fatherhood, black brotherhood seems achievable and desirable. Implicit in brotherhood is the ideal of equality (though ambiguously: equality between blacks or between all?). Brotherhood suggests the horizontal rather than the vertical. Instead of receiving the wisdom of the past and passing it down to those who come after, brotherhood suggests collective endeavor defined by us, here, now. Yet brotherhood faces the same basic antinomy of transmission for black Americans: it is both essential and impossible. The historical prohibitions on black sociality and the consequent pathologies of those black communities that do exist result in what Cornel West has diagnosed as "Black nihilism."[7] The rhetoric of brotherhood conceals the (forced) reality of suspicion and atomization, the ontological reality that black being is impossible, and the consequence that collectivities recognizing black beings are, too, impossible. Brotherhood is also essential: when the white world denies the possibility of black life, the only way for black life to be affirmed is by creating the black collectivities that reject that denial, that affirm the impossible (that this could be done individually, existentially, is obviously a deception of whiteness).

Not only does the ideal of brotherhood give rise to the same antinomies as transmission, it also represses the relationship to the past, flattening the past from a living presence into, at most, a list of lessons to be accepted or rejected as need be. Narratives of transmission, in contrast, fold into themselves narratives of sociality. The relationship to the past is always shared (put too pithily: brotherhood implies shared fatherhood). This is why (white) America must find freedom and equality in the past just as freedom and equality define the present polity: the present polity needs affirmation from its parent. Black counternarratives of transmission, those stories of lost parents, create fraternities of orphans, joined in their shared mourning. Curiously, narratives of black sociality have received much more critical attention than narratives of black transmission, but my contention is that the latter has primacy. It is by working through the antinomies of transmission that the consequent antinomies of sociality can then be clarified and then that new visions of black politics can begin to emerge. Community supervenes on tradition.

Theological Transmission

In the opening pages of *The Souls of Black Folk*, W. E. B. Du Bois announces his project in that majestic book, and he announces it in terms that sound like transmission: "[T]he spiritual striving of the freedmen's sons is the travail of the souls whose burden is almost beyond the measure of their strength, but who bear it in the name of an historical race, in the name of this the land of their fathers' fathers."[8] There are sons and fathers, there is past and future, and there is a present that bears the responsibility of passing meaning down through the generations. But note how these fathers and sons are configured. In fact *we*, contemporary black Americans, are the sons, the "freedmen's sons," whose inner lives Du Bois will describe. It is not our fathers, or our father's fathers, who transmit wisdom to us. Rather, it is *their land* (America) and *their race* that motivate black Americans in the present. Finally, and crucially, we ourselves are not merely a conduit for the past to sweep into the future. We, black Americans, have "souls." We are three-dimensional, as it were. We ourselves, the "sons," have desires. These desires are hampered by racism, but we are motivated nonetheless by the past (*not* by our fathers). In short, Du Bois does not present a story of smooth transition from past to present to future. He does put past, present, and future in relation to each other, but the force of the past is not overbearing; racism is overbearing. This alternative approach to transmission Du Bois gives religious names, here "spiritual strivings."

Thinking transmission differently, or thinking an alternative to transmission, is a theme that recurs in Du Bois's writings under the banner of the theological. It is vividly present in his juxtaposition of a chapter entitled, "Of the Faith of the Fathers" and the next, "Of the Passing of the First-Born," in *Souls*.[9] In the former, Du Bois describes the African American religious life he encounters in the rural South as involving "pythian madness," "stamping, shrieking, and shouting."[10] But he also describes the role black churches play as the social centers of communities, offering education, insurance societies, opportunities for women's leadership, a space for mass meetings, and more. Du Bois tells a history of black religion and its repression that contextualizes these two extremes, and he suggests that a middle way ought to be found. But the realization of such a middle path is entirely unpredictable, he asserts; it will come "some day," but no one knows which day, and no one can cause it to come today or tomorrow. This "awakening" Du Bois describes as emerging once "the deep religious feeling of the real Negro heart, the stirring, unguided might of powerful human souls who have lost the guiding star of the past and are seeking in the great night a new religious idea" is finally loosed.[11] For Du Bois, then, blacks are unmoored from the past, although it is important for us to understand the past, and we await an unpredictable moment in the future when we will emerge "out of the Valley of the Shadow of Death." In our souls in the present we already have a foretaste of this future to come, in our "deep religious feeling"—a feeling often distorted in the past. Rejecting (or reimagining) transmission, Du Bois finds discontinuity between past, present, and future, discontinuity that can only be expressed theologically, "the faith of the fathers," a messianic "awakening" in the future. In the present, ineffably linking the present with past and future, is a "deep religious feeling" that "broods silently."

Du Bois uses religion to remedy the antinomies of transmission, to express the impossibility and necessity of transmission for blacks. He uses a specific type of theological language: the messianic. Too often the messianic is confused with the prophetic in studies of black culture.[12] The latter has attracted much attention as a description of the intersection of black religion and politics, as popularized by Cornel West. According to West, who is in fact (not so humbly) describing his own position, "[P]rophetic pragmatism acknowledges the inescapable and inexpungible character of tradition, the burden and buoyancy of that which is transmitted from the past to the present. The process of transmittance is one of socialization and appropriation, of acculturation and construction."[13] Prophecy is about continuity: discerning the values of the past, showing how they mismatch the present, and pointing to the consequences of that mismatch for the future. The consequences could be good, reaching the land of milk and honey, or they could be dire, fire and brimstone, if the mismatch persists. In other words, prophecy is about knowing fathers rightly, knowing the wisdom of our forefathers, and it is about raising sons rightly, passing that wisdom down to them.

The messianic, in contrast, is about discontinuity, about those elements of the past that do not fit into historical narratives and those elements of the future that are not thinkable in the present.[14] From the perspective of the messianic, there is no clear path from here to the land of milk and honey, but there is work to do: the work of preparing ourselves for when the Messiah arrives, whenever that may be. This preparatory work includes cleansing ourselves of all that distorts our souls, which includes looking rightly at our past. It does not mean dwelling on the past, or thinking that we bear a responsibility to transmit the wisdom of our fathers to our sons. The lives of our sons are always underdetermined, from the messianic perspective, and we should not wish to pass on to them anything of ours with one exception, that ineffable "deep religious feeling" that characterizes the human (or black?) soul. Politically, the messianic is open to revolution, to the world being turned upside down. Moreover, while prophecy is practiced by the elite and consumed by the masses, the messianic names a practice accessible to the masses, a practice of preparation for radical transformation.

Du Bois develops his account of the messianic in varied places in his many writings, including, notably, in his short stories about the coming of a dark Jesus to the South (the world is not prepared for the messiah, who is rejected) and in *Dark Princess*, which culminates in the birth of the protagonists' child, proclaimed, in the novel's final line, "Messenger and Messiah to all the Darker Worlds!" In two of Du Bois's most famous texts, "Conservation of the Races" and his Fisk Commencement speech, he quotes from the final lines of Tennyson's "In Memoriam." The poem, which commemorates the death of a friend, concludes:

That God, which ever lives and loves,
One God, one law, one element,
And one far-off divine event,
To which the whole creation moves.

The messianic event animates all of the world, even if it is "far-off." Faith in God is faith in this event, faith that transmission will be disrupted, that radical transformation is possible, that a foretaste of this radical transformation is already present in human souls or black souls. In "Conservation of the Races," Du Bois writes that blacks have "a spiritual message" to offer civilization. This message is not the wisdom of fathers but the hope of mothers. Blacks "*must* be inspired with the Divine faith of our black mothers, that out of the blood and dust of battle will march a victorious host, a mighty nation, a peculiar people, to speak to the nations of earth a Divine truth that shall make them free."[15] Unlike fathers, who transmit norms and values, mothers witness to the divine; they have an infectious "deep religious feeling" that entails a stance toward a future triumphant. The proper response to these mothers is preparation for this coming messianic age. Du Bois has specific prescriptions for this preparation: "[I]t is our duty to conserve our physical powers, our intellectual endowments, our spiritual ideals; as a race we must strive by race organization, race solidarity, by race unity to the realization of that broader humanity."[16] Organizing our community is how we must prepare for the messiah. This is difficult work, as Du Bois describes in his 1898 commencement address at Fisk: "It is not easy to guard the sacred image, to keep alive holy fire that lights and lightens life."[17] Yet it is necessary, for if this work is abandoned, if the coming of the messiah is forgotten, "life is death."[18]

"Of the Passing of the First Born" is Du Bois's most dramatic and personal articulation of the messianic. It begins with an epigraph from Swinburn that reads, in part,

> The voice of the child's blood crying yet,
> WHO HATH REMEMBERED ME? WHO HATH FORGOTTEN?
> Thou hast forgotten, O summer swallow,
> But the world shall end when I forget.[19]

In these lines we see transmission upside down. Now it is the future, the child, who must be remembered. It is the coming of that child who will, one day, transform our horizon of possibility, who will allow our "deep religious feeling" to encompass our whole lives, that keeps our world in the present alive. In the short life of his own son, in remembering that life, Du Bois models such remembrance of the future. The messianism of his text is unmistakable, clearly drawing on the Christian tradition. The chapter opens, "Unto you a child is born"; Du Bois describes his wife, the child's mother, as "a transfigured woman"; and Du Bois declares that he and his wife "were not far from worshipping this revelation of the divine."[20] This image of divinity was so different from the world Du Bois had known, so strange that his son's existence was "ludicrous." The child's eyes "peer into my soul," Du Bois reports, and he later reflects, "[T]hat yonder deep unworldly look that ever and anon floated past his eyes was peering far beyond this narrow Now."[21] Looking back at those eyes, Du Bois saw "a land whose freedom is to us a mockery."[22] The child was at once inside and outside of the world, inside and outside of time. With his death, that embodied window into a world would come closed; our world was unready, unwilling to accept it. At his son's funeral, onlookers shouted, "Niggers!" While Du Bois puts his son's story at the heart of *Souls*, his own father is notably absent. Du Bois did elsewhere tell the story of his own past—for example, in *Dusk of Dawn*, sharing his family tree in the service of describing the complicated mixings that make up the experience of race in America. Yet Du Bois did not seek out his own father, who had left his mother when he was a child, preferring instead to represent his past abstracted, unlike his vivid depiction of his lost son.[23] Du Bois's writing, embracing the messianic, faced forward, not backward.

If the messianic is an attempt to address, to suture, the antinomies of transmission in black America, does it succeed? The messianic names both the impossibility and the necessity of transmission into the future. The messiah cannot be welcomed based on the wisdom of the world, yet the messiah *will* come, thwarting the wisdom of the world. What of transmission from the past to the present? A messianic orientation toward the future results in a pragmatic orientation toward the past, appropriating what is useful, discarding what is not. This seems inadequate to describe the hold the past has on us, a hold that is not exhausted by calculating appropriation. For Du Bois there is one point of continuity between past, present, and future: the "deep religious feeling" that is an essential part of the soul. But this is a deeply individual, and deeply mysterious, feeling. It is unlike the "Faith of Our Fathers"—Du Bois understands but remains suspicious of both excessive enthusiasm and religion reduced to community organizing. Messianic accounts of transmission like Du Bois's do not address the sociality encompassed by transmission, the way that a relationship to past and future are constitutive of community in the present. The ubiquitous "deep religious feeling" oriented toward the messianic described so eloquently by Du Bois is a feeling of individuals. If they join together to cooperate in their preparations for the messiah they do so only for pragmatic reasons, reasons not connected to their relationship to the past or future. Indeed, all of the present is approached instrumentally in such a view, for the messianic, which will bring meaning and truth to the world, bears no ascertainable relationship to the existing world. If our task is to prepare for the unknowable, we must use those things and people around us as efficiently as possible for that task.

The Black Fantastic

We live in "an era characterized by the dismissal of any possibilities beyond the already existing," writes Richard Iton.[24] Our response, according to Iton, should be to look for new sites of politics, sites that are often dismissed as apolitical. He points, in particular, to elements of the black public sphere—necessarily fugitive spaces given white hegemony—including comedy and writing workshops, the black press, and, most importantly for Iton, black music. White hegemony once excluded black sound and now welcomes it, even forces its spectacular overinclusion, just so long as black sounds fit the expectations of white ideology. Politically successful black music, politically *radical* black music, must thwart and expose these white expectations—for example, through "aesthetic humilities, ablative disjunctions, intentional silences, hesitations, and invisibilities."[25] In his book *In Search of the Black Fantastic*, Iton turns to the register of the fantastic, a particular way of understanding black popular-cultural production, to supplement and reorient the study of black politics. He proposes that the fantastic "destabilizes, at least momentarily, our understandings of the distinctions between the reasonable and the unreasonable, and reason itself, the proper and the improper, and propriety itself, by bringing into the field of play those potentials we have forgotten, or did not believe accessible or feasible."²⁶

Might Iton's fantastic be understood as another response to the antinomies of transmission? Might he be suggesting a theological aesthetics of black tradition? In other words, might black popular culture give us a way of thinking about the relationship between past, present, and future that both acknowledges continuities and opens space for dramatic discontinuities, that both acknowledges the political imperative to make these connections backward and forward, but also acknowledges the political imperative to underscore the ontological erasure of black humanity? Moreover, might the black fantastic suggest a way of thinking these issues that does not lean on the misogynistic and heteronormative framework that makes us take transmission to be the work of fathers for sons?

Solidarity Blues, Iton's first book, includes a chapter on popular culture framed as an adjunct to politics: "The making and remaking of cultural forms with which different constituencies can identify and through which they can process and come to terms with the various aspects of their alienation are relevant to the left because these public goods allow for the formation of solidaristic conceptions of community, the kinds of understandings that are crucial to successful leftist enterprises and campaigns."²⁷ Iton's analysis in this book is focused on politics in a traditional sense: institutions, elections, policies, and so on. Popular culture is relevant insofar as it shapes how people engage with politics; popular culture is not itself political. Popular culture can articulate the desires of those without a voice and so mobilize the disenfranchised for political action. In this early work Iton is still pessimistic about popular culture's political potential, at least in the American context. "Despite the transgressive elements contained in American popular culture, ultimately significant is the historical tendency of these forms to reinforce and uphold racial categories and attitudes and to delegitimize more inclusive conceptions of community."²⁸

Such pessimism will transform into ambivalence in *In Search of the Black Fantastic* and into something like optimism in Iton's final article, "Still Life." What motivates this change in attitude is Iton's shifting understanding of the relationship between popular culture and politics. After *Solidarity Blues*, Iton no longer subordinates popular culture to politics; he reads them together, as one. He writes of his subject as the "politics/popular culture matrix."²⁹ Recognizing the way hegemonic ideology manages popular culture, sometimes through the hypervisibility in popular culture of minorities, Iton's "search" is specifically for the "black fantastic," instances of popular culture that elude this hegemony—"the minor-key sensibilities generated from the experiences of the underground, the vagabond, and those constituencies marked as deviant."[30] The black fantastic marks sites of potentiality rather than actuality, for if they were fully actualized in a world of white hegemony they would lose their disruptive, radical force. Thus Iton is careful to distinguish the fantastic not only from popular culture but also from "aesthetics," which he views as a category always already corrupted by hegemonic ideology. However, being attentive to aesthetics is how the black fantastic can be found, for it is in discordant aesthetic practice that the potentialities of the black fantastic are revealed, how we can hear their "minor-key sensibilities." The plot of Iton's book, the search, involves reading black popular culture together with contemporaneous political developments, mindful of the aesthetic dimension of popular culture, motivated by a desire to find hints of those "minor-key sensibilities."

Framing Iton's project in this way, as a search for the black fantastic within the politics/popular culture matrix, elides his work's diachronic dimension—and, I will argue, the possibility that it can be read as a response to the antinomies of transmission. *In Search of the Black Fantastic* proceeds chronologically, and one of the book's arguments is that reading politics and popular culture together allows for better historical explanations. For example, in the book's second chapter, Iton tracks how Paul Robeson's race, labor, and internationalist public stances informed the politics of the artists of the next generation, artists such as Harry Belafonte and Sidney Poitier, who would go on to lend their support to Martin Luther King Jr. We should not read such descriptions as simply a history of black political artists. To do so would already accept the separation of the cultural and the political. When Iton describes Robeson telling Belafonte not to share a stage with him in order to protect the younger artist's career, Iton is also describing how the black fantastic replicates itself, how it passes from the older to the young (notably, not from father to son).[31] It is also important to remember that the politics/popular culture matrix is not only the domain of elites. Just as ideology interpellates individuals into subjects, and there are no subjects outside of ideology, the politics/popular culture matrix forms dark-skinned individuals into black Americans, and there are no black Americans outside of this matrix. From this perspective, each specific example of artistic transmission that Iton tracks—and tracking such examples forms the substance of *In Search of the Black Fantastic*—serves as a metonym for transmission in black life generally. This transmission is sometimes explicit, sometimes furtive, sometimes dangerous, sometimes self-interested. But Iton's project also has a normative dimension, the dimension that motivates the search. In addition to the descriptive work of tracking the unfolding of politics/popular culture, Iton attempts to discern which elements qualify as the fantastic, finding them amidst the broader array of elements of politics/popular culture that merely replicate ideology. In other words, the transmission that Iton describes (that broader array) is not something he extols; it is, like Obama's narrative, a story of white America. Iton is searching for something more, for something that cannot be expressed in terms of transmission but that continues to have an impact on black life, continues to make itself manifest, and to disrupt: the black fantastic.

It appears, from a certain angle, that Iton's black fantastic is simply the messianic in secular guise. Our orderly, modern world is inexplicably interrupted by that which we cannot grasp, the black fantastic. These interruptions point toward something like the awakening described by Du Bois. Recall how Iton writes that the black fantastic "destabilizes, at least momentarily, our understandings of the distinctions between the reasonable and the unreasonable, and reason itself, the proper and improper, and propriety itself, by bringing into the field of play those potentials we have forgotten."[32] In much the same way that Walter Benjamin extols "setting alight the sparks of hope in the past" in order to prepare for the Messiah who will explode hegemonic ideology, Iton sees his task as holding up subversive moments of the black political/popular culture matrix, holding them up together, and beckoning a future where all worldly distinctions (those distinctions that support and constitute hegemonic ideology) will fall away.[33] Iton remains theologically agnostic: all he says is that we glimpse the other-worldliness he describes "at least momentarily." Messianism could be read as motivating Iton's search, making it a religious quest, ultimately a quest for redemption. As in the writings of Du Bois and the tradition of black theology, black culture would serve as a privileged site for finding redemption, as the divine dwells with the most disenfranchised.

Yet Iton's account of the black fantastic does not quite fit the messianic mold for two reasons. First, he is too interested in stories of transmission. Perhaps we could put it this way: Iton is interested in the way that transmission and messianism are always already intertwined, the way stories of fathers and sons always contain lurking within them sparks of the wholly other. Iton's privileged term "matrix" is helpful here, suggestive of complex internal relations on a plane of immanence. The apparently messianic transforms the matrix (its rows of reasonableness and its columns of propriety) rather than acting perpendicular to the matrix. The second reason messianism does not quite fit is that Iton is much more deeply committed to the uniqueness of blackness than would be permitted by a messianism that simply searches the darker corners of culture and history. It is blackness not as physical characteristic or even as culture that Iton is invested in; rather, he is invested in blackness as a structuring principle of modernity: "a broad, global phenomenon, a marker of the divide between 'Europe' and 'non-Europe,' with intimate connections to the colonial order and cultural, epistemological, and governmental implications that far exceed historical, localized, and corporeal boundaries."[34] Blackness and black America, then, are not privileged quantitatively but qualitatively. At the very core of hegemonic ideology is the degradation of the black; to be degraded is the ontological position of the black. Iton aligns himself with Afro-pessimists who define blackness as impossible humanity, subjectivity always under erasure.[35] Against this background, the language of the messianic obscures the specificity of earthly evil. It is not that we live in a fallen world needing redemption; it is that the world is fundamentally structured around the dehumanization of black bodies, and that is what needs to change.

It is important to distinguish Iton's development of the black fantastic from Fred Moten's "aesthetics of the black radical tradition."[36] Both read together the political, the cultural, and the aesthetic. Both find radical political potential in moments of disjunction, in minor-key sensibilities. But transmission is not a pressing concern for Moten, only the debasement of blackness. For Moten, black aesthetics have their radical potential precisely because of the ontological negation of the black. As always already excluded, blackness represents a dangerous supplement, threatening to subvert every site where it appears. Recall that Iton refuses aesthetics as a radical category, seeing aesthetics as complicit in the project of modernity-coloniality-whiteness. If whiteness defines beauty, defines it deeply, in the very structure of our world, proclaiming that black is beautiful can only lead to the cooptation of blackness by whiteness, can only lead to hyperbolic performances of blackness commissioned for a white audience. Moten struggles to reconcile Afro-pessimism and his own black aesthetic optimism, but this is territory that has already been charted by Iton. Black aesthetics do not happen in metaphysical space (as it often seems for Moten) but in performances by specific individuals, at specific times and places, influenced by some, influencing others. Moten might worry that contextualizing deradicalizes, mutes—maybe even whitens—the disruptive potential of black performances. Iton would agree, but add: that is precisely why we need to contextualize, for acknowledging the specifics of transmission make it possible for us to refuse the allure of false messiahs, of idols in blackface. Grappling with transmission allows us to see icons, to see those performances that qualify for the register of the fantastic, that bring us out of ourselves and our worlds and into communion with others displaced from their worlds, into a communion that is necessarily political because it is by definition opposed to the order of the day.[37]

Stuntin' on Martin Luther

Memorabilia is widely sold in the black community that features an image of Barack Obama, so often seen as fulfilling the hopes of generations that came before him, facing an image of his forefather, Martin Luther King Jr. In his version of the song "My President," Jay-Z sets this image to music: "Rosa Parks sat/So Martin Luther could walk/Martin Luther walked/So Barack Obama could run/Barack Obama ran/So all the children could fly."[38] Jay-Z's remix of Young Jeezy's "My President" not only transforms the latter's Lamborghini into a Maybach, it also removes Young Jeezy's ambivalence about the presidency and about transmission.[39] Jay-Z sings, "My money's dark green/And my Porsche is light gray," replacing Young Jeezy's original words: "My momma ain't home, and daddy's still in jail." Jay-Z's version is an affirmation of the past and future, identifying himself with the direction of progress. He stands with Obama, and he will reap the rewards: "I'm headed for D.C./Anybody feel me," he sings. In contrast, Young Jeezy uncomfortably juxtaposes Obama's election and the singer's own car, placing both against the background of continuing injustice—significantly, the fact that the singer's father remains in chains. This theme from the chorus is maintained in the first verse, where the election is a "good day" and the singer hopes he himself will have "a great night," yet he quickly and ominously spots "great white" and asks rhetorically, "who knew what came with prison/Just 'cause you got opinions." When Nas joins for the third and final verse, he makes this theme even more explicit: "Then they put us in jail, now a nigga can't go vote/So I spend dough, on these hoes's strippin'." Conspicuous consumption is not just against the background of injustice; it is caused by injustice. Nas, too, is excited but also concerned for Obama. He accepts that Obama is "for real" (like himself, he notes) but also implores him, "Never lose your integrity."

Fitting with his general ambivalence, Young Jeezy does not take transmission from generation to generation for granted. Invoking memories of lynching, the rap marks the precariousness of Obama's situation: "at the top will be the same place you hang from." Obama's blackness does not mean all black children will excel (Young Jeezy describes his own son as "addicted to polos"). Nor does it mean that Obama inherits the virtues of his forefathers. Rather than Martin Luther King making Obama's ascent possible, for Young Jeezy Obama is "Stuntin' on Martin Luther, feelin' just like a king." Again we find ambivalence. "Stuntin'" and "feelin'" suggest appearances rather than realities, showing off and exalting oneself. The messianic makes an explicit appearance in the rap as Young Jeezy sings, "we need a miracle," explaining that "this shit is hysterical." The way to procure a miracle, according to the rap, is to "email Jesus." When forefathers cannot be relied on to make the present predictable and the future better, the only person to whom we can appeal is outside of the world: God.

The tenuous lyrics of Young Jeezy's rap might be explained by its release after Obama had won the Democratic primary but before he had won the presidential election. Yet the accompanying video was released after the presidential election, and that is when the song's popularity peaked (it was also January 2009 when Jay-Z recorded his remix). Young Jeezy's video emulates an outdoor campaign rally, with supporters holding the signs one would expect to find at a political convention indicating state delegations. But in the video, there are signs not only for states but also for cities and neighborhoods (including Vegas and Watts), countries and regions (including Haiti, Iraq, and Africa), colonial possessions (Virgin Islands), rappers (Tupac), and political leaders (including Malcolm X and Che Guevara). Most of the crowd is composed of African Americans, though there are a few people of other races also moving with the beat. In alternate cuts, Young Jeezy and Nas are wearing golden crosses around their necks. As Young Jeezy is singing, "we need a miracle," a young black child raises his right hand in the air. During the next line, the young boy's hand is closed into a fist. The camera zooms out, and we see that now everyone in the crowd has their fists raised in the black power salute. A symbol of the past passes to the future, to youth, yet this passage is highly precarious. The "My President" video refuses an easy identification of our forefathers, and it refuses easy transmission of wisdom to our sons and daughters. It longs for a miracle and manifests that longing in practices of black solidarity—sometimes joined by others, but always black-led. It hints at the black fantastic within the aesthetic, within a genre so often incorporated into the contemporary (white) neoliberal order. It hints at a black theological aesthetics.

CHAPTER 6

What Is Black Organizing?

"Nowhere is the promise of organizing more apparent than in the traditional black churches."[1] This is the conclusion reached by Barack Obama after three years of organizing on the far South Side of Chicago. Black churches had financial resources, membership, and moral authority that could be mobilized to do more than charity. They could foster grassroots leadership and direct action, building power in black communities to demand justice for black communities. Moreover, according to Obama, "organizing teaches as nothing else does the beauty and the strength of everyday people." This revelatory power, which Obama sees exemplified, in "the songs of the church and the talk on the stoop," woven by an organizer into a shared vision, hints at a religious significance to community organizing. Indeed, Obama himself came to Chicago because he found in organizing "the promise of redemption."[2] In other words, it is not just religious institutions that might facilitate organizing; organizing itself might be understood as a religious practice.

There is an increasing amount of scholarship examining not only the sociological and political significance of faith-based community organizing, but its ethical and theological significance.[3] This scholarship reflects on how organizing might be viewed from within a religious tradition, particularly Protestantism. Community organizers have long appealed to Bible verses and religiously inflected concepts of justice and love. The seminal book on organizing, Alinsky's *Rules for Radicals*, aligns organizing with "those rights and values propounded by Judaeo-Christianity and the democratic political tradition."[4] Such appeals are easy to view as instrumental in the service of organizing. In recent scholarship, religion is taken as more than a resource to be tapped, more than a repertoire of symbols and stories that can motivate action.

In contrast, there has not been a similar deepening of reflection on the significance of race in community organizing, and there has been little if any reflection on the way that the entanglement of religion and race should affect our understanding of organizing. This is perplexing, given the way that the civil rights movement is so often central to the story of organizing in the United States and how civil rights movement history is told as a religious story. Further, community organizing is frequently held up as an exemplary and relatively unique site of interracial cooperation just as it is a site of interfaith cooperation. In most of what follows I track the absence of substantial reflection on race in faith-based community organizing as well as the presence of shifting conceptions of race. Following the change from what Jodi Melamed has termed the era of "racial liberalism" to our current era of "neoliberal multiculturalism," I argue that faith-based community organizing often participates in a style of management of difference characteristic of contemporary culture—better, contemporary ideology.[5] Unmanageable dimensions of difference are muzzled. Finally, I reflect on how a more substantial account of race may be insinuated in discussions of faith-based community organizing in a way that advances the early promise of black theology.

Organizing for Civil Rights

A shift in the historiography of the civil rights movement in the United States has caused a shift in the way organizing, race, and religion are thought to intersect. The three were once said to reach a grand convergence in the 1950s and 1960s, embodied in Rev. Dr. Martin Luther King Jr.[6] In this account, the momentous Montgomery bus boycott was catalyzed by church networks that offered lines of communication with the black community, financial resources, and leaders. It was ministers who called the boycott. It was at a church-style mass meeting that the black community of Montgomery ratified the boycott and began to organize committees and mobilize resources to support the boycott. With the success in Montgomery, King and other religious leaders founded the Southern Christian Leadership Council (SCLC) to replicate the successful religious organizing model developed in the year after Rosa Parks was arrested, with its techniques for communicating, fundraising, carpooling, and negotiating. According to this older version of the historical narrative, the civil rights movement began to decline when the religiously committed leadership of the SCLC was displaced by more secular, more radical protesters, proclaiming an allegiance to black power that substituted rhetorical flourish for organizing effort. With King's assassination, faith-based organizing for the rights of black Americans effectively ended.

Critics have charged that this account of the civil rights movement focuses too much on the top-down leadership of charismatic figures, much loved by the (white-controlled) media, such as King. They have charged that it overlooks grassroots leadership, both from older generations of black activists and as it developed organically within the movement. Further, these critics charge that the term "organizing" is misused when it is applied to charismatic preachers calling for a protest or leading a march, activities that differ from the relationship-building work that is essential to organizing. Historians have uncovered intergenerational networks of local grassroots activists existing well before protests captured the national spotlight, and they have shown the central, but rarely visible, role of women as organizers in the movement. In this revised version of civil rights movement history, it is the Student Nonviolent Coordinating Committee (SNCC) that takes center stage, with its emphasis on facilitating the development of local leadership through sustained organizing using techniques with closer affinities to the labor movement than to black churches. Organizers went house to house, listened to community members' stories, explained how the organizing effort was in their interest, and carefully chose tactics to confront the powers that be. A result of this shifting emphasis is that organizing in the civil rights movement is now portrayed as a secular activity, with the young, overall-clad SNCC worker living in an attic replacing the immaculately clad preacher as the paradigmatic organizer. While the most famous of this type of organizer, including Ella Baker and Bob Moses, are sometimes portrayed with a spiritual aura, they have none of the Christian commitments of King, Rev. Joseph Lowery, or Rev. Ralph Abernathy.[7]

The subsequent story of race and organizing, told as a story of decline, rarely includes religion. The urban uprisings of the late 1960s entailed chaos and destruction, the opposite of organizing. In Oakland and then nationally, the Black Panther Party tapped and channeled this energy. They combined flashy, media-friendly images of berets, leather jackets, and guns with a commitment to freeing black communities from American "internal colonialism." This commitment manifested as organizing alternative institutions for the black community: patrols to prevent attack from the police, a free breakfast program for children, and a medical program focusing on diseases particularly affecting black Americans. Despite the religious background of key Panthers, the party spoke in a Marxist idiom, and it was sometimes severely critical of organized religion. However, religious institutions offered the infrastructure for some of the Panthers' social programs. Many free breakfasts were cooked in church kitchens and served in church halls, to take but one instance.[8]

In the 1970s, the task of building community institutions as a concrete manifestation of the "black power" slogan required funding. The foundations that had once supported civil rights organizing along with the federal government's anti-poverty programs channeled funds into institution-building. So did some church organizations, in part as a reaction to James Forman's demand—dramatically announced through a statement he read when he interrupted the service at Riverside Memorial Church—for $500 billion in reparations to black Americans from white churches and synagogues. That much money did not materialize, but some church and government coffers were opened, with funding going to develop industrial parks, cultural institutes, and community service projects. Organizing became institutionalized, professionalized, and subsidized by outside forces that were not at all interested in supporting challenges to the powers that be.[9]

With this next act in the story of organizing for racial justice came a decline in the reputation of race-based community organizing and a redescription of earlier organizing projects. Organizing was increasingly transformed into social service subsidized by and used as a tool of the growing number of black elected officials. The civil rights movement, both from SCLC-centric and SNCC-centric perspectives, came to be remembered not as an example of race-based organizing but as an example of organizing against unjust laws, an entirely different project than the easily corruptible, already sullied project of black cultural nationalism. The civil rights movement became the organizing project that preceded feminist organizing and followed labor organizing, with lessons on offer for the organizing projects of today and tomorrow. In this narrative of the American Left, race is one difference among many, one site of struggle among many. Faith-based organizers today learning about organizing history track the involvement of religious communities in each of these endeavors, and they track the way that religious values guided these organizers of earlier generations.

Eliding the specificity of race in the history of organizing is worrying. It complements and reinforces contemporary multiculturalism's muzzling of the critical and unmanageable aspects of difference.[10] But it also obscures the long and rich history of black community institutions such as freemasons, fraternal orders, and women's church groups that have been committed to race-based organizing and that should be understood in continuity with the civil rights movement.[11] When this history is obscured, the effect is a sense of "nihilism in black America," to again invoke Cornel West's phrase, with no institutions seeming to offer visions of the future or values for the present.[12] When black America is understood to be devoid of institutions and traditions, the only hope to address problems of the black community is to form coalitions with those whose institutions appear stronger and whose traditions appear to run deeper.

The Alinsky Organizing Tradition

In 1964, the city of Rochester, New York, experienced a race riot. In response, liberal white clergy decided to ask for outside help in addressing the city's race problem. They did not turn to the SCLC; they turned to Saul Alinsky.[13] Since pioneering neighborhood organizing on Chicago's South Side two decades earlier, Alinsky had gained a national reputation for mobilizing the diverse people and resources of a community to address its problems. His pugnacious and often crude manner was accompanied by an abiding commitment to American ideals of freedom and equality—the determined effort that he labeled "radical." As he wrote in 1946, "The Radical believes completely in *real* equality of opportunity for all peoples regardless of race, color, or creed."[14] Alinsky condemned unions for their racial discrimination, which he considered "an attack on the very soul of America," and he made sure the bylaws of his first organization began by stating that the group was concerned with all, across the color line and across religious divides. What organizing meant for Alinsky was bringing people together, particularly bringing together those who were already leaders in some way in their community, whether they were leaders of a city park or a choir or a group of youths. By joining resources and identifying shared concerns, these local leaders could advance the interests of their community in the face of opposition from the wealthy and the powerful. Alinsky or another professional organizer would simply catalyze the natural process of leadership development and cooperation. He writes, "[M]ankind from time immemorial has always organized, regardless of what race or color they were, whenever they wanted to bring about change."[15]

Alinsky did not immediately pack his bags and move to Rochester when he was called. He responded that organizers "were not a colonial power like the churches who sent their missionaries everywhere whether they were invited or not," and he waited for an invitation from Rochester's black religious leaders, which came soon thereafter.[16] In Rochester, as in Chicago and elsewhere, religious leaders were central to Alinsky's organizing efforts. Alinsky himself was a secular Jew, but he wove references to Jewish and Christian sources into his writings. The first epigraph to his 1971 *Rules for Radicals* is from Rabbi Hillel, "Where there are no men, be thou a man." He describes the professional organizer as "reaching for the highest level for which man can reach—to create, to be a 'great creator,' to play God."[17] Alinsky really believed that Judeo-Christian values are integral to American democratic politics, that they entail ideals to fight for, not just weapons to wield in the struggle.

For Alinsky, religion or race could define a community; they were not just a box to check on a demographics form or part of a tossed salad of many cultures. After Alinsky, and after a decade of decline, several community organizing networks formalized Alinsky's process and made a major change. Now, community organizations would be funded by churches that would become members and whose parishioners would become organization leaders. Additionally, organizing became "broad based," reaching many communities across a city rather than being defined by a neighborhood. This helped address the increased mobility of families—living in one part of a city, shopping in another, and working in another—and it also made possible alliances of very different sorts of people. White suburban churches and Latino Catholic churches and inner-city black Pentecostal churches could all be members of the same organization, pooling resources and developing leadership to address the ills of their city.

Describing this new organizing model as one aimed at "reweaving the social fabric," Ernesto Cortes embraces the culture of multiculturalism.[18] Where Alinsky went to Rochester to help blacks address discrimination, Cortes, who led the growth of faith-based organizing in the 1990s, sees organizing in grander terms, building trust across racial and ethnic lines. Moreover, in his account organizing is motivated by a shared faith, which Cortes explains as not being "a particular system of religious beliefs, but a more general affirmation that life has meaning." This reduction of religion to affirmation accompanies a sociological reduction of religious institutions: they are "built on networks of family and neighborhood." Religion and race come together, for Cortes, in a magnificent unity: "The best elements in our religious traditions are inclusive—respecting diversity, and conveying a plurality of symbols which incorporate the experiences of diverse peoples. The mixed multitudes in Sinai and Pentecost are central to the Judeo-Christian tradition; they represent the constant incorporation of different traditions in our social and political fabric." Good religion brings "diverse peoples" (presumably a euphemism for racial or ethnic difference) together in harmony, many voices singing together. It is hard not to read this as a theological, or crypto-theological, claim: that all difference ultimately resolves in unity—and if it cannot, then we must be misunderstanding the difference in question. In this way, proper racial difference is difference that can be submerged in unity, presumably in something like the affirmation of common humanity to which religious difference is reduced.

According to a survey conducted in 2011, faith-based community organizing groups exhibit an impressive degree of diversity at every level.[19] Five million Americans belong to a congregation or organization that is a member of one of these groups, and predominantly black congregations make up 30 percent of this membership, more than twice their representation in the population. More than half of the staff and board of director members of these groups are nonwhite, with 32 percent of board members and 21 percent of staff African American. In sum, the surveyors conclude, these groups create spaces where cross-racial and cross-ethnic collaboration really happens.

In the 1990s, racial difference was rarely discussed in faith-based organizing groups, even though issues of racism were often addressed by these groups—discussed in nonracial terms.[20] The poor education offered at a predominantly black school might be an issue around which there was organizing energy, but it was not condemned as racist. It was shared religious faith, even if that faith had little content besides the proclamation that one "has faith," that was seen as uniting a community, allowing divisive issues of racial difference to be put to the side. Sociologist Mark Warren summarizes the groups' views at this time: "In a society so fractured along racial lines, people from different racial groups often have difficulty seeing a common interest. A set of common beliefs, a shared identity as people of God, helps people to identify themselves as members of the same community."[21]

This silencing of racial difference led to tension in some organizations. For example, Warren examines the 1993 case of a racially motivated murder outside of Fort Worth, Texas, that prompted protests organized by some of the African American clergy participating in the Fort Worth organizing group. This multiracial group as a whole did not respond to the murder. Warren suggests that "Anglo and Hispanic leaders, and the white lead organizer, may not have grasped quickly enough the unique importance of the verdict to the black community." The group had its strongest roots in the Latino community but had cultivated African American participation. According to Warren, "[T]he event revealed a significant weakness in the organization's level of multiracial understanding."[22] Over the next years, the network of organizing groups of which the Fort Worth group was a part, led by Ernesto Cortes, offered a series of seminars for group leaders on African American issues, bringing in speakers including Cornel West and James Cone.

By 2011, race was often discussed explicitly by community organizing groups. Indeed, 29 percent of faith-based community organizing groups tackled issues directly concerned with racism. In comparison, 70 percent tackled poverty issues, 66 percent education issues, and 54 percent immigration issues.[23] Some organizing networks, such as the Gamaliel Foundation, have established national African American leadership teams. Yet the way race was discussed by these groups ensured that racial difference would remain manageable. For example, a group in New Orleans addressing the myriad issues raised by the aftermath of Katrina avoided framing these issues in terms of race. As Jeffrey Stout reports, "I found no reluctance among them to discuss the racial dimension of the situation. They present it, however, as one dimension among others; and they present it in this way, as far as I can tell, because they see it in this way, not merely because they are trying to draw whites, Asians, and Hispanics into the coalition."[24] Stout further concludes that the shift to broad-based organizing from community- or race-based organizing ensures that successful campaigns do not become overly invested in defending their newly achieved place of power, since they are not competing for that seat at the table with other communities or minority groups.

Participants in faith-based organizing groups report a sense of difference subsumed into unity, just as Cortes announced. Political scientist Heidi Swarts reports her experience on the last day of an organizer training: "An African American female participant expressed the 'high' of solidarity that the training had produced for her as 'a glimpse of heaven. This is God.' A Filipino man became emotional about experiencing 'so many religions come together: to see black, Hispanic, Asian, Filipino all together—if we can do it here, up on the hill, why can't we do it down there?'"[25] In the first case, the African American woman is offering a naturalized theological vision: God as (the feeling of) solidarity among different people with different stories. In the second case, the Filipino man's slippage between religious and racial identities mirrors Cortes's implicit suggestion that race and religion are two of the many differences that define who we are and that all are subsumed under a larger, implicitly theological vision of unity "up on the hill." Just as some theologians have contrasted the Christian mythos of fleeting violence within an essentially peaceful world to the secular liberal mythos of a fundamentally violent world in need of restraint by the state, this Filipino man has been shown the organizing mythos of unity in difference, and he is ready to go back to his community to make converts.[26] Given the convenient way that this crypto-theological position coincides with the unity-in-difference prescribed by the contemporary cultural-economic order, we might venture to call the theological commitments of this Filipino man, and perhaps of the organizing network training him, a *theology of neoliberal multiculturalism*. Significantly, this theology does not see itself as accountable to tradition or authority. It is taken as self-evident.

Taking Difference Seriously

In recent years, the way that difference is understood in community organizing has been called into question from two quarters: theologians and religious ethicists taking religious difference seriously and feminists taking gender difference seriously. Melissa Snarr's recent examination of community-labor-religion coalitions supporting living-wage campaigns is an example of the former. Rather than filling out a theological position that supports an organizing campaign, Snarr develops an account of the religious meaning of the practice of organizing from a Christian perspective. In other words, she rejects the split between specific religious commitments, reduced to general affirmation of "faith," and the generic crypto-theology supporting the practice of organizing, unity in difference without tradition or authority. Encounters with difference do play an important role for Snarr. They are a crucial part of organizing not because they are needed to build power and win campaigns but because they enlarge the moral agency of those participating in organizing. Through struggling with difference while working on a joint project advancing shared goals, participants build their capacity to be sensitive to difference in the future. Furthermore, organizing across difference makes participants more aware of their interdependence, conceived theologically as "our creation by God as social beings," mirroring "God's own nature, in Trinitarian formulation."[27] Participants do not wallow in their unity or interdependence: they act on it, working together in pursuit of the common good. In this collective action, each has her or his calling; each can contribute (and develop) her or his skills in a specific way. But collective action gives all a way to share their stories, to have a voice.

For Snarr, the activity of organizing also builds moral agency by teaching suspicion of the powers that be and of the way the world is ordered. By identifying injustices and searching for their causes, organizing helps participants see that the ways of the world can be deeply corrupt and that collective action can offer an effective remedy. Put another way, organizing shows that laws can be unjust, but that a commitment to justice shared with fellow citizens can transform the law, can make it more just. The meaning of justice is not revealed from on high but discerned through collective reflection—with neighbors, fellow congregants, coworkers, and with those one might never have thought to talk to before. Organizing for justice always meets resistance, and this resistance, too, serves a pedagogical function. The distortions propagated by the powerful are a reminder of the dangers of idolatry, the need for suspicion and critical examination of the messaging one encounters in the media and in our habits of thought. Organizing builds virtue: it cultivates the disposition to commit oneself to the common good despite serious obstacles. This virtue is instilled regardless of whether a particular organizing campaign wins or loses, for it is the process of organizing that holds ethical and theological significance, not the outcome.

Reading Alinsky with Augustine, Luke Bretherton suggests that organizing offers a model of faithful citizenship in the secular world—by which he means the world between Christ's resurrection and his return.[28] This world is deeply ambivalent, with both human and divine authorities having pull. Bretherton understands Alinsky and Augustine as optimistic realists, acknowledging the difficult, messy work of politics necessary in this world and yet committed to a vision of peace and justice in the future. Both do not look for salvation from the state; they urge citizens to faithfully work together toward the world of justice they deeply desire. In the process, according to Bretherton, difference must not dissolve. Organizing resists "the spirit of capitalism that precisely demands the dissolution of particularity and the formation of liquid identities in order to aid capital flows."[29] By listening carefully to the stories of others, by witnessing their passions, and by glimpsing the depths of their traditions, participants in organizing projects are able to appreciate the complexity of the world in a time before Christ's return, refusing to simplify it under the gaze of ostensibly neutral liberalism.

Snarr and Bretherton take religion as more than one identity category, more than one set of propositions to believe about matters of ultimate concern. For them, religion involves a way of seeing the world and acting in it, informed by resources from the past and animated by a shared vision for the future. If religious difference can be understood in this way, can other differences be so understood, as well? Before turning to racial difference, a review of feminist critiques of Alinsky-style organizing will help set the stage. Feminists have pointed out that the process of Alinsky-style organizing, with its focus on demonizing an opponent, wielding power against that opponent, and the cultivation of indigenous leadership by outsiders is antithetical to feminist values and to many existing women-led forms of organizing.[30] Even if a majority of professional organizers in Alinsky-style groups are now women, the world of practices, values, and dispositions opened by a gendered perspective may still be ignored as gender is treated as one difference among many to be unified—or so these feminist critics charge.

Saul Alinsky's model of community organizing is premised on organizing being an action in the public sphere, not the private sphere. This public-private distinction is contested by feminists who argue that it is always artificial and that it serves particular interests. When the distinction is ignored, new sorts of practices can be understood as practices of community organizing: friendship networks, breastfeeding support groups, family reunions, block clubs, and even gossip. I think of my own mother, who has started newsletters for her neighborhood in each place she has lived, allowing neighbors to get to know each other, allowing them to share their passions and concerns, and alerting them to issues affecting the neighborhood. Such practices are neither purely private nor public. They can start informally in the home then lead to demands on the state, such as demands for changes in school curricula. Susan Stall and Randy Stoecker point to settlement houses and consciousness-raising groups of an earlier era, and more recently to tenant and welfare rights organizing, as employing what they call a "woman-centered" model. As opposed to the rigid procedures, slogans, and technical jargon deployed by Alinsky-style organizing groups ("one-to-ones," "accountability sessions," "leaders," the countless acronyms), woman-centered organizing is more informal. A human catalyst is not added to existing community relationships in the form of a professional organizer. The relationships already existing between women, often begun over a coffee table in the home, lead to demands for action against the powers that be. These deep relationships, unlike the artificially cultivated relationships of Alinsky-style organizing, are capable of sustaining an organizing effort over the long haul.

Note how this feminist critique of organizing does not simply urge that gender difference be discussed in organizing efforts or that staff members be sent to diversity trainings to be sensitized to women's issues. The feminist challenge runs much deeper: the very way the activity of organizing is conceived needs to be rethought from a perspective that sees and values the world differently. The question of efficacy is bracketed. Both Alinsky-style and woman-centered organizing campaigns have had their successes and failures. What matters are the sorts of relationships that are visible in a community and that are seen as having the potential to affect change. Melissa Snarr writes of the sacrifices made by the predominantly female organizers in Alinsky-style groups, working long hours for low pay.[31] From the feminist perspective, another misfortune can be added to these organizers' basket, that of false consciousness. As outsiders entering a community and seeing themselves as possessing the formula for organizing success, the key players and relationships they chart out overlook the already strong and potentially fecund bonds between women and families in that community.

Taking Race Seriously

Can a black critique of organizing efforts be made along the same lines as the feminist critique? This would mean pointing out distinctive features of organizing among black communities, and it would mean pointing out the limitations of organizing models that do not take seriously the way blackness is not just one issue among many but is constitutive of social worlds. In the history of civil rights organizing, there was, in fact, a long and distinctive race-based organizing tradition. In some ways, this tradition resonates with the woman-centered organizing tradition.[32] Because blacks were excluded from the mainstream public sphere, it was through alternative institutions (such as churches, newspapers, and fraternal societies) and informal relationships that organizing could get its start. Bob Moses once described the key to starting the organizing process as bouncing a ball, literally.[33] Soon children will come to watch, and eventually the ball will need to be retrieved from someone's yard, starting the process of building informal relationships.

Those black institutions and leaders that did exist before the civil rights movement were always precarious, their positions and often lives threatened if they challenged the powers that be. One reading of the tragedy of post–civil rights black politics is that the alternative public sphere created by segregation collapsed, leaving leaders with no base, thus even more dependent on white patronage than ever before. Cornel West labels this the "crisis of black leadership," and he argues that broad-based (not race-based) organizing is the antidote, citing Alinsky's Industrial Areas Foundation (IAF) as an example of the sort of "grassroots organization in principled coalitions that bring power and pressure to bear on specific issues" he recommends.[34] West also argues that black leaders must be "race-transcending," critical of both black and white wielders of power while promoting a vision of social justice for all.[35] But such a position refuses to contemplate the possibility that there might be distinctively black forms of organizing. Moreover, rather than seeking to rebuild black institutions desiccating since integration, West concedes their demise and, by urging the formation of broad coalitions, forecloses the space for their reemergence.

Taking racial difference seriously is precisely the intent of the Center for Third World Organizing, a network of groups organizing in communities of color. Sociologist Richard Wood compared the organizing techniques of this race-based style of organizing to an Alinsky-style group.[36] Both groups Wood examined organized in the same neighborhoods of Oakland, both had similar levels of racial diversity represented among their participants, and both addressed similar social justice issues in their campaigns. While the Alinsky-style group drew participants from member congregations, the race-based group drew participants from people of color (and a few whites) living in downtrodden neighborhoods of Oakland. Where the Alinsky-style group's members' commitments to the group grew out of their commitment to their congregations, the race-based group not only organized campaigns for social justice but also cultivated commitment among its members by organizing cultural events with them. Wood asserts that, sadly, the strongest bond racial minorities in the United States have is a shared consumer culture, and he views race-based organizing as a way to foster bonds between minorities independent of that consumer culture.

Because the participants in the Center for Third World Organizing were, in fact, of many races, cultural events (in which all participated) ranged from Kwanzaa to Cinco de Mayo and beyond. This group's goal is "a future American society that is not only multiracial in its demographic composition, but that values and celebrates the diverse cultural expressions of minority communities and somehow fuses them into a shared political culture."[37] To achieve that desired future, race needs to be acknowledged and embraced in the present. Class and gender are also important, and their connections with race as "interlocking systems of oppression" are acknowledged by the group, but race is considered a "first among equals."[38]

Wood concludes that race-based organizing is likely to remain marginal to American political life. While that marginality allows it to address more controversial issues, such as racial profiling and abortion, it is unlikely to build the power necessary to hold institutions accountable in a sustained manner—a possibility that is more realistic for Alinsky-style faith-based organizing groups.[39]

Yet what Wood labels "race-based" organizing is not exactly that. It would be better labeled "multicultural" organizing, for racial difference is essentially reduced to cultural difference. Stories about a culture's history, a meal with their cuisine, and a celebration of their most visible holidays are seen as sufficing to build bonds within a minority group and between minority groups. Indeed, the distinction between race, ethnicity, and culture is further blurred by the term around which organizing occurs, "people of color." The term would seem to refer to biologically determined race, but it is actually used to refer to socially designated nonwhite groups ranging from Asian immigrants to Native Americans to Latinos to African Americans. To assert that each of these groups even has a fixed, monolithic culture that can be embraced and shared with others buys into a problematic story about American pluralism. Analogizing from the feminist critique, race-based organizing should not mean embracing culture and then using the same organizing process as everyone else. Rather, it means allowing a racially marked set of values and ideals to shape the practice of organizing itself, with culture relevant only secondarily.

One of the impediments to imagining race-based organizing in the contemporary United States is the very ambiguity between race and ethnicity, given the large and growing size of the country's Latino population and their ambiguous racial/ethnic status. Latinos' status near the bottom of the socioeconomic ladder has made organizers and funders particularly keen to organize in, or with, this community. Sometimes the issue of Latinos' place in the U.S. ethnic/racial landscape is entirely averted by considering Latinos under the rubric of "immigrants," and immigration has received much attention from faith-based organizing groups. To consider Latinos as a race is not just to complicate the binary American racial landscape. Nor is it just to displace African Americans from their symbolic location as most denigrated and so to divert resources away from blacks. To consider Latinos a race is to embrace a pessimism concerning their status in the United States. The cultural connotation of race is intractable hardship, a condemnation to eternal subordination, permanence in the position of "other."[40] The cultural connotation of ethnicity, in contrast, is optimism. It connotes hardship to endure now, but rewards later on. It connotes a rich culture, with tasty foods and colorful clothes. Ultimately, it connotes something to be proud of. Ethnicity, then, can be reduced to culture with minimal remainder—that remainder being ethnic beauty, a nose or eyes or skin color that marks assimilated difference. Mixing race and ethnicity, as the Center for Third World Organizing does, obscures the most fundamental workings of American racism: the pessimism so deep it might even warrant the label theology that accompanies racialization. Such pessimism requires a unique organizing process, one that does not merely demand a seat at the table but demands a new sort of table.

Race, Religion, Organizing

In sociologist Mark Warren's account of the varieties of congregations participating in faith-based organizing, he concludes that, compared with other religious traditions, the "African American religious tradition has not been as readily available for IAF organizing . . . because the black tradition has been focused primarily towards racial justice."[41] Black churches have been primarily concerned with a message of liberation, but such a message does not fit with the more pragmatic concerns of broad-based community organizing. Professional organizers, like many black churches, take Exodus to be an important text in thinking about religious involvement in the contemporary world, but where black churches have interpreted the Exodus story as one of liberation from enslavement, professional organizers emphasize "the themes of inclusion and community building."[42] Further, according to Warren, the "authoritarian leadership styles" of ministers in black churches pose a challenge for organizers invested in the democratic process.[43]

This misfit between the expectations and values of professional organizers and those of black churches underscores the need to take race seriously in faith-based community organizing. Given the deeply entwined histories of religion and race, and particularly of Christian theology and the subordination of blacks, such an account would need to think about how both categories, religion and race, can be taken seriously together, how both can refuse the bounds set on them by the ideology of neoliberal multiculturalism. From within the always already racialized tradition of Christianity, what meaning does organizing take on? Is it a religious or an ethical practice? Does organizing look different when it is seen as part of a black tradition? I do not propose to fully answer these questions here. My interest in this chapter is primarily drawing our attention to them and in the process pondering why they so often go unasked.

The challenge for black churches, according to Warren, is to reconcile an emphasis on grand narratives of liberation with the practical tasks of building power in a community in order to challenge the powers that be. This task of reconciliation is precisely what one would expect to find in the writings of black liberation theologians, but it is rarely found there (a major exception is Jeremiah Wright). The first generation of black theologians was more concerned with abstract questions, both theological and political, than in community organizing, swept up as they were in the militant rhetoric of the black power movement. Indeed, the heavy emphasis that James Cone places on liberation at times seems antithetical to organizing. For example, in one of his first essays, from 1968, Cone describes the urban uprisings happening around him as "not a conscious organized attempt of black people to take over; it is an attempt to say *yes* to their own dignity even in death."[44] During this early, existentialist-influenced phase, Cone saw pure rebellion and pure liberation as linked, with both receiving divine sanction. He emphasized raw anger and emotion leading to action, unmediated by the processes or structures of organizing. Cone does not mention organizing again in his published writings until 1991, long after his seminal writings on black theology. He discerns a shared quality of Malcolm X and Martin Luther King Jr.: the ability "to teach the people how to organize themselves for the purpose of achieving their freedom. Organizing for freedom requires thinking about the meaning of freedom and developing strategies to implement it in the society."[45] Even in this case, organizing is not an organic activity, already occurring and in need of catalysts. It is something new that must be taught from above, from someone with the time to contemplate the big theological and philosophical questions.

But perhaps the seemingly simpleminded message of liberation is just what is needed. Given the intractable pessimism that race connotes, not to mention facts on the ground like the nearly one million black men currently imprisoned in the United States, smiling families with skin of all shades holding hands is not the right image of our future. If the world has in store only suffering and death, and worse for our children, and worse still for their children, the language of liberation rings true. This is liberation without content, liberation that means overturning the table, radically reconfiguring the social world in a way unimaginable from the perspective of the present. Any content attributed to liberation evinces optimism and so false consciousness, a refusal to acknowledge the depths of racial injustice in America.

But is Warren's worry justified, that such a commitment to liberation is depoliticizing, or at least inappropriate in the context of organizing? No. A theological emphasis on liberation fits with the suspicion of worldly wisdom that is taught by organizing, as Melissa Snarr has shown. In the shadow of future liberation, the institutions and systems of the present are necessarily misguided in fundamental ways. That suspicion of worldly wisdom extends to the worldly wisdom conveyed by organizing manuals and trainings, to the processes and tactics entailed by faith-based community organizations. With pessimism about the present and a commitment to liberation in the future, black theology does not aspire to offer justification for particular campaigns or tactics, does not attempt to hallow what is ultimately profane. Put another way, black theology trusts the grassroots, trusts the wisdom of ordinary black people to continue doing what they have been doing for generations: working together, listening to each other's stories, consulting with community elders, and collectively confronting what strikes them as unjust.

The black theological vision of organizing moves beyond this austere silence when it proclaims that God is working through history. James Cone describes faith as "the perspective which enables human beings to recognize God's actions in human history."[46] It is from this perspective that the black organizing tradition should be read: it should be understood theologically. Whether or not organizers understood themselves as Christian, the movement toward liberation is God acting in the world. That means telling a story of black organizing, from freemasons to Ida Wells's anti-lynching crusade to SNCC and SCLC to the Panthers, is telling a theological story, one in which we are all invited to participate. Faith illuminates that tradition and calls for participation. It does not dictate tactics or opponents—all of these are choices made fallibly by individuals working together in the world, aspiring to participate in the spirit of God's work in the world. Faith involves discernment. Not all community organizing efforts are working toward liberation. Many are blinded by optimism, ignoring the depths of American racism. Some electoral campaigns may fit with the organizing tradition, with God's work in the world. Chokwe Lumumba's successful campaign to become mayor of Jackson, Mississippi, in 2013 built on and reinvigorated an ostensibly secular tradition of black organizing, supported by the Malcolm X Grassroots Movement.[47]

This particularly black perspective on faith-based community organizing invites us to read differently the stories told about such organizing. Rev. Claude Black was reluctant to bring his congregation into the San

Antonio affiliate of the Industrial Areas Foundation. In Texas, the driving force in the network had been Latinos. Rev. Black wanted to start an all-black community organizing effort. Eventually, as the neighborhood around his church shifted from black to Latino, Rev. Black concluded that joining the broad-based organizing group was in his congregation's best interest. His thinking was that "integration has changed our community structure. There is no way to improve this community as a black community. It must be improved as a biracial community."[48] Read through the racial lens developed by black theology, this is a story about a minister refusing to persist in despair, turning too quickly toward a helping hand. The tradition of black organizing knows a thing or two about the dangers that come with helping hands of different colors. What Rev. Black should have done is to see himself as part of this tradition, to invite his congregation to discern how God is acting in their world, and to remember that peaks and valleys are a necessary part of how God works in the world. And then he should have begun a prayerful wait.

When we take race seriously in organizing, just as when we take religion or gender seriously, we can no longer measure success by the speed at which specific community goals are accomplished. Indeed, the notion that organizing is a way of efficiently achieving discrete desires is very much a symptom of our neoliberal moment. It might be objected that there are other reasons to organize in broad-based coalitions. Negotiating the many differences encountered in such coalitions forces participants to question their own beliefs and values. Diverse coalitions provide space for diverse voices within minority groups to be heard—for example, black atheists or Latino lesbians. But the pessimism of race, a pessimism so deep it may properly be understood as ontological (or theological) overwhelms these concerns. As Frank Wilderson puts it, "If the position of the Black is . . . a paradigmatic impossibility in the Western Hemisphere, indeed, in the world, in other words, if a Black is the very antithesis of a Human subject . . . then his or her paradigmatic exile is not simply a function of repressive practices on the part of institutions."[49] Race, understood as inextricably entangled with religion, marks non-being and so marks an ontological rather than an ontic difference, marks a difference that fundamentally structures the worlds not just of blacks but also of whites. To have faith in lives denied the status of human, to resurrect being out of non-being—that is the project of black theology. It is the horizon on which virtues can develop and on which the plurality of human differences can unfold. But it must be taken as decisive for how we organize.

CHAPTER 7

For What Are Blacks to Hope?

In a world of violence and suffering, it is hard enough to have faith. It is hard enough to believe, without evidence provided by the world, that there is a God who is good, who assures peace. Yet Christians are called not only to have faith but also to have hope. In other words, Christians are to be committed to a vision of the future in which goodness prevails, a time when violence and suffering end. This vision produces an uncannily bright disposition, a disposition discordant with the violence and suffering that surrounds. Christians are called to do more than endure or persevere in a world of wretchedness. They are called to thrive, to have a radiance guaranteed by the eternal happiness they know is to come—to have a radiance that itself participates in that happiness.

Hope is the definitive experience of the Christian: more definitive, we might even say, than prayer or creed or sacrament (in a sense, it is all three). It is Christianity in practice, lived, embodied. Adversity allows for Christian hope to be made visible. In comfortable circumstances, Christian hope and worldly hope are difficult to distinguish. But in the face of sustained adversity, worldly hope retreats. After all, worldly hope is really optimism, a disposition enabled and sustained by worldly circumstances.[1]

Optimism is a precarious individual disposition; Christian hope is a virtue involving affect that circulates, that swirls amidst the Body of Christ. Comfortable circumstances bring with them the performance of optimism: this is part of the spirit of late capitalism, a Christian simulacrum. There will always be more, or better, or cleaner, or smarter. In these comfortable circumstances, we will inevitably be disappointed, but we will inevitably find a new site to imagine more, better, cleaner, smarter: what Lauren Berlant has called "cruel optimism."[2] In deep adversity, away from the comforts of the consumer class, the hollowness of such optimistic performance becomes unsustainable. If there is any hope left, it is theological.

To put it strongly, Christian hope is normative for theology, and we can see Christian hope most clearly among the wretched of the earth: the martyrs and the colonized, the saints and the paupers. Blackness names one category of wretchedness, and it names wretchedness as such. In what follows, I will explore the possibilities and perils of blackness as a site for theological reflection on hope. By tracking the dialectics of black theological development, there are vital lessons to be learned about Christian hope—and so lessons to be learned for Christian theology as such. Secular theorists have also grappled with how to understand hope in the most dire circumstances, but I conclude that it is a dialogue between black theology and a Catholic theologian, Edward Schillebeeckx, that can help orient us toward hoping rightly.

Hope in Black Theology

Hope has been a remarkably consistent feature of black Christianity, and hope has often been a topic of black theological reflection. However, recent work on black theology has focused particularly on the apparent hopelessness of the black condition, leaving as an open question what role hope may play as black theology continues to develop. Before examining these recent developments, let us examine how past generations of black theologians have understood hope. Black theology can be divided into three generations. Blackness, as a category, and black theology, as a project, emerged at the same time, in the late 1960s, in the United States. The shift from "Negro" to "black" at this time was a political shift, an effort to reject a name that the group had been given by their oppressors with a name blacks gave themselves, with pride. In this atmosphere black theology meant doing theology that, at least in principle, rejected white idioms and named God in blacks' own language, as it were. This is the project of black theology, but this was only part of the project of the first generation of black theologians. For them, as for the secular proponents of black power, blackness was more than an identity in need of affirmation. Blackness was a privileged mode of existence.

To understand this claim, and to understand how it is theologically plausible, let us reframe it. Christ identifies with the "least of these," so theology should start with reflection on the experiences of the "least of these." Or, more strongly, the religious insights of the "least of these" are authoritative for theology because they represent those through whom we can hear God speaking the most clearly today. In Matthew 25, Christ labels "the least of these" the hungry, the stranger, the naked, the ill, and the prisoner. The first generation of black theologians argued that "the least of these" today are blacks (often with an expansive sense of the African diaspora). The word "black," then, took on two senses at once: it named a specific group of individuals experiencing oppression, and it named the oppressed as such.[3] Black theology is not just theology in a black idiom but a uniquely insightful mode of theology. If Christians want to learn about how to speak rightly about Christ, the church, liturgy, hell, or hope, they should listen to black theologians—or so this first generation claimed. This is what James Cone meant when he wrote that blackness refers both to an "ontological symbol" and to a "visible reality."[4] Black theology attends to the Christian faith of those with dark skin, but it also speaks to Christian faith as such, since, when blackness is understood as an "ontological symbol," it is obvious that God is black.

What insights does this first generation of black theologians offer regarding hope? To learn about the theological meaning of hope, we are to turn to the experiences of blacks—to slavery, segregation, colonialism, and racial violence. In such dire circumstances, blacks produced stories and songs that expressed faith and hope.[5] This was not just belief in an other-worldly God and a commitment to endure worldly travails—that would be faith without hope. The stories and songs of blacks expressed a belief in better things to come, both in the next world and in this world, as well as a belief that these worldly and other-worldly futures are connected but not identical. Representative of this heritage is the North Star, featured frequently in black stories and songs. The North Star stands for both the heavens, a world beyond the miseries of the present, and the Northern states and Canada, viewed as a place of safety for those in the Southern states. There is hope in the future, and this future is both other-worldly and this-worldly. Faith in God and other-worldly hope fuel this-worldly hope. Indeed, the heavens quite literally offer a practical route to a better future in this world: by "reading" the heavens rightly, by locating the

North Star and following it, racial violence could be evaded. Similarly, the famous slave spiritual "Swing Low, Sweet Chariot" includes the line "Steal away to Jesus," commonly understood to refer to escape from slavery in addition to its more obvious religious meaning. The spiritual "Canaan" likewise includes the equivocal lines "Run to Jesus—shun the danger" and "I am bound for the land of Canaan."

While the hope expressed in slave stories and songs can certainly be inspirational, what seems most useful for theological reflection is the clarity such expressions can bring regarding the relationship between this-worldly hope and other-worldly hope. It is tempting to understand other-worldly hope expressed as exoteric and this-worldly hope expressed as esoteric, protected from broader view because of the looming threat of racial violence. In other words, it is tempting to dismiss the religious language of black stories and songs as simply expressing secular concerns—and secular hope. But this quick dismissal reflects a misunderstanding of hope, a reduction of hope to either a plan for the future or a desire for an improbable but fantasized future. Neither view captures hope as a disposition or virtue, hope as a way of responding to dire circumstances, without despair. Such a virtue necessarily finds expression in concrete, worldly terms: desires for *this* and *that*, obtainable through *these* channels. But such a virtue is not exhausted by such expressions—just as blackness may be a concrete, worldly expression of the "least of these," even though the experiences of blacks do not offer an exhaustive account of who God is. In the songs and stories of those enslaved, the irreducible equivocation between the this-worldly and the other-worldly is a marker of hope's irreducibility to specific desires or fantasies. Indeed, this is another marker of the paradox at the heart of Christianity: the divine and the human together yet distinct, the supernatural inhering in the natural. It is tempting to forget this essential paradox when discussing hope, a concept that seems at first so unequivocal, but black theology reminds us that hope, to be Christian, must contain paradox within it.

Yet this is only the first moment in the development of black theology, and tracking the dialectical development of black theology will offer further insights into hope. The initial development of black theology was precarious for two reasons. First, the world is in motion. Once one group in particular is identified with the "least of these," what happens when circumstances change and that group no longer counts, empirically, as "least"? What happens when slavery ends, when colonialism ends, when de jure segregation ends? Or, what happens when new forms of oppression take aim at a similar, but not exactly the same, community as had previously suffered deep oppression? Once a theological endeavor takes hold and becomes institutionalized in the academy and the church, it reproduces itself rather than responding to dynamic conditions on the ground. In other words, a theology built on any particular "least of these" has a tendency to lag behind the actual experiences of worldly suffering and so has a tendency to say things about God that are systematically amiss. The second problem faced by initial endeavors in black theology was that choosing any particular name for the "least of these" elides the internal differences and complications within the group to which that name refers. A growing body of scholarly literature on multiple marginalization and intersectionality points to the way that, for example, treating the experiences of black women simply under the heading of "black experience" significantly misrepresents black women's experiences and could even amplify the violence of whiteness and patriarchy. In short, naming blacks as the "least of these" is a blunt instrument that can itself do violence; more nuance is necessary to describe the world and its ills as they really are.

These concerns with the initial thrust of black theology spawned a second wave of black theologians who saw the project of black theology as one among many forms of contextual theology, all important and all interlinked. While this might be called a "second generation" of black theology, as I showed in Chapter 1, even the most recognizable figure from the first generation, James Cone, began to redescribe black theology as simply explicating the Christian faith of the black community. Among the consequences of this shift was a change in emphasis from politics to culture, from struggle against oppression to embrace of African American history and values. Through the late 1970s and 1980s and beyond, theologians explicated the Christianity of black women, immigrants, queers, and multiracial individuals, among others. Each of these groups was also marginalized and also resilient. Myriad differences—a rainbow of differences—no longer had to be subsumed under monolithic labels like "blackness." Indeed, everyone qualifies, in some way, as part of a group that has been among the "least of these," and we can now learn to embrace these aspects of ourselves. Each community speaks of hope in its own way, based on its own history, its own struggles, its own insights—literally or figuratively, in its own language. Black theologians are among the many voices that can enrich our conversation about hope, or so this second wave of black theologians suggested.

Afro-Pessimism

Over the past decade, several currents in black studies have been consolidated under the name "Afro-pessimism."[6] These currents have been both theological and secular; they have also challenged the division between the theological and the secular. They have been consolidated by black studies scholars, and their consolidation has given new justification to the existence of black studies departments: Afro-pessimism names a complex global problem that can be addressed with many disciplinary methodologies, but, most essentially, it is a problem that has to do with blackness. In other words, black studies does not have to justify its existence by modeling itself on Latino or Asian American or Native American studies. Afro-pessimism is now inflecting the work of black theologians, pushing the conversation in black theology beyond the contextual focus of the second wave. Afro-pessimism promises to renew the importance, authority, and intellectual ferment of black theology as it has for black studies.

What is Afro-pessimism? Bringing together elements of the thought of Frantz Fanon, Sylvia Wynter, Hortense Spillers, and Achille Mbembe, among others, Afro-pessimism makes four basic claims. First, blackness is not like other differences—not like racial or ethnic differences nor like the differences of gender, sexuality, or disability. Second, blackness does not assimilate and fade away. Integration, at least as conventionally understood, is impossible. Third, blackness is an ontological condition. It names the condition faced by a person for whom the very possibility of being is foreclosed. Fourth and finally, blackness is woven deeply into the fabric of Western metaphysics. In other words, the oppression of blacks may be an empirical condition, but it is also much deeper, so addressing that oppression requires much more than reducing present suffering. Altogether, Afro-pessimism is so labeled because it points to the depth and gravity of black oppression, and it suggests that the many efforts at ameliorating that oppression over the years and decades have been in vain.

The claims of Afro-pessimism are supported by appeals to empirical evidence, by accounts of the history of Western thought, and, in some cases, by theological engagement. Empirically, Afro-pessimists point to data showing how, for example, the end of de jure segregation did not improve the conditions of blacks in the United States (or how the end of colonialism did not improve the conditions of blacks in Africa). They point to continuities between the treatment of blacks during slavery, during segregation, and today, in what has been dubbed the era of mass incarceration.

The cultural currency of such arguments has increased dramatically in recent years as police brutality and racial violence have again caught the attention of the American public: Trayvon Martin, Ferguson, stop-and-frisk. Yet the hard numbers and painful experiences have been there for any to see for years. There is a one-in-three chance that a black boy will go to jail, the percentage of black children in segregated schools has stayed around seventy-five for the last fifty years, and the average wealth of black households stands at around $6,000 compared to around $110,000 for white households. There are similarly stark empirical differences when comparing blacks to other minority ethnic groups within the United States. Those groups show significantly greater signs of upward mobility, just as other "developing" regions show greater economic gains than Africa. The severity and apparent permanence of these many disparities motivate Afro-pessimists to posit deep roots for black oppression.

Those deep roots of anti-blackness are located, by many Afro-pessimists, in the history of Western thought. In the secular philosophical tradition, Enlightenment thinkers including David Hume, Immanuel Kant, and Georg Wilhelm Friedrich Hegel all held deeply negative views of blacks.[7] Even when these views are ostensibly distinct from philosophical claims, Afro-pessimists argue that racism still infects the philosophical ideas that have come to dominate the West. Ideas that ostensibly proclaimed liberty also ensured servitude for blacks. In the theological register, Afro-pessimists argue that Christian anti-Judaism continued in a new guise with anti-black racism.[8] Explicitly or implicitly supersessionist theology, even when it has little to say about blacks, functions to authorize racial violence. To combat anti-blackness, Afro-pessimists seek to reconfigure the philosophical or theological tradition in a way that affirms all humanity, not just white, European "man."[9] Until that task is complete, until the very structures of thought that shape our world are revamped, the dire empirical conditions that blacks face will persist, no matter how much effort goes into racial reconciliation and "reform."

Black theologians indebted to Afro-pessimist thought are unsatisfied with the felicitous diversity embraced by their second-wave predecessors. Put starkly, framing theology in terms of the rhetoric, really the ideology, of diversity seems troublingly untheological. Not only is it untheological, it apparently buys into neoliberalism's characteristic style of identity management: identities are choices, desires, never fixed or mandatory, always fluid, always subordinate to the individual free agent. Cultural specificities add richness to life—tasty food and music, curious customs and gregarious neighbors—but they never bring with them normativity. Further, and even more theologically troubling, the ideology of multiculturalism goes hand in hand with the ideology of secularism: religion ("religious identity") is managed by the same mechanisms as race ("racial identity"), both allowed as entertainment, forbidden as anything more.[10] Second-wave black theologians took their task to be explicating the Christianity of a community, but is this not, ultimately, a form of diversity divertissement? And is not theology, after all, supposed to be about God, not about humans?

Today we are witnessing a third wave of black theology, and it is not simply a return to the first wave. While both agree on the privileged, authoritative place of black experience in the theological enterprise, for the first wave this role is contingent while for the third wave this role is necessary. Anti-blackness, as a continuation of supersessionism, is the paradigmatic heresy, not just one more manifestation of marginalization. Put another way, if the first wave of black theology was political and the second wave was cultural, the third wave is metaphysical, though the metaphysics at stake has clear and powerful political implications. The turn to culture, from the perspective of the third wave, is premature, for black cultural production, like black sociality, is always born out of pathology and offers no hope for redemption. At most, black culture offers reminders that white or colorblind hegemonic culture is incomplete and unsatisfying.[11]

What can Afro-pessimism and third-wave black theology teach us about hope? Unlike the first and second waves of black theology, the third wave has remained relatively silent on hope. Whether or not the claims of Afro-pessimism are ultimately correct—thinking through the complications of race in a context like Europe or the persistent nexus of Islamophobia and race does urge caution—it is a sufficiently plausible theory to pose a dramatic problem for how we understand hope, perhaps accounting for the silence of recent black theological writing on the topic. The depth of the challenge posed by Afro-pessimism suggests that this is an especially productive site for theological reflection. The Afro-pessimist bottom line is that hope for improvements in the lives of blacks has been misplaced. Does this mean that the only hope possible is other-worldly, that the earlier black theological insights about the paradoxical connection between this-worldly and other-worldly hope were misguided? Before turning to further theological reflection on this question, it will be helpful to review how deep pessimism has resulted in novel accounts of hope in recent secular scholarship.

Deep Racism and Secular Hope

Afro-pessimist scholarship itself rarely turns toward practical questions and rarely asks, *What are we to do?*, or, *How are we to hope?*[12] This scholarship consists largely in descriptive work, taking political events (lynchings and police shootings, for example) as symptoms of a deeper, racialized metaphysics. There is, however, a broader scholarly conversation about deep pessimism caused by difference that may be instructive. Scholars of Native American studies, immigration, and queer studies have also explored how these categories of difference are deeply embedded in Western culture, but in some cases they have grappled more explicitly with questions of hope.

Jonathan Lear has identified a virtue he labels "radical hope" in Native American communities facing the elimination of their ways of life.[13] Focusing on Plenty Coups, the last chief of the Crow, Lear studies a context where the social practices that constituted the Crow world were no longer possible. For example, with lands stolen by the U.S. government and traditional means of resolving conflicts disrupted by firearms, the practice of bravery in battle was no longer possible. Bravery had involved face painting by a wife, care for horses, and recounting the victory post-battle; it was thoroughly woven into Crow life, and with the disappearance of the material conditions for Crow life, bravery, too, disappeared. To be a Crow meant to do the social practices of the Crow, but when those social practices are foreclosed, Lear echoes Plenty Coups in concluding that "nothing happened." The Crow continued to live, but with their culture gone it was only the barest form of biological existence. The good life, its meaning culturally determined, could no longer be pursued; practical reasoning went haywire when there were no longer specific goods to be pursued. However, all was not lost. As Lear tells it, Plenty Coup had a dream (this medium indicating a break with practical reason) that the chief interpreted to mean that the Crow must acknowledge their traditional way of life was coming to an end, but they also must be committed to the notion that the Crow will survive and new social practices and new goods will come about, even if it is impossible to know what they are or how they will come about now. This radical hope rejected as futile practical reasoning, self-destruction, and fantasy. Soberly assessing the world as it is, radical hope persists in acting as if a wholly new world is possible—and so exercises the virtues of adaptability and perceptiveness. Yet radical hope only works, Lear argues, because of the Crow's premise that God exists and is good.

Might radical hope offer a way for black theology to respond to the problem of Afro-pessimism? There are clear similarities between the cultural devastation faced by the Native American community that Lear studies and the cultural devastation wrought on blacks through, among other things, the slave trade and the prison system. Unlike the Crow, black cultural devastation was not a one-off event but, according to the Afro-pessimist critique, is an ongoing process inherent in Euro-American culture itself, continually grinding away at the social practices of blacks. Or, put another way, the continual pressures on black individuals and communities tend not simply to take away social practices but to corrupt them, changing them at times from incubators of virtue to incubators of vice (one thinks of the corporate appropriation of black music or the performance of black respectability necessary for success in the white business world). Lear's account of radical hope depends on a robust culture that once, in the not-too-distant past, existed to fuel hope for the future. This past is the source of the chickadee, the symbol of hope in Plenty Coups' dream, along with the Crow view of God and the crucial practice of dream interpretation. The Afro-pessimist charges that Western anti-blackness is so deep-seated that there was never a robust culture from which such a radical hope could flow; even if there was, the centuries of fruitless hope and embattled community would surely lead to the collapse of the virtue.

Another approach to deep racism is to reject hope altogether, favoring instead two different sorts of alternatives: an embrace of grief or an embrace of the present. Anne Cheng's *The Melancholy of Race* exemplifies the former approach. She agrees that racialization has an enormous, persistent impact—in the context of her study, on African Americans and Asian Americans. She agrees that race shapes the ideological foundations of the West. In her view, the usual response to racism, articulating grievances and pressing for them to be addressed, does not adequately address the depths of the problem; indeed, it masks those depths. By formulating a list of grievances and putting one's hopes in the possibility that they will be rectified, the racialized subject imagines that she will achieve equality and dignity. Then, she will be just like everyone else. The world will be postracial. Cheng argues that grievances obscure grief, the deeper process that afflicts the psyche of racialized subjects who know they will never be "normal." Grief distorts the psyche of white subjects, as well, since white identity is constituted in relation to the racialized other. In the face of deep pessimism, the proper response, in this view, is to look beyond the specific grievances (and hopes) of a racial minority and instead explore the varied ways that the wound of racism sabotages the affective economy of that minority. Acknowledging and interrogating rather than rejecting grief—

racial melancholia—is the only way to see the world rightly and so is the prerequisite for any properly directed social or political action.

Cheng's response to deep racial pessimism is decidedly secular and decidedly individualist. Her critique of grievance, which could be read as a critique of hope directed at specific objects or as a critique of desires for specific goals masked as hope, is in a sense a critique of idolatry, but her response to idolatry is to reject transcendence altogether in favor of the folds and wrinkles of immanence—of our affective economies. But what if we consider grievances not as ends in themselves but as instrumentally used in collective (anti-racist) struggle? Might the process of collective struggle, and not any particular goal, provide a means of healing psyches damaged by racism? Tracking and probing this damage seems less important than commending the forms of collective practice and community organizing that could cultivate the virtues that serve as a buffer against disabling grief. Indeed, this is a point made forcefully by first- and second-generation black theologians: black communities are essentially communities of struggle and, as such, shape character in a way that holds off despair.

Like Cheng, Lee Edelman rejects hope and acknowledges the radical exclusions faced by minority communities.[14] Edelman is particularly concerned with queer men, and for him queer identity is fundamentally opposed to any future orientation—and so to any hope. The normative, heterosexual world is concerned with the future because it is concerned with reproduction: individuals with reproducing themselves through their children and societies with reproducing themselves from generation to generation. The figure of the child is sanctified, according to Edelman, because she or he represents this reproduction of the way things are. Yet queers, as incapable of reproduction, are excluded from this heteronormative way of seeing the world. Indeed, queers disrupt the smooth reproduction of the ways of the world—and, Edelman contends, they ought to embrace this role. They will not suffer now so that a child can have a better life, and they ought to embrace pleasure in the moment rather than pleasure deferred to the next generation. In short, queers are a minority structurally excluded from Western metaphysics, with its implicit commitment to procreation, and the proper response for such a minority is to happily embrace hopelessness along with temporality centered on the *now*.

Edelman helpfully demonstrates the way that interest in the future is closely tied to self-interest and to the powers that be in the present. He also helpfully demonstrates the way that minority groups whose exclusion is fundamental to regnant ideology can potentially short-circuit that ideology by refusing to participate in normative, future-directed practices. Indeed, there is at times a messianic tone to Edelman's project as he finds the fullness of time in the present moment. Yet the heart of Edelman's project is an extension of Cheng's, an extension from the critique of idolatry to the critique of ideology. Where Cheng took issue with specific hopes, Edelman presents himself as taking issue with hope as such—but in fact he is taking issue with hope motivated by present social structures and institutions. In other words, Edelman is warning against hope that is really not about the wholly new, warning against hope that advances the interests of the old with the rhetoric of the wholly new. For Edelman, as for Cheng, the only alternative is making ourselves into gods: an even deeper form of idolatry (an even subtler rouse of ideology). Black theologians grappling with Afro-pessimism can learn much from these secular efforts and their sharp critical perspectives, but black theologians also bring to the problem of racism a view of hope directed toward a God who is irreducible to worldly terms or desires.

God the Future of Blacks

The quick and easy response of black theologians to Afro-pessimism is to simply present Christ as the solution. In the Afro-pessimist framework, black being is an oxymoron: blackness has no being; it is defined by its exclusion from being. Christ raises the dead, turning non-being into being, flesh defined by death into flesh defined by life. Participation in Christ means participation in his resurrection: denying the world's denial of being. Such a stance does not take the form of overcoming blackness, of becoming white. That blackness is defined by death does not mean that whiteness is defined by life. To the contrary, whiteness hubristically claims life, being, on its own—whiteness claims ontology without theology, and that is idolatry. Blackness is not outside of being but paradoxically inside and outside at once, being that is not counted as being, that thus disturbs the regime that would hubristically define being. J. Kameron Carter, working along these lines, thus labels blackness "paraontological."[15]

Concealing the being of the slave, or the prisoner, or the native takes much ideological work, for the principle of black non-being must overcome the stubbornness of lived reality. Blackness points to the precariousness of ontology, reminds us that the present order of being is not natural, not universal. Blackness essentially destabilizes the order of things, so the resurrection of black being is not the assimilation of blackness into the order of things, into whiteness, but rather is the triumph of the theological over the ontological. What does this mean concretely? The resurrection of black being means black agency: black writing, black art, black rhetoric, and black creativity that are unexpected, unauthorized, and, from the perspective of the white world, often unintelligible. The slave writes, the prisoner paints, or the native imagines. The objects of these verbs, these acts, need not be God—indeed cannot be God, for that would be idolatry. Independent of their object, these verbs represent participation in God because they represent the resurrection of non-being into being, blackness triumphant, Christ triumphant.

This account of black theology responsive to Afro-pessimism is appealing but ultimately deeply flawed. It suffers from individualism, a profoundly secular ailment—the ailment that defines the secular. The creativity and strength of the black man (for such creative agency is gendered) will save the world from itself. In this theology there is no space for community, for love, or, crucially, for hope. There are no virtues of blackness developed in community, just the act of individual rebellion against the powers that be. And there is no vision of a future world transformed, just a set of disconnected black men doing art in their attics, as it were. The black theologian inclined to such a view may respond that "church" would consist of the informal networks created among these, what Stefano Harney and Fred Moten call "the undercommons."[16] But such networks seem a far cry from communities of virtue that could nurture, sustain, and properly order the black rebellious spirit. Indeed, such a theological perspective suffers from an extreme Christocentrism, the theological vice corresponding to the secular vice of individualism. Christ cleaved from God and Spirit defines all value; indeed, what matters on this account is not even a Christ who loves or suffers but exclusively a Christ who is risen.

What we need is a black theology responsive to Afro-pessimism but also concerned with the social world, with love, and with justice. The theological reflections of Edward Schillebeeckx offer a useful, if unexpected, resource to accomplish this task. Of Schillebeeckx's extensive, learned corpus, I will focus exclusively on one essay, "The New Image of God, Secularization and Man's Future on Earth," the final chapter of *God the Future of Man*.[17] This is a particularly important essay, consolidating much of Schillebeeckx's thought and clearly developing the themes that are central to much of his writing over the decades before and after its 1968 publication. It is essentially an essay about secularity. Schillebeeckx makes three key points. First, he offers a new way to think about secularization. Christians, instead of lamenting declining church membership rolls, should see secularization as part of a reorientation away from the past and toward the future. Science and technology hold new possibilities, while changing social arrangements create new ways of living. Life no longer consists of repeating the past or interpreting the past for lessons on the present. Instead of looking backward, we now look forward. To determine what ought to be done now we look less to what has always been done than to what might eventually be done. We act on our hopes instead of on our memories.

Schillebeeckx's second point is that God is, as his book's title suggests, our future. Where the Christian tradition has embraced the slogan that God is the first and the last, the emphasis has too often been on the first, *in the beginning*, according to Schillebeeckx. Shifting this emphasis, Schillebeeckx encourages us to think of God as the "wholly New," that which is to come, and he encourages us to think of Christ as demonstrating that we ourselves can participate in God by creating anew, leaving behind the sins of our past. For Schillebeeckx, God is the future not of any individual but of humanity collectively: *our* future. Given this second point, Schillebeeckx is able to view modernization and secularization cheerfully. Instead of mourning a decline in religiosity, Schillebeeckx sees secularization bringing with it a better religiosity, one based on a more correct understanding of God. Secularization strips away old idols that tied Christianity to this world—that made God an object of this world, determined by history. The shift in human orientation toward the future that happens with secularization is a shift in orientation toward God.

The problem with an orientation toward the future is that humans find themselves unmoored from norms of the past, so it would seem as though anything goes. It is clear how to look backward for normativity, to judge based on what has been done before, but it is not clear what it would mean to look forward for normativity. If God is the future of humankind, must this be a God without standards or morality? Schillebeeckx's third point is meant to address this worry: "The Christian inspiration in socio-economic and political life is therefore directed, by its 'critical negativity,' against every image of man whose lines are strictly drawn or which presents itself as a positive and total definition and against the illusory expectation that science and technology are capable of solving the ultimate problems of man's existence."[18] In short, Schillebeeckx embraces negative theology, or theology as the critique of idolatry (and ideology). The future must remain unnamable. If it is named, as so often happens when humans are oriented toward the future, this must be criticized by theology because such naming ascribes a worldly identity to the divine. Christian hope is distinguished from secular optimism because the former refuses to be sated with any object or concept. Secularization's reorientation of humans toward the future can be a proper orientation toward God, or it can be another form of idolatry, like the orientation to the past. Schillebeeckx's third point, about negative theology, is necessary to render judgment on whether this future orientation is properly theological. Such judgment is rendered in a community that keeps alive the vision of God as wholly new: in church.

Might we think of black experience as involving a form of secularization? Might the experiences of slavery, segregation, and imprisonment offer the possibility of shifting black orientation from the past to the future? Where the social transformations accompanying modernity severed the normative force of the past for whites, the normative force of the past was severed much more directly for blacks: through violent displacement, incarceration, and death. Mothers and fathers, grandmothers and grandfathers, were taken away—are being taken away. One response is a nostalgic turn backward to an impossible past: fantasy images of Africa, newly created rituals to remember "the ancestors," and, at the intellectual level, a fixation on the experience of slavery as overdetermining black experience.[19] Another response is to hope. Here hope means an orientation toward the future, necessitated by the inaccessibility of the past. When God is understood as wholly new, as God is for Schillebeeckx, experience can be said to orient blacks toward God. Moreover, Schillebeeckx offers "critical negativity," nurtured in loving community, as a tool to determine when this orientation goes wrong. In dialogue with the insights of Schillebeeckx, black theology is essentially negative theology on the conceptual level; on the level of practice, it embraces the theological virtues. Moreover, the sudden, severe breaks with the past experienced by blacks suggest that, from Schillebeeckx's perspective, black theology ought to be paradigmatic for all theology: it offers a much more intense version of the gradual reorientation from backward-looking to forward-looking that Schillebeeckx identifies and commends in European modernity.

This Schillebeeckxian inflection of black theology is responsive to the worries of Afro-pessimism because it takes as its starting point that the denial of black being is deeply entwined with the metaphysics of the West. This is the mechanism, in the realm of ideas, resulting in the violence, in the realm of practice, that severs blacks from the past. A missing father can be found; an impossible father is irretrievable—resulting in melancholy or in an orientation toward the future.[20] The foreclosure of black being is not just about police stops and incarceration rates, moments when humans are treated as less than human. Those practices are authorized by a metaphysics: this is the Afro-pessimist insight. According to such metaphysics, blacks have no history; blacks are excluded from the unfolding of being through world history. Black community, and particularly black religious community—church—gathers individuals who cannot be oriented toward the past and negotiates an orientation toward the future—toward God. That community is founded on the memory and real presence of Jesus Christ: the possibility for black being to be resurrected. Christ offers the foundational norm for that community, a model of how death can become life and how false hopes (in objects, in law, in self) are to be quashed. Together, as community, as Body of Christ, the black church negotiates proper orientation toward the future—and so properly worships God.

Unlike the first generation of black theology, this Schillebeeckxian inflection of black theology accounts for the depths of anti-blackness in the West. Unlike the second generation of black theology, this Schillebeeckxian approach does not take culture or community as an end point. Culture and community do not provide the norms for black theology; Jesus Christ does. But culture and community, for those forcibly detached from their past, provide a way to maintain proper orientation toward the future—to hope rightly. Like the secular theories of deep racism already discussed, the approach outlined here acknowledges how problematic hope is for those enduring intractable wretchedness, but unlike the secular theories, theological hope can now be cleaved from idolatrous hope.

Is this Schillebeeckxian inflection of black theology at all political, or is the hope it commends simply a religious-ethical practice? The critique of idolatry and ideology is always political, and such critique is, first and foremost, the task commended by this account. This critique goes hand in hand with hope. It is a critique of those who would turn police into gods, prisons into hell, and settlers into saviors. The virtue of hope is political because it is inextricable from such critique, but hope also fuels the activity of communities oriented toward the future, committed to building new practices and institutions together. It is not for theology to specify in advance what those practices and institutions will be. That would be idolatry. The task for the theologian, rather, is to clear the intellectual space necessary for this essential, life-giving work to be sustained.

CHAPTER 8

For What Are Whites to Hope?

There has now been an astounding transformation in racial politics in the United States. Trayvon Martin was a moment, but with the addition of Eric Garner and Michael Brown we now have a movement. These names stand for both a change in consciousness and concrete mobilizations. I never saw as many black students gathered together on my campus as I did in front of our chapel to honor the memory of Trayvon Martin and to call for action. I never heard so many black and white students on my campus naming police violence as a problem, not only in the halls but on posters at marches, as I did after the deaths of Eric Garner and Michael Brown. Something is happening that is unprecedented in my generation. The careful management of blackness by the apparatus of diversity has been exposed as a farce, chief diversity officers and cultural awareness programming concealing the daily violence and humiliation that never was hidden from "the least of these." Anti-blackness was concealed from those who were anti-black, and the story of multicultural harmony was sold to blacks themselves. It was bought by some middle-class blacks but never really believed. False consciousness can only go so far down when faced with the realities of the police and courts. Even so, false consciousness is powerful, maintaining the inertia of the status quo, until it doesn't. Those names—Trayvon, Eric, Michael—gather those memories of official violence, violence that had gone unnamed, and so interrupting the inertia of the status quo.

James Cone describes the interruption that was the black power movement, an interruption that caused him to set aside his dissertation on Karl Barth, to step away from his white liberal professors, and to reimagine theology from the perspective of blacks.[1] Three decades have passed, and that interruption, like the interruption effected by Martin Luther King Jr., has been incorporated into the status quo. King represents diversity for the nation; Cone represents diversity for the theological guild. We are in an era of neoliberal multiculturalism.[2] Today, diversity means multicolored Band-Aids on the six gunshot wounds in Michael Brown's dead body. It is easy to say, hopelessly, that the institutional incorporation and subsequent political impotence of those names, King and Cone, was inevitable. They performed an appealing—because safe: short, high-pitched—form of black masculinity that was ostensibly directed at black audiences but actually did its work among white audiences. In King's case, this critique of black leadership is by now well worn by scholars and activists. Black people did not need a leader to tell them that they were oppressed and that change could, someday, come. Black people in the United States have known this since the Middle Passage. Black people did not need to be told where to march; grassroots organizers had been unglamorously organizing for years, since time immemorial. In short, charismatic leadership is more likely to bring manipulation than salvation.[3] It manipulates hopes, attracting people to divinized worldly leaders and away from both the concrete and the other-worldly.

It would be uncharitable and unrealistic to extrapolate conclusions about Cone from reflections on King. As we have seen in Chapter 1, Cone stridently affirmed the unique power of black theological vision in his earliest writings; later, Cone embraced black theology as contextual theology, as one vantage point among many from which to speak of God. With King killed, it was the public, or the powers that be, that did the work of diversifying King, of ushering him into our era of neoliberal multiculturalism. Cone did this work himself, changing his views with the changing times. Yet Cone's theological reflections were never as easily assimilable into a multicultural mainstream as King's theological vision. In a sense, it is lucky that there was Cone to do the assimilating himself. My worry, to state it bluntly, is that Cone's personal embodiment as black theology functions as King's personal embodiment as integration. Black Christians have been doing black theology since time immemorial; it is whites who need a James Cone, and it is whites to whom he essentially speaks.

My point in these reflections on Cone and King is to warn against a certain response to our current moment of racial crises, to warn against a certain style of hope. We do not need a leader, an Al Sharpton—who conveniently presents himself as both King and Cone at once. We do not need black elites telling black folks about black oppression or urging black folks to organize or to pray. What black elites—black scholars and black theologians—can do is weaken the intellectual defenses of white supremacy. This means ideology critique: challenging the hold that certain ideas have, certain ideas that make the status quo seem natural. In other words, rather than black elites performing their blackness for a white audience, black elites ought to directly address that white audience, naming what is taken for granted by those whites, naming that conventional wisdom that is actually constitutive of whiteness. In ideology critique (in theological terms this is the critique of idolatry), the space is cleared for the ongoing organizing efforts of ordinary blacks to flourish and for the ongoing prayers of ordinary black Christians to be voiced. For this the black theologian should hope: to weaken the hold of the idols of white supremacy so that the least of these can speak for themselves. It is only in their voices, in their movements, that we are sure to find the divine.

This has been my apologia for conceptual work, for what might seem like a venture into the realm of abstraction on a topic that calls for the practical. The question—for what are whites to hope—would seem to call for a specific, concrete answer, but I am more concerned with how this question is approached, how it is understood, and why it is deemed pressing. In what follows I sketch conceptual terrain. I hypothesize that hope often functions to support the status quo—specifically in a racial context, this means supporting white supremacy.[4] Hope does this in various ways, for hope is used variously, and I see no reason to suppose that all usages point to the same concept. My efforts are intended to be more suggestive than conclusive, asking new questions rather than providing new answers. But I do think these reflections have practical significance, at least in the negative. Religious communities, and specifically Christian communities, have a tendency to sanctify profane hopes, or profane styles of hoping, and this deserves the name "idolatry." To be clear, I am not arguing that all secular hopes are idolatrous, just as it would be absurd to argue that all secular loves are idolatrous. Rather, hopes are idolatrous if they are not oriented by our relationship to the good, or God, just as loves are idolatrous if they are not so oriented. Aquinas puts it strongly: God is the ultimate object of all our proper hopes, as of our proper loves, even when those hopes or loves seem directed at worldly objects or people. But whiteness has nothing to do with godliness, and hope understood in such a way as to secure the mythology of white supremacy must not be understood as theological.

Hope as Desire

In nearly all secular philosophical accounts of hope today, hope is analyzed as a desire that is not certain to be fulfilled.[5] Understood in this way, hope is not oriented toward the good. Hope is a descriptive rather than a normative term. Or, if hopes are to be judged, they are to be judged based on whether an individual has reason to so desire, not whether the object hoped for is good in itself. This approach admirably links hope and reason, ensuring that hope does not float freely in an imagined realm of pure feeling. But by tethering hope to reason and desire, hope becomes isolated from the broader context of a life and a world. Analyzing hope becomes a matter of counting and weighing discrete reasons and desires at a particular moment in a particular life. The individual is imagined as an abstracted bundle of desire—a desire for friends, a desire for money, or a desire to live in a warm climate. One does not habitually hope, repeatedly aiming one's passion in certain directions; hope is simply a fact about what one is doing at a particular moment. Community is effectively irrelevant for hope as desire; hopes are accountable to nothing beyond the individual. If a hope is to be judged wrong, it could only be because an individual makes errors of reasoning or perception concerning her own desires.

When hope is understood in this way, we forget that hope is cultivated in community and that hopes may be evaluated in terms other than rational self-interest. A hope for equality or for racial justice would be motivated by an individual desire, not by the goodness of the end desired. This individual desire would be motivated by reasons, and it could be challenged or refined by exchanging reasons with others. Hope understood in this way does not result in a disposition to act in certain ways. A reason for action is one reason among many; there are also many reasons not to act in ways that advance racial justice (for example, desires for social stability, desires to preserve status, desires to maintain the economic benefits that whites derive from racism). Because reasons are weighed differently at each moment, there is no sense of hope as a habit in this view. Yet we have a strong intuition that hope does resemble a disposition and that it cannot be confined to the bounds of the atomized self. What are the consequences of understanding hope as desire in this way? When hope is taken to be a desire for a specific state of affairs—racial justice conceived in a particular way, for example—it is invested in and secures the ways that we see the world today. That hoped-for state of affairs is hoped for in the language, as it were, that we speak here, now. But the language that we speak here, now, is deeply distorted by racial injustice. The reasons we have for our current desires are based on what we consider facts about the world, but these facts are seen through racializing lenses. The dramatic transformation that is necessary to free ourselves from racialized ways of perceiving and acting cannot be plotted from the perspective of the present.

Hope as Affect

Hope is sometimes taken to be in the head, but at other times it is taken to be in the heart, as it were, as an affect. Understood in this way, hope becomes a personality type and a mood. There are some people who are hopeful. They see the glass half full. Others are not hopeful, seeing the glass half empty. After a string of successes an individual is more hopeful than after a string of defeats. In youth an individual is more hopeful than in middle age. Further, affects circulate; they are contagious.[6] To be surrounded by hopeful people increases the hopefulness of one who is otherwise not particularly hopeful. There are cultures that might be said to include a robust swirl of hopefulness: elite high schools preparing students for Ivy League colleges, for instance, or a running club training for a marathon, or the fans of a sports team, or the supporters of a political candidate. Some have argued recently that capitalism depends on and cultivates the circulation of hope, with the individual consumer or worker perennially seeing her economic glass half full.[7] Understood as affect, hope is not essentially a belief about the future but rather a feeling about the future; if it seems that hopeful people believe things about the future it is because that is how their feeling manifests itself. Moreover, as an affect, hope in this view is not reducible to a disposition. It is not that a hopeful individual tends to respond to adverse circumstances by persevering (that is the virtue of faith).[8] Rather, affects are deeper than any of their visible manifestations in dispositions; an affect names the passions of the heart. Affects sometimes, but not always, express themselves in words or actions; they do not necessarily do so consistently.

Hope, in this view, is not directed at a certain object. Circumstances may be dire, but there remains a feeling that they will certainly improve. Racism may be trenchant and cruel, but it will not last forever. Such a feeling is cultivated as it circulates: listening to King's "I Have a Dream" speech, reading tweets, or participating in an interracial dialogue group. Yet the connection between affect and action is tenuous, and particularly so when affect circulates in a space that necessarily downplays actually existing racial disparities. When hope for racial justice is cultivated by being around others who hope for racial justice, the problem of racial justice is understood as being out there, something for us, who are racially unmarked, to go work toward. In addition to eliding the complicity of those who hope, this way of understanding hope tends to mask precisely the questions of judgment, and the process of exchanging reasons, over which the account of hope as desire obsessed. If hope circulates as affect, how is it to be challenged, refined, or made actionable?[9] Further, the feeling of hope from a position of privilege is qualitatively different from the feeling of hope from a marginal position. The former tends toward optimism while the latter interrupts a world of despair. Seeing a glass half full is quite a different experience when you are at a restaurant and when you are trudging through a desert. Christopher Lasch has compellingly argued that optimism is a different creature than hope: optimism entrenches the interests of the wealthy and powerful by assuring all that the way society is structured is the way it ought to be structured.[10] What seems amiss now will soon be corrected.

Hope as Rhetoric

When we hear someone proclaim that they hope for the end to racial injustice, this statement may be interpreted in three ways. It can be interpreted as expressing hope as desire or affect, already discussed, or it can be interpreted as rhetoric, a speech act intended to persuade. Hope's rhetorical power is famous, or infamous: it stood metonymically for all of Barack Obama's rhetorical skill in his 2008 presidential campaign. Obama was using language to mobilize the masses, not representing any desire he held about the future (his desires were notoriously realist) and not describing his affective state (which was notoriously flat). Certainly rhetoric works to persuade by tapping the affect of listeners and by catalyzing the circulation of affect, but rhetoric itself is distinct from affect, and rhetoric uses both reason and affect to persuade.[11] Most of the time we hear the word "hope" used, at least in public discourse in the United States, it connotes the rhetoric of hope rather than hope as affect or desire.

It is tempting to cynically dismiss all of the language of hope as it concerns race, as it concerns whites desiring racial progress, as *mere* rhetoric. At least as used in the white public sphere, the language of hope regarding race suggests neither an affect nor a desire on the part of the speaker. It attempts to persuade listeners first and foremost that the problem of race is not intractable, that a solution will inevitably be found. A solution will inevitably be found because the rhetoric of hope relies on a commitment to historical progress. All worldly problems will, sooner or later, be resolved because of human ingenuity. Further, the language of hope in the white public sphere, whether employed by whites or blacks, persuades blacks that racial injustice will come to an end. For both audiences, ironically, hope as rhetoric at once implies that humans have the capacity to rectify racial injustices and absolves individual humans of the responsibility to fight racial injustice. Because history is moving in the direction of racial equality, does it really matter whether I personally join the struggle? Why would history need me to move it along? Some would object that the rhetoric of hope is meant to disrupt stasis. Things would remain the same indefinitely if there were not a sense that they could change, and change for the better. But on questions of racial justice and of white involvement in racial justice struggles, both doing nothing and doing something from a position of privilege are problematic. The something that could be done from a position of privilege is something shaped by the perspective of that privilege, acting on one of the options visible to those privileged. More often than not, such courses of action preserve privilege and systemic racial injustice.

Hope as Novelty

That hope often has regressive rather than progressive effects has not gone unnoticed. Hope as desire, as affect, and as rhetoric affirms the status quo, but might there be a way to understand hope differently, more theologically? In the wake of the Nazi genocide, some European thinkers sought to rejuvenate hope, conceiving of it in new ways that intentionally challenged the status quo. The Marxist social theorist Ernst Bloch and the Protestant theologian Jürgen Moltmann sought to retrieve a sense of hope as the radically new that they found in Christianity.[12] It was not so much the Christian intellectual tradition to which Bloch and Moltmann turned as it was to the Bible. Bloch himself was of Jewish ancestry, and he, like Walter Benjamin, introduced into Marxist social theory a sense of the messianic. Moltmann was deeply influenced by Bloch's theoretical work and found in the New Testament evidence for a sense of the messianic animating Christianity. Concisely, this sense of the messianic is the radically new and unexpected breaking into history. To hope means to refuse to be limited to the possibilities of the present, to the apparent configuration of the world today. In other words, in response to the complicity of many conceptions of hope with the status quo, hope was now defined simply as an orientation toward that which is different from the status quo. In this account, hope means orienting a life around the sense that dramatic change will come and around a further commitment that we cannot know when or where or how this change will come. At most we can make ourselves ready. Hope, in this view, is not desire or affect or rhetoric but something deeper, something that inheres in the experience of life itself. We humans have a deep longing that cannot be sated by anything around us, no matter how many of our specific desires are fulfilled. That deep longing is a reminder that the world can and will be radically different in the future, radically new. It is a longing that may be expressed in specific desires, or in affect, or in rhetoric, but it is more than any of these. Hope must be investigated by means of phenomenology, examining the phenomenon of hope beyond its manifestations.

Moltmann spent the 1967–68 academic year at Duke, visiting the U.S. South at the height of racial turmoil. He dedicated the lectures he gave during that year, *Religion, Revolution, and the Future*, to Martin Luther King Jr., and he befriended James Cone.[13] In an essay provocatively entitled, "Black Theology for Whites," Moltmann summarizes the theological project he encountered: "Black theology opens up for the theology of the whites the unique chance to free itself from the constitutional blindness of white society, and to become Christian theology."[14] In other words, black theology can allow Christian theology to become postracial, to overcome the problem of race. Such a conclusion follows naturally from the view of hope developed by Bloch and Moltmann. In their view, hope disregards the terms of the present world, welcoming the radically new—and so disregards whiteness and blackness, welcoming a world where race plays no role. While the election of Barack Obama seemed to open a postracial era in the United States, the years since his election have demonstrated that anti-black racism is alive and well, raising difficult questions about whether hope for a postracial world might actually elide and so reinforce deep-seated, virulent racism.

Those who would understand hope as novelty may dismiss this worry by arguing that an orientation toward future possibility manifests as challenges to the specific practices and institutions that maintain the status quo. Specifically, in the case of race, dismantling white supremacy would be the way an eschatological vision of postracialism manifests. Moltmann, after all, thinks black suffering reveals "the constitutional blindness of white society." However, as soon as there is a process to get from here to there, from our current world to the reconfigured, colorblind world for which we hope, radical newness is no longer involved. The new world is no longer unexpected. We are back to the rhetoric of hope—of the new, of progress—combined with an individual's hope as desire for this or that reform. Once again, we have a conception of hope that allows whites to see themselves as committed to racial transformation, to achieving a colorblind society, while actually reinforcing the status quo.

Hope as Poverty

Frustrated with the social and political limitations of hope conceived as novelty, liberation theologians sought a conception of hope more clearly aligned with genuine social transformation.[15] According to this even more oppositional understanding of hope, genuine hope means the hope to become poor—or, in the case of black theology, the hope to become black.[16] God is present among the poor and black, among "the least of these," so hoping to become poor or black means hoping to participate more fully in God. Privilege distorts perception and personality; because of this, any desires or affect or rhetoric of the bourgeoisie will be misguided. Middle-class hope is, in a theological idiom, directed away from God. Moreover, from this perspective hope understood as novelty, as an orientation toward the radically new, will go wrong unless the material conditions of the one who hopes change. What counts as radically new for the bourgeoisie is not actually radically new because the bourgeoisie misperceives the status quo; the bourgeoisie is so invested, consciously or unconsciously, in maintaining the worldly order that the world appears to them different than it really is. The poor have an epistemic privilege because the poor, broadly conceived to include all marginalized communities, are not invested in the status quo—it is the status quo that marginalizes them—so their hope can turn away from worldly things, toward the truly other, toward the divine.[17]

What does it mean to hope to become poor or black? On the one hand, it is tempting to avoid the apparent difficulties of this question by considering poverty and blackness as symbolic. What they symbolize is marginalization. But the argument here is more subtle. God dwells with "the least of these," but who "the least of these" refers to varies by time and place. Disclaiming privilege is not enough: dwelling with the most disadvantaged is necessary. And what does this mean? It may mean living in a certain neighborhood, shopping at certain stores, eating at certain restaurants, wearing certain clothes, or choosing certain careers. Privilege is not an abstract quantum but maintained by its exercise: the habitus must be lived to be a habitus.[18] White skin will not darken, but whiteness has never really been about skin color; skin color only serves as a proxy for race.

The formation provided by a privileged upbringing will never entirely stop shaping one's life, but that is why such renunciation requires hope—hope that, one day, the rich woman will be mistaken for a poor woman and the white man mistaken for a black man. This is hope for a postracial, postclass world, for a world that is radically otherwise, but it is hope that is only possible from the position of poverty.

This understanding of hope is oriented by God: it is hope to participate in God by taking the earthly form that is closest to God—that of the poor, understood broadly. The specific desires entailed by the hope to be poor, such as the desire to live in a certain place or to eat a certain food, are desires that are oriented by the overarching hope to participate in God. This understanding of hope also makes clear how hope is a gift of God: to hope to become poor requires a renunciation of worldly hopes. When hope is understood as the hope for poverty, hope is also understood as a virtue: it is the disposition to act as the poor would in whatever circumstances present themselves. However, it is not quite right to call this understanding of hope a virtue, because virtue implies a disposition cultivated in community. For the wealthy who would become poor, hope requires detaching oneself from community, severing bonds to those who shaped one's self. Yes, new relationships are to be built and a new community is to be formed, with the poor or black or otherwise marginal, but that community can never become fully one's own because of the residuum of privilege. This residuum makes the hope of the wealthy renouncer and the "naturally" poor manifest differently. The hope of the privileged manifests, first and foremost, as the desire to renounce privilege; the hope of the marginalized manifests, first and foremost, as the desire to overturn the social and political structures that secure privilege. The hope to renounce privilege is a lonely hope, for it by definition cannot tolerate a community of those who similarly hope. Yet when there is no community to nurture such hope, the hope degrades, threatening to become a desire to identify with titillating otherness. Such hope can become vicious: witness the case of Rachel Dolezal, the white woman from Montana who, ostensibly out of commitment to racial justice, "became" black. The possible nobility of her intentions was obscured by her pathologically confused statements and farcical self-presentation because she did not have a community to whom she could be held continually accountable. Her privilege was never fully renounced—she became a local leader of the National Association for the Advancement of Colored People—and the publicity she eventually garnered called into question the sincerity of all who wish to renounce their privilege.

Hope as Theological Virtue

What if the four accounts of hope limned previously are all ways that hope is viewed from the perspective of our secular age, degradations of a once robust understanding of hope as a theological virtue? I do not intend to argue that this is the case, only to float the possibility in the interest of motivating reflection on what a postsecular, or theological, understanding of hope might look like. As a theological virtue, hope is a disposition to have one's passion directed toward the good—where the good is that which images God, the highest good. As a theological virtue, hope is not entirely learned through community practice; it is also infused by God. Members of a community may desire things that are possible but not certain; this is not enough to teach a young person growing up in the community to hope, for there are many such worldly desires that are not good (getting away with cheating, for example). Without God's gift of hope, human passion is directed at objects both good and bad; with God's gift of hope, human passion is oriented toward good objects. Although enculturation is not sufficient to learn the virtue of hope, participation in a community of those who hope, of those who share in the divine gift of hope, nurtures the virtue of hope. Even with the divine gift of hope, worldly pressures can distort the virtue, if not properly nurtured through the church. These are the key features of hope as understood in the Christian theological tradition.

When hope is considered as a theological virtue it is aimed at objects that are good because they reflect the image of God, not because of individual preference and not because of community consensus. If racial justice is a good, as it certainly must be, then those who have the virtue of hope would be disposed to direct their passion toward racial justice naturally, as it were, not as a result of balancing reasons for and against. It is only in extraordinary circumstances when dispositions are short-circuited. Hope as a theological virtue promises a way of understanding the church as a community sharing a hope for racial justice in opposition to mainstream society. Indeed, as a place where hope is nurtured, the church would scrutinize hopes for racial reform articulated by liberals whose hopes were not fully directed at the good. Of course churches are not *the* church, and actual existing churches never nurture hope perfectly. But perhaps we can see in the civil rights movement (or the anti-apartheid struggle, or the nascent Black Lives Matter campaign) a moment when something like the church invisible manifests, nurturing the virtue of hope rather than affirming individualized, secular hopes.

Understanding hope as a theological virtue means rejecting the individualism of other conceptions of hope. It means appreciating that hope is a disposition nurtured in community—in the racial context, in a community struggling against racial injustice. But the insights tracked as the understanding of hope has been refined, from desire or affect to novelty or poverty, should not be forgotten. They are insights about how to preserve hope from contamination by worldly interests. Yet the accounts of hope as novelty and poverty are still invested in an aspect of worldliness, of secularity: they leave a focus on the individual that prevents hope from being understood as cultivated in community. The question, then, is how to bring together hope as a theological virtue with the insights of those who would understand hope as novelty or as poverty. Put another way, in the context of anti-black racism, what would a community of whites committed to renouncing privilege look like? It seems we have reached an antinomy, for when the privileged act in concert, whatever their goal, the result is to further privilege: social capital, like all capital, is fecund. Perhaps we are left hopeless.

White Tears

At least since Trayvon Martin was killed in 2012, black commenters on social media have used the phrase, or hashtag, "white tears" to denote two distinct phenomena: (1) white complaints about the difficulties they encounter, oblivious to the enormous privilege they wield and oblivious to the difficulties an order of magnitude more grave faced by blacks; and (2) ostensibly progressive whites taking offense at being labeled "racist" by blacks, for instance, when blacks ask white supporters to take a secondary role at an anti-racism protest. Although these two usages are distinct, they both suggest frustration combined with naïveté. In the first case, whites who know little about the depths of racism struggle to understand why everyone is not just treated as equal. In the second case, whites who do know, intellectually, about the depths of racism are so accustomed to exercising their privilege that an explicit refusal of this privilege causes barely repressed guilt to surface—in tears. Those tears are themselves a reassertion of privilege, a performance of privilege. Social scripts dictate that crying people, especially crying white people, and most especially crying white women, must be comforted. To comfort usually means to apologize, or to say that you really didn't mean to offend, or that everything will be all right—each of these a reaffirmation of white supremacy. How, then, are whites to despair?

This question may seem corollary to the question of white hope, but the two are actually much more closely related. Despair, after all, is hopelessness. Kierkegaard compellingly inserts despair at the very center of religious life.[19] He argues that one must first despair before one can truly have faith, or love, or hope. Despair wipes out false gods and focuses our attention solely on one true God, on a God qualitatively different from the world. Before we despair, our hopes are oriented by the world, by the secular rhetoric of hope and by our own desires and feelings. After we despair, hope becomes a virtue, a disposition oriented by God, repeatedly expressed in the circumstances we encounter. Of course, despair is not encountered only once in a lifetime; that story is a heuristic. Despair is encountered repeatedly, cleansing us of idolatrous hopes and reorienting our hopes toward the ultimate good, God. In other words, to hope properly one must despair properly.

Formal instruction in despair is unnecessary for the marginalized and oppressed; life offers them plenty of opportunities to learn about despair naturally, as it were. The policeman stops them for no reason, or the underfunded bus system makes them perpetually late for work and costs them their job, or the only grocery store in the neighborhood moves to the suburbs. In contrast, privilege mutes despair. It prevents situations from occurring that might give rise to despair, and it reduces the severity of those situations that do arise. An ill child gets the best medical care money can buy, or at least that is how it is marketed. A lost job might require a second mortgage, but owning a house makes that possible; a family member's drug arrest is resolved with the help of a savvy lawyer. The power of the phrase "white tears" is in capturing this distinction between the despair of the poor and the despair of the privileged. The phrase names the superficiality of white misfortune: "white tears" vaguely echoes "crocodile tears." White tears mark the simulacrum of despair. White misfortune seems grave, warranting tears, but this is nowhere near the depths of despair that would cleanse the self of its belief in idols and orient the self toward the divine. One who is shedding white tears seems impossibly trapped between good intentions to help and the violence done by that help, since it flows from a position of privilege. From the perspective of the white person in tears, it feels as if there is no hope. And in both cases this is an illusion: it is an affect worn rather than existentially felt, Braxton Hicks contractions rather than labor pains. Kierkegaard offers the felicitous phrase "inauthentic despair."

How are whites to despair? The answer is closely tied with the suggestion that whites are to hope to become black—which is to say, to entirely renounce race privilege, not just in this moment, for this rally, or in this meeting. The realization that renouncing privilege, in the context of the United States in the twenty-first century, requires whites to become black (and poor) does warrant genuine despair. After all, skin color overdetermines race, and for a white to become black is nearly impossible. But together with this despair at the difficulty of renouncing privilege is the hope that the good might be pursued, that whites now may be able to participate in God as long as all idols are abandoned—a hope against hope. The hope to become poor, or black, must be accompanied by despair so that this hope does not become fantasy, so that it does not become yet another idol. The hope to become poor, or black—that is to say, the proper hope of whites—is a despairing hope, a hope for hopelessness.

This way of understanding hope, as a hope for hopelessness through the renunciation of privilege, offers a means to bring together hope as a theological virtue, practiced in community, and hope as poverty. It seemed as though the desire to become poor, or black, foreclosed hope in community, making hope nearly impossible to maintain, compounding despair. But now we can see that despair is not a bad thing; it teaches. It offers training in hope. There may be no community to nurture the imperative to become poor, or black, but despair can serve as substitute teacher, purging errors and making possible proper dispositions. That there is no community to support the imperatives of the privileged is yet another reason for the privileged to despair, but this despair need not be fatal. Indeed, despair promises to open new possibilities for faith, hope, and love, and for community. But these are new possibilities that cannot be the object of hope: they are divine gifts given once human hubris is abandoned. To reject such hubris means rejecting the desire to get hope right, to know the object or mechanism of hope, and instead to hope only for despair. Rachel Dolezal thought she could hope rightly on her own, to become black—hubris. When renouncing privilege is the prerequisite for hope, hope is impossible. This impossibility fuels despair: that for which whites should hope.

Although the hope for despair may seem a lonely hope, it is in fact a hope oriented toward and accountable to a community. This is not an existing community; it is a community not yet in existence, a community of those who now despair singularly—an eschatological community.[20] In other words, community must be understood theologically, not empirically, with the faith that this theological vision of community will become clearer only as despair becomes deeper, only as worldly hopes are lost. Yes, this eschatological community is postracial, but what a postracial community would look like is impossible to see from the perspective from the present—and racism digs in deeper every time well-meaning whites forget that.

PART III

Exempla

CHAPTER 9

The Revelation of Race: On Steve Biko

South Africa in the 1970s witnessed a phenomenon that was unique in many ways. The Black Consciousness Movement, led by Steve Biko, combined a philosophy of empowerment education and community building with the introduction of a novel, inclusive use of the term "black." In doing so, Biko was able to bring into question fundamental assumptions about the significance of race while also altering the political landscape in a way that advantaged anti-apartheid forces. Cultural theorist Slavoj Žižek has provided an innovative model for thinking about naming as a political intervention, and by combining his theoretical model with notions of performativity developed by feminist theorists, Biko's significance and successes can be better understood as transcending and thwarting secular race politics. He refuses the options on the table; he rejects how political questions are framed. He has faith and hope that the table can be overturned, that the terms of the conversation can be transformed into something unknowable from the perspective of the present. In secular terms, race is a worldly fact; in theological terms, blackness is revealed. It is revealed in a way that thwarts the secular, that challenges the wisdom of the world and the powers that be. Blackness was revealed by Biko, through Biko, for Biko—from beyond the world.

Steve Biko

In 1960, when Bantu Stephen Biko was thirteen years old, the African National Congress and the Pan-African Congress, the two largest anti-apartheid political movements in South Africa, were made illegal. In 1977, at the age of 30, Biko died in police custody, and the organizations he was instrumental in founding and forming, collectively known as the Black Consciousness Movement, were made illegal. In between, Biko injected energy and ingenuity into anti-apartheid organizing in South Africa.[1] The name "Bantu" translates as "people"; it was the name Biko was given by his parents. He spent his youth in King William's Town in the Eastern Cape, raised by his widowed mother, who worked as a domestic to support her four children. Biko showed academic promise, and to fund his secondary education his community gave him money they had been saving to build new classrooms. Shortly after his arrival at boarding school, Biko was arrested with his older brother, who was suspected of involvement with the Pan-African Congress. Although released after interrogation, Biko was expelled from school. It was not until the following year that he could continue his education, attending a boarding school in Natal and later attending the University of Natal Non-European Section to study medicine. It was there that he became involved in politics, and for the next several years his dormitory room served as an office, lounge, and haven for the Black Consciousness Movement.

At the University of Natal, Biko first became active in the National Union of South African Students (NUSAS), a multiracial organization to which the student government groups on many campuses were affiliated. He attended the 1967 NUSAS national meeting held at Rhodes University. There, Rhodes forced Indian and Colored (mixed race) delegates to stay off-campus in Grahamstown, and African delegates had to stay in a church hall some distance from the university; white delegates were allowed to stay in university dormitories on the campus. During the meeting Biko moved that the conference adjourn until a "non-racist venue" could be found; the discussion that followed, lasting well into the morning, led Biko to conclude that the presence of white liberals in the anti-apartheid struggle was detrimental to the movement. Some white liberals were only half-heartedly committed to fighting racism on the micro level; they were more interested in being activists *for* blacks. Further, the de facto result of the presence of whites in anti-apartheid organizations was that they would dominate the debate and the leadership, mirroring the very system against which they claimed to be fighting. This was reinforced by practical realities: Biko noted that, in the organizations in which blacks and whites worked together, many whites were much more fluent and articulate in English, their first language, than the blacks, for whom English was a second or third language.

Working through the University Christian Movement, Biko formed a network of black students dissatisfied with NUSAS. In 1969 they created the South African Students' Organization (SASO), an all-black parallel organization to NUSAS that was the core from which the other black consciousness organizations later grew—the grassroots, empowerment-oriented Black Community Programmes, the political Black People's Convention, and others. SASO expanded rapidly, becoming an—and then the—important force in black anti-apartheid activism in the 1970s. This was due in part to the void that existed because the primary black political organizations, the ANC and PAC, had been made illegal in 1960, a void that was filled by the Black Consciousness Movement. Many leaders of organizations that would later become prominent in the struggle, including the United Democratic Front and the Azanian Peoples Organization, spent their formative years as SASO activists.

Informed by the anti-colonial existentialist tradition embodied by Frantz Fanon, the ideas of empowerment education advanced by Paolo Freire, and the black power movement in the United States, Biko and those surrounding him formulated the intellectual foundations of black consciousness. SASO's statement of goals began with its mission "to crystallize the needs and aspirations of the non-white students and to seek to make known their grievances." The organization's mission also included attempting "to establish a solid identity amongst the non-white students" and "to boost up the morale of the non-white students, to heighten their own confidence in themselves."[2] As part of this mission, Biko discouraged blacks from making close alliances even on a personal level with whites. He condemned blacks who, "instead of directing themselves at their black brothers and looking at their common problems from a common platform," choose to complain to their white liberal friends about the injustices that they face. Biko describes those who would do this as "dull-witted, self-centered blacks" who are just as guilty of maintaining the apartheid regime as whites.[3]

The critical moves that Biko makes and that are formulated in the founding statements of the Black Consciousness Movement are twofold. First, "black" is redefined to include not only those who the apartheid government had named Africans but also those whom the government had named "Colored" and "Indians." In Biko's address as the newly elected president of SASO in 1969, he had already made this move, but he referred to the group of Colored, Indians, and Africans as "non-whites." In a letter from the following year, Biko begins to positively define all these groups as "blacks." Second, "black" is made to describe a new set of positive characteristics: assertiveness, self-reliance, independence. The identification of these traits with blackness was fostered through community development programs meant to empower blacks at the grassroots level.

In 1973, Biko was "banned" under the Suppression of Communism Act—forbidden from participating in political events and meeting with groups of people, and his life was restricted to King William's Town. Despite the restrictions, Black Consciousness–affiliated programs sprang up in the King William's Town area, including a new community medical center, and many of the movement leaders continued to consult with Biko. After the 1976 Soweto uprising in which empowered black youths resisted the apartheid government on a large scale, the government increasingly began to harass and restrict the Black Consciousness organizations, which had been thought of as benign or even helpful (supporting segregation) by the government in the early 1970s. In August 1977, Biko was arrested while returning from Cape Town, outside of the magisterial district to which he was restricted. On September 12, Biko died. The events surrounding his death are still not entirely clear. He suffered a severe blow to the head while being interrogated on September 6, and his health deteriorated thereafter. Doctors finally recommended that he be brought to a hospital; he was transported handcuffed and naked in the back of a truck nearly seven hundred miles from Port Elizabeth to Pretoria. Biko died less than a day later. A government inquest concluded that his death was the result of "a scuffle" and that "the available evidence does not prove that the death was brought about by any act or omission involving . . . an offence on the part of any person."[4]

Revealing Names

The cultural theorist Slavoj Žižek identifies a theoretical move (made in different forms by the German philosopher Georg Wilhelm Friedrich Hegel, the French psychoanalyst Jacques Lacan, and the American analytic philosopher Saul Kripke) that serves as a resource for his analyses of ideology as expressed in popular culture. Žižek points to the significance of the "return of a thing to itself" for Hegel: "After we decompose an object into its ingredients, we look in vain in them for some specific feature which holds together this multitude and makes of it a unique, self-identical thing." Many ingredients may be present, but without the positing of a name, they do not make a thing. The name takes a bundle of characteristics and turns them into "a unique, self-identical thing," although this is clearly only a creature of the symbolic realm.[5] Furthermore, with naming comes "presupposing the existence of ground which holds together this multitude of conditions": naming not only gives an identity to a cluster of characteristics, but it also asserts the legitimacy and essential existence of that identity.[6]

The parallel process in Lacan is that of "quilting." Instead of the simple Saussurean picture of the relationship between signifier and signified in which "the linear progression of the signified runs parallel to the linear articulation of the signifier," Lacan envisions a more complex double movement: the movement from signifier to signified is quilted by a mythical intention of the subject that is "sewn" into the signification chain at the *point de capiton*. This process has a retroactive character in that meaning is always produced backward, before the subjective intent. For instance, in the case of ideological signifiers like "freedom," "state," or "peace," the meaning is retroactively determined by that which is quilted—for instance, "Communism." In this case, "the 'state' is the means by which the ruling class guarantees the conditions of its rule . . . only the socialist revolution can bring about lasting 'peace,'" etc.[7] Is there anything in common between the notion of "democracy" as informed by a Communist ideology and the notion of "democracy" as informed by a liberal democratic ideology? Not at all. Lacan, like Hegel, is suggesting that a set of disparate characteristics only gains meaning and an imagined essence through its naming—but for Lacan, this naming process is governed by the dominant ideology.

Kripke makes a similar argument about the significance of naming in his seminal *Naming and Necessity*. Instead of viewing a name as describing a set of characteristics of the object it points to, Kripke suggests that a name is identified with a certain person or object through a "primal baptism"—that is, the first use of the name. The name then stays in usage through the transmission of it from individual to individual. A name would still be associated with the same person or object even if the descriptions of its object changed. In contrast to those who would argue that "Kurt Gödel" might refer to the person who put forth a proof of the incompleteness of arithmetic (or a more complex but similar description), Kripke points out that Gödel would still be Gödel if the person who had in fact discovered the incompleteness theorem had been murdered by Gödel, who claimed the credit. The implications of this observation are not limited to proper names: if a substance were discovered that had "all the identifying marks we commonly attributed to gold and used to identify it in the first place, but which is not the same kind of thing, which is not the same substance, [w]e would say of such a thing that though it has all the appearances we initially used to identify gold, it is not gold."[8] The same would hold true for unicorns: if scientific evidence were discovered for the existence of prehistoric creatures that fit the description of unicorns, they would not be unicorns, since "unicorn" was fixed in a primal baptism to a mythical creature. Kripke calls names "rigid designators": as in the Hegelian and Lacanian accounts, they unify a set of independent characteristics through the functioning of the name itself.

Synthesizing these accounts, Žižek argues that names structure ideological space into a unified field. "What is at stake in the ideological struggle," he writes, "is which of the 'nodal points,' *points de capiton*, will totalize, include in its series of equivalence these free-floating elements."[9] In other words, ideology secures itself by organizing disparate elements together with a set of privileged names, and whether those names will successfully capture those disparate elements is a site of contest. Going beyond Kripke, who leans on a "primal baptism" that fixes meaning, Žižek argues that "guaranteeing the identity of an object in all counterfactual situations, that is, through a change of all its descriptive features, is the *retroactive effect of naming* itself: it is the name itself, the signifier, which supports the identity of the object."[10] In popular culture, the character of "Jaws" (from the Spielberg movie) can be seen as a privileged name, Žižek suggests. "The accomplishment of *Jaws* consists in an act of purely formal conversion which provides a common 'container' for . . . free-floating, inconsistent fears by way of anchoring them, 'reifying' them, in the figure of the shark."[11] These fears may be fears of a variety of phenomena, but the shark functions not to symbolize but to block further inquiry into these fears. The shark annuls the fears by occupying their place, rendering the fears invisible while becoming the feared "thing itself."

Žižek identifies a less benign example of this process in the anti-Semitic construction of the figure of the "Jew." Similar to "Jaws," the name "Jew" does not add any content to the process of signification: the fears (moral degradation, unemployment) already exist; "the name 'Jew' is only the supplementary feature which accomplishes a kind of transubstantiation, changing all these elements into so many manifestations of the same *ground*, the 'Jewish plot.'"[12] "Jew" ostensibly signifies a cluster of (negative) properties, but to achieve "anti-Semitism proper," as Žižek puts it, "we must *invert* the relation and say: they are like that (greedy, intriguing . . .) *because they are Jews*." This latter use of "Jew" does not signify a cluster of properties but rather what Žižek calls "that unattainable X," "the impossible-real kernel."¹³ This Real (a technical Lacanian term) is that which evades symbolization, a signifier without a signified that functions to fix meaning. This evasion of symbolization is a blockage "which prevents the society from achieving its full identity as a closed, homogenous totality."¹⁴

Ideology functions by concealing its use of naming to unify disparate elements and so stabilize itself—in a sense, the use of names as idols. Žižek charges critics of ideology with the task of demystifying names, exposing the artificial unities they construct and so making vulnerable ideology as such. But on Žižek's account the privileged political role is reserved for the theorist or cultural critic, exposing the machinations of the powers that be, of those who would establish themselves as gods. But what about those at the grassroots? Might they also be capable of using the power to name? In more theological terms, might the negative theology that accompanies critique be complemented by an openness to revelation that could radically reshape our world's conceptual terrain? Might the new names that emerge from below create blockages in the working of ideology that could prevent a society from becoming a "homogenous totality"?

Feminist theorist Judith Butler's account of gender envisions performances that could create just such blockages. Butler searches for a place to locate agency that does not presuppose a Cartesian (secular) subject but rather that takes into account why individuals are shaped by the world around them, and particularly the world as structured by language, discourse. While discourse shapes the individual, it does not determine who the individual is or what she does. Furthermore, discourse cannot be thought of as being exterior to the subject—it is not a medium "into which I pour a self and from which I glean a reflection of that self"; rather, identity exists through a set of linguistic signifying practices.¹⁵ The question of agency then becomes a question of resignification: subjects are not determined by discourse because discourse is a *process* of repeated signification, and agency "is to be located within the possibility of a variation on that repetition."¹⁶ This is relevant for Butler's project because the location of agency in resignification allows her to posit a potential for subverting the existing gender binary and creating new possibilities for gendered existence by toying with the rules of signification and, ultimately, through parodic performance achieving resignification.

Butler is critical of Žižek's argument that naming (in the sense he develops from Hegel, Lacan, and Kripke) structures ideology precisely because it does not leave space for creative performances with potentially transformative affects. She worries that the reliance on a "primal baptism" that once fixed the meaning of a name with a worldly description, even if that "primal baptism" is acknowledged as a post facto illusion, ascribes more stability to ideology than it deserves. Furthermore, Butler points to the potentially problematic fixity of names over time—from generation to generation. Does Kripke's theory not imply that "it is God the father who patronymically extends his putative kingdom through the reiterative fixing of the referent?"[17] Whereas a performative theory of naming would imply that the use of the name constitutes that which it signifies, Butler suggests that this cannot be the case with names in Žižek's sense, understood as rigid designators, because they do have a meaning that is fixed (and fixed rigidly). The consequence, she charges, is particularly problematic for feminism: if "woman" is a name that is a rigid designator, does this not imply that there is some primal, unnamable, and yet fixed meaning to the term? Does this not close off "woman" as a site of continuing political contest?

Butler and Žižek are not as distant as they may seem, for it is really Kripke's account of naming, and not Žižek's synthesis of Hegel, Lacan, and Kripke, that is Butler's target. In Žižek's own account, the moment of primal baptism is neither pushed back to time immemorial nor simply a fantasy. There are specific, analyzable forces that bring together a set of descriptions with a name at a particular moment—for example, "Jews" and "Jaws" and "democracy." It is possible to witness the baptism of these names, so to speak. In Žižek's account, agency does not matter because names are in the service of ideology, protecting the interests of the powers that be. Ideology perpetuates itself, at once impersonal and enlisting us all as its agents. Butler's focus on performances that disrupt discourse, altering a seemingly fixed ideological landscape, is not in opposition to Žižek's account but complementary to it, emphasizing potential disruptions to ideology. Indeed, Žižek's explication of the importance of naming provides a more concrete account of how the "re-signifying" performances Butler lauds (most famously, drag) might actually effect political transformation. Rather than just reminding those who view such performances that the way we view the world (and, specifically, concepts such as gender) is contingent and open to radical transformation, successfully introducing a new name in Žižek's sense reshapes the ideological landscape, creating new potential alliances—though this possibility is ignored by Žižek. In short, using the frameworks of Žižek and Butler together, we can see just how radical the political work of Steve Biko was. We can see that the subaltern can baptize, that names can reveal.

The political potential in the idea of a name without a fixed referent is that it might be held up as a rallying point for political mobilization, bringing together individuals or groups who previously did not see themselves as at all connected to each other.[18] But this is also the risk: the name under which mobilization is occurring can become a homogenizing force—exactly the elimination of difference in the category "woman" against which Butler was rebelling with her book *Gender Trouble*. This danger comes when certain characteristics are thought to be essential to the name, when the special status of the name as exceeding any set of descriptions is forgotten. Biko's appropriation of the political signifier "black" was efficacious and, moreover, particularly subversive because on its face it undermined any pretensions the hearer might have to tie descriptions with the name because, quite literally, many "blacks" were not black. This had two effects: first, it created a tension in the mind of the hearer when confronted with the expected and actual referent in a manner analogous to the tension created in the viewer who sees a woman or man wearing drag. Butler writes in praise of the subversive potential of drag precisely for this reason: the tension that is created leads the viewer to question the integrity of the categories with which she or he is used to making classifications—gender in Butler's case, race in Biko's. Secondly, by severing any connection between political sign and a supposed physically descriptive referent, the Black Consciousness Movement was able to avoid literalistic understandings of its name dictating political tactics. Rather than embracing fluidity and difference unlimited, Biko's new naming of blackness embraced paradox and so humility. Front and center was the fact that political claims must be made in the name of a group, but such a group is only constituted by making political claims.

White power in South Africa was maintained by white ideology, and that ideology had much heavy lifting to do, given the nation's majority non-white population. In a process carefully analyzed by Biko himself, white apartheid ideology—before the Black Consciousness Movement—maintained its illusion of impenetrability by loading the name "African" with a series of connotations that induced fear and distress. For this process to succeed, apartheid ideology first stripped "African" of its previous connotations: the history of Africans was negated with the dominant ideology's assertion that Africans had no history. Then, content from the apartheid ideology was poured onto "African." Whites "have deliberately arrested our culture at the tribal stage to perpetuate the myth that African people were near-cannibals, had no real ambitions in life, and were preoccupied with sex and drink," Biko writes.[19] Indeed, the workings of apartheid ideology to create racial labels were quite clear: in 1950 the National Party passed the Population Registration Act, which "set the foundation for apartheid by establishing distinct racial categorization of the population according to subjective interpretations of reputation and 'appearance.'"[20] Such a procedure bordered on a literal baptism, establishing who was African, Colored, or Indian, at times dividing members of the same family. This legal framework complemented workings of apartheid ideology in culture, and the Black Consciousness Movement stood in opposition to both. When a black South African says, "This is a black man's country; any white man who does not like it must pack up and go," Biko argues that "the myth of the invincibility of the white man [is] exposed."[21] It is this vulnerability of the ideological construction that Biko and the Black Consciousness Movement are able to exploit.

By beginning to use the term "black" in a new way, Biko and the Black Consciousness Movement moved from secular politics through theological critique (the position of Žižek) to something like revelation. Biko's use of the name "black" is more than simply a subversive rearticulation; rather, it is a rebaptism of "black" because of the radical dissimilarity between the usage of the term after the rebaptism and the usage of the term— or equivalent terms—before. "Black" was rarely used in South Africa before the Black Consciousness Movement adopted it in 1970, and the term "non-white" as it was used by the apartheid government to describe people of a certain race did not correspond to the new use of the term "black." Non-white represented a negation of being, Biko felt, whereas black could be used—rebaptised—as a positive, affirmative term, a sign under which a new political movement could be formed. The term "non-white" hinted at a specific characteristic of reality that would determine its meaning— namely, skin pigmentation—whereas the new term, "black," used to label people of many skin colors, did not.

For Biko, "black" refers to those "who are by law or tradition politically, economically and socially discriminated against as a group in South African society" and who identify "themselves as a unit in the struggle towards the realization of their aspirations." Thus, "Being black is not a matter of pigmentation—being black is a reflection of a mental attitude."[22] In this baptismal text, Biko is asserting a new referent for the name "black." It has nothing to do with skin pigmentation but rather is a name for a legal and psychological state. Further, "black" is invested with positive content: a black person is one who is not content with his or her status as defined by the apartheid government and is actively asserting himself or herself in such a way that the system is being challenged. "[T]he term black is not necessarily all-inclusive ... the fact we are all *not white* does not necessarily mean that we are all *black*." Biko defines "non-whites" as those who work in the government security forces and broadly anyone "who calls a white man 'Baas,'" the term more or less analogous to "Master" for blacks in the United States. "Black people—real black people—are those who can manage to hold their heads high in defiance rather than willingly surrender their souls to the white man."[23]

In May 1976, Biko testified at the trial of nine Black Consciousness leaders accused of conspiring to bring about revolutionary change and to "cause, encourage or further feelings of hostility between the White and other inhabitants of the Republic" under the infamous Terrorism Act. Biko skillfully outlined black consciousness as a positive philosophy encouraging black empowerment and community development, not unconstitutional revolutionary change. While his testimony was clearly shaped by the short-term goal of winning the court case, one courtroom exchange was particularly illuminating. On the second day of Biko's testimony, the prosecutor asked him to explain what he meant when he wrote, "Any Black man who props the System up actively has lost the right to be considered part of the Black world. . . . They are extensions of the enemy into our ranks."[24] Biko replied that what the prosecutor referred to was a political definition of blackness, as opposed to a definition "which implies purely an observation of the external factors." He continues, "I could look at you [Advocate Atwell, the white prosecutor] and because of your short hair think that you are a Colored and therefore call you Black [laughter]—that is purely descriptive. I haven't gone into your political thinking."[25]

Whereas the apartheid government's baptism of "African" (and "non-white") was purely descriptive—if the government official assigning identities in 1950 thought someone looked "African," then they were African—the rebaptised term "black" was fixed at baptism with a fundamentally political meaning: those oppressed by the apartheid system who hold their heads up high in the face of the violence it imposes were named "black." To the prosecutor, the representative of the apartheid ideology, it was an unquestionable reality that race terms were meaningful because they described a certain set of characteristics. In Biko's response he is able to shake the confidence of the prosecutor, destabilizing the old symbolic through its confrontation with the new symbolic, a political terrain defined by the rebaptised articulation of blackness.[26] The confrontation between apartheid ideology and Biko's new use of language causes tension and precipitates "[laughter]." In the face of the apartheid government's seriousness in racial labeling by which an African is an African and is certainly not Colored, a seriousness founded on a commitment to (ideological) language mapping perfectly onto reality, Biko displays that which is beyond this rationality. He reveals that the ideological empire stands in the nude. *And he laughs.*

Disrupting the solemnity of the courtroom, what Biko shows is that in a politics defined by their rebaptised identity, physiognomy is irrelevant for black consciousness. When the new name refers to a set of political and not physical characteristics, what appeared to be fixed boundaries of "race" gave way to the flux. A "white" man with short hair can become Colored; a Colored man with light skin can become white. It is here that the subversive power of resignification through rebaptism lies: by the subaltern structuring the symbolic differently, those categories that were previously unquestionable become unthinkable. What can "race" mean anymore?

Grabbing the Phallus

The process of what we might call "radical rebaptism" that we see in the Black Consciousness Movement is described, in a quite different context, in Sharon Marcus's essay "Fighting Bodies, Fighting Words: A Theory and Politics of Rape Prevention." Marcus, writing in 1992, suggests that contemporary feminist theorists often see rape as an inevitable reality of women's lives. This leads to a sense that rape cannot be fought, only feared. The political efforts of feminists concerned about rape were centered in the judicial system—a system already heavily biased, especially with respect to race in the case of rape—while little if any effort was being put into rape prevention. Marcus suggested that we think about rape not exclusively as an act of physical violence, but also as enacting cultural scripts in a way that "shapes both the verbal *and* physical interactions of a woman and her would-be assailant," leading to "the would-be rapist's feelings of powerfulness and our commonplace sense of paralysis when threatened with rape."[27]

A rapist is successful, Marcus argues, not because he is overwhelmingly stronger than his victim. Rather, the rapist is following cultural scripts dictating that gendered interactions must involve unequal power and position. The power of men and the powerlessness of women is not the cause of rape; rather, in the process of rape women are feminized. A rapist must maneuver his victim into the status of victim; the victim is not preconstituted: "By defining rape as a scripted performance, we enable a gap between script and actress which can allow us to rewrite the script" in such a way that the name "woman" is rebaptised so as to no longer be a product of a patriarchal ideology.[28] "Woman" names the scripted role in the performance of rape that will inevitably guarantee the success of the assailant. But, rephrasing Marcus's conclusions, if "woman" is rebaptised in a different (but equally imaginary) way by those outside the dominant, patriarchal ideology, the success of the script of rape will no longer be guaranteed. Clearly, this is not simply a subversive resignification of the form Butler advocates but rather a new baptism—a new name (or an old name, "woman," stripped and repurposed) under which a new grouping of characteristics may assemble.

There are real, practical consequences of the meaning of "woman," the cultural scripts of rape among them—and real consequences to the proposed rebaptism of "woman." As Marcus tells it, in contemporary culture penises are seen as weapons, offering near invincibility, so a woman's only reasonable response to a threat accompanying a penis is passive avoidance. She shows how police manuals, if they suggest self-defense at all to rape victims, often advocate using "flimsy and obsolete accessories such as hatpins," and they "often neglect to mention male genitalia when they designate the vulnerable points of a potential rapist's body, thus perpetuating the myth of the unassailably powerful penis."[29] She points to studies that conclude there is no relationship between whether or not a woman physically resists a rapist and how much force the rapist uses, so active resistance actually is quite reasonable. When the cultural script that results from the passivity of "woman" is ignored—in the case of rape, by screaming, fleeing, pushing, defecating, etc.—then the unquestioned logic of subordination is destabilized; the rapist may be confused and forget his line on the script. Simply verbal self-defense, such as "treating the threat as a joke; chiding the rapist; bargaining to move to a different place . . . wisecracking, scolding, [being] bossy" can sufficiently disrupt the script to stop a rape, Marcus asserts.[30] Further, she focuses on those potential rape victims who attack that element most central to gendered cultural scripts, the penis itself. Marcus cites the experience of one such woman who had been threatened with death if she did not cooperate with her rapist:

> If he's going to kill me he'll just have to kill me. I will not let this happen to me. And I grabbed him by his penis, I was trying to break it, and he was beating me all over the head with his fists, I mean, just as hard as he could. I couldn't let go. I was just determined I was going to yank it out of the socket. And then he lost his erection . . . pushed me away and grabbed his coat and ran.[31]

What Marcus describes here is not just one more effective form of rape resistance that has been overlooked. She describes grabbing the phallus, that real object that functions in the psyche to hold together the realm of discourse itself, where discourse is shaped by ideology. By zeroing in on that privileged marker that holds together the (patriarchal) structure of the world, those who are acting based on that structure (rapists) are disoriented. This example illustrates that ideology is held together by certain privileged hinges, what Žižek describes as names, and that the real violence that accompanies ideology (e.g., rape) is best disrupted by focusing on those vital points rather than by endorsing any sort of creatively nonnormative performance (as Butler's work sometimes suggests).

Just as meanings attributed to "woman" and "man," as well as "penis," function to hold together patriarchy, race labels functioned to hold together the apartheid regime. The result was not only direct discrimination but also a deformation of the horizon of possibilities for blacks. Biko writes that in the "old approach" of anti-apartheid student activism "blacks were made to fit into a pattern largely and often wholly determined by white students. Hence our originality and imagination have been dulled."[32] More specifically, as Africans, Coloreds, and Indians the prescribed role is passivity, but with a new name, *blacks* are active participants in the struggle. Biko writes that "blacks should work themselves into a powerful group so as to go forth and stake their rightful claim in the open society."[33] With their new name, Biko is saying, those who are signified by "black" now have the potential to enact new social practices that were previously unimaginable. Biko insisted that care must be taken to fully void blackness of any old connotations before ascribing new ones so that the new horizon of possibility that was to be created for blacks did not have lingering debts to the old regime.[34] This was part of the Paolo Freire–inspired "conscientization" that Biko advocated: "a process whereby individuals or groups living within a given social and political setting are made aware of their situation . . . conscientization implies a desire to engage people in an emancipatory process, in an attempt to free one from a situation of bondage."[35] Through this process, the positive content given in the new term "black" could be genuinely transformative.

Biko addresses the question that the white liberal would pose to him: If I accept your position, what am I as a white to do? "If you ask him to do something like stopping to use segregated facilities or dropping out of varsity to work at menial jobs like all blacks or defying and denouncing all provisions that make him privileged, you always get the answer—'but that's unrealistic!'"[36] The Black Consciousness Movement was later forced to address this issue more directly as radical whites increasingly became interested in Biko's style of anti-apartheid activism. Whites were encouraged to work within their own communities in programs of "white consciousness," creating justice-oriented white communities whose social practices would no longer be thought of as "unrealistic" by the rest of the whites in the nation.[37] Reframing the issue in Marcus's terms: the script can be rewritten by the victim, but it is also possible for the potential rapist—or white South African—to problematize the script. As Lacan points out, the phallus, as representative of the symbolic order, of ideology, is not identical with the penis. In the account of the assertive woman who escaped rape cited by Marcus, the entire symbolic order is destabilized with the forced disidentification of the penis with the phallus—when she grabs her assailant's penis and he loses his erection. The assailant himself can attempt to force such a disidentification, whether he is a rapist or a white in apartheid South Africa, and white consciousness is the process through which the ordering principles of the symbolic, of the ideology that supports white superiority, are renounced.

Beyond South Africa

Although the racial language applied to blacks in the United States has changed several times over the past century, there has never been a transformation of the sort that the South African Black Consciousness Movement effected. In contrast to the black consciousness political redefinition of "black" that resulted in a racial openness, bringing those previously classed in different races into the anti-apartheid struggle with a newly shared racial label, the changes in racial labels in the United States have resulted in increasingly narrow definitions of the black race. Moreover, changing racial labels in the United States have generally striven to more successfully represent reality, moving toward names with meanings fixed to a (physical) description rather than the creation of new names that would allow a totally new referent to be created. In short, black racial politics in the United States has embraced secularism.

A number of racial terms were used in Colonial America: "Negro," "colored," "black," and "African American" were all in circulation. By the mid-nineteenth century, "colored" had become the dominant term, and it was used not only for the descendants of African slaves but also for people of mixed ancestry and Asians. As the nineteenth century drew to a close, W. E. B. Du Bois and Booker T. Washington joined forces in an effort to replace the term "colored" with "Negro." "Negro" was seen as a stronger term and had a more specific denotation, but it also was used in a derogatory sense by whites. Even after the term had gained dominance, it took more time for the first "N" to become capitalized in print, seen as a mark of respectability. In 1930, the *New York Times* announced in an editorial that, "In our 'style book' 'Negro' is now added to the list of words to be capitalized. It is not merely a typographical change; it is an act of recognition of racial self-respect for those who have been for generations in the 'lower case.'"[38] Such a "recognition" eerily resonates with the sort of recognition decried by Biko: the sort of recognition by which the governing ideology reinforces the terms by which the myth of its totality is secured.

With the surge in civil rights activism in the 1950s and 1960s, the term "Negro" increasingly came under scrutiny by civil rights advocates. It was thought that the symmetry between "black" and "white" would be productive in creating a connotation with "black" that would be the opposite of the (negative) connotation many blacks had with "white." The introduction of "black" was pushed by the more militant among the civil rights advocates—Black Muslims and the black power movement. In Martin Luther King's "I Have a Dream" speech, he uses "Negro" fifteen times and "black" (the adjective) four times, each time in parallel with "white."[39] By the late 1960s the term had taken off, with slogans such as "black is beautiful" and "black pride" coming into vogue.

It is instructive to examine the use of the label "black" in the black power movement more closely, since it comes the closest to the type of usage that Biko introduces, perhaps because of the influences of U.S. black power on the South African Black Consciousness Movement. In the U.S. context, the new label "black" initially marked a politicized working class in contrast with an increasingly sizable middle class. "Black brothers and sisters . . . are emancipating themselves," while Negroes were "still in Whitey's bag."[40] Similarly, Malcolm X's equation of "White" with "Oppressor" and "Black" with "Oppressed" in his *Autobiography* reinforced the political rather than descriptive definition of what blackness meant. This is the point at which American anti-racist movements approach most closely the twin theoretical moves made by Biko of refusing the identification of race with specific physical characteristics and infusing blackness with positive meaning. While the latter move was made successfully by the U.S. black power movement, the former did not occur, since the referent of race language only narrowed by excluding those not participating in the struggle against oppression; it failed to correspondingly widen to include others who also faced oppression but who had not been described by "colored" or "Negro."

On December 21, 1989, U.S. civil rights advocate and public persona Jesse Jackson called a press conference to announce that blacks would thenceforth like to be known as "African American." Many leaders of the black community quickly joined in Jackson's call for the new terminology, and over the next few years "African American" equaled and then surpassed "black" as the term of choice, both in the media and among blacks themselves. Jackson's proposal was meant to put blacks on an equal footing with other ethnic groups in the United States—Asian Americans, Arab Americans, Italian Americans, and so on. Furthermore, Jackson said that it just made sense: "Black does not describe our situation. In my household there are seven people and none of us have the same complexion. We are of African American heritage."[41] The new name would also encourage renewed emphasis on the African heritage of blacks in America, promoting solidarity and a sense of tradition by reminding blacks of their dual African and American identities. The seven people in Jackson's household obviously all have *something* in common; Jackson just needs to come up with the term best suited to describe what this is and to affirm its value. Yet it is the dominant, white ideology that determines who seems to have *something* in common, so the label "African American" does not fundamentally disrupt the way that white ideology divides up the world.

In recent years, while the middle-class black establishment in the United States has been laboring to promote the use of "African American," fundamentally subversive murmurings have been coming from urban, lower-class black communities expressed in the medium of hip-hop music. Tupac Shakur, in his first album, suggested that "Nigga" stands for "Never Ignorant, Getting Goals Accomplished." Historian Robin Kelley proposes that the reappropriation of this formerly negative term represents the use of a race name "to describe a condition rather than skin color or culture . . . the character of inner-city space, police repression, poverty, and the constant threat of intraracial violence."[42] The black bourgeoisie does not qualify to be called "nigger"—it is a representation of a shared urban, underclass experience. Although Kelley goes on to say that by using "nigger" as a racial label "gangsta rappers implicitly acknowledge the limitations of racial politics, including black middle-class reformism as well as black nationalism," it is not clear that this term has the inclusive as well as exclusive character that black, in the South African context, carries.[43]

During each of the transitions from one race term to another in the United States, the new term was initially one of militancy, and often the first to use the new term were the young and those who felt that they had been particularly badly treated by white society.[44] With each change, the new term brought with it a sense of independence, confidence, and pride that had been lacking in the old term—as that old term had become so closely identified with the management of racial difference by white culture and the state. That the same ordering of race nonetheless persists as it did two centuries and four racial labels earlier is illustrated by Tom Smith's 1992 claim, "For Blacks in the 1979–1980 National Black Survey and the 1982 General Social Survey there is no association between skin color (very light to very dark) and preferred racial term."[45] The absurdity of this statement does not seem to bother Smith in the least. How is it that he can overlook the obvious problem that the data he cites suggest that such a thing as a "Black" with "very light skin color" somehow is a coherent concept, while data for a person classified as "White" with "very dark skin color" (or even documented African ancestry) is not even collected? Smith illustrates precisely the dominant ideology's reliance on a specific type of connection between racial labels and physical descriptions that Biko sought to subvert. After all of the transformations in racial labels lauded by the black community in the United States, the political landscape in which black struggles against oppression operate is still defined by terms with meanings fixed by white ideology.

The assumptions implicit in Smith's statement serve as a reminder that "whiteness"—in both South Africa and the United States—is itself a name that does not correspondent to any specific descriptions, certainly not skin color. "White" had not been a primary identity label before the encounter with "non-whites"; with the term's introduction, previously disparate ethnic communities were joined together in an essentially political project (white supremacy).[46] It is no longer possible to say that "white" corresponds precisely to any description: for instance, in the time since the baptism of this term in both South Africa and the United States, substantial Jewish populations—not included in the original baptism—have become white, while some South Africans and Americans of primarily but not entirely European origin have been excluded from the category "white." In other words, whiteness has long functioned at the behest of the dominant ideology in the same way that Biko would have blackness function at the behest of the marginalized: consolidating varied individuals and communities in order to secure political power. The difference is that whiteness serves the interests of the powers that be, strengthening their control, and making the wisdom of the world seem as if it is eternal and unchangeable. Blackness, as introduced by Biko, is orthogonal to the ways of the world, illegible by the powers that be (and their courts), and bringing with it the potential for radical redistribution of power—the potential to end white supremacy.

CHAPTER 10

The Racial Messiah: On Huey P. Newton

Panther, the Mario and Melvin Van Peebles film fictionalizing the early days of the Black Panther Party, begins with the familiar sounds of "We Shall Overcome" and the familiar voice of Rev. Martin Luther King Jr.[1] Soon the images turn to documentary footage of the violent repression of civil rights marches and the voice of Malcolm X talking about the right to self-defense. The film switches from black and white to color, from documentary to fiction. We see a young black boy bicycling through a friendly community of fast-talking black people of familiar types—informal merchants, knowing elders, curvy and colorful women, corner boys, and a well-dressed preacher. The young bicyclist is hit by a car, and the motley community members gather around his bloody corpse to mourn. Reverend Slocum, we are told, is holding "another vigil," but a group of twenty-something black men propose to their friends that they should respond differently—that they should put pressure on the police by following police patrols. They propose to respond to the tragedy "not by praying, but by watching." "You think City Hall really cares about a bunch of black people holding another prayer vigil at some God-damned church?" the character played by Chris Rock queries. We see a prayer vigil: a road filled with candle-holding black people, led by Reverend Slocum, singing, "We Shall Not Be Moved." They are confronted and beaten by billy-club-wielding police while the nascent Panthers scramble to record police badge numbers.

In jail, Reverend Slocum interrupts the Panthers' planning, interjecting, "Remember, we must turn the other cheek, brothers. . . . What we need to do is pray for their forgiveness." After further exchange, the minister, played by Dick Gregory, queries of whites, "Lord, why don't they show us no respect?" Huey Newton, played by Marcus Chong, responds, "Because they don't have to. They can brutalize us and lock us up without a jury of our peers because we are ignorant of the law. What we need to do is organize and keep our shit correct and exercise our Constitutional rights as citizens to defend ourselves and arm ourselves." Exiting the jail with a golden cross in his hand, Reverend Slocum exclaims to the waiting crowd, "Free at last, my brothers and sisters. God hath delivered us from the lion's den." He is embraced by an adoring crowd of young black women. Behind him, the Newton character ponders, "As the good reverend says, God helps those who help themselves." The Black Panther Party creates a human stoplight at the intersection where the boy was killed, and their membership grows.

This dramatized origins myth leans on the commonly held view that black power, and the Black Panthers in particular, emerged as the limits of religiously inspired nonviolent protest became evident. The iconic songs and prayers of the civil rights movement were met with billy clubs and bullets from the police. Initially, the televised images of these confrontations mobilized support for civil rights in many parts of the United States and internationally. But after years of protest and little substantial progress, younger movement leaders grew frustrated, culminating in Stokely Carmichael's decisive rhetorical shift, in 1966 during the "March Against Fear," to the language of "black power." The Van Peebles's fictionalization captures this trajectory as it manifests at the local level in Oakland. An older generation of civil rights leader (the gray-haired and gray-bearded Reverend Slocum) is superseded by a younger generation without the patience to pray. This new generation, the Van Peebles's suggest, was also more deeply rooted in the lived realities of black life, emerging from the community rather than leveraging positions of religious leadership. These youths' language is sprinkled with expletives, and they talk politics on the basketball court rather than in the sanctuary. The civil rights–to–black power narrative concludes in tragedy, as the transition provoked such a virulent response from the police and the Federal Bureau of Investigation that black power was finally an empty spectacle, making none of the political gains of the civil rights movement and resulting in little more than an affirmation of black and African culture—with the ultimate result being the ascendance of apolitical multiculturalism in the 1980s and 1990s. Christianity had become atheism, which had, in turn, become some vague sense of African spirituality. "We Shall Overcome" was replaced by "Power to the People," which was replaced by African dance classes at the local fitness center. Or so the story goes.

But *Panther* also hints that the shift from civil rights to black power may involve a transformation, rather than rejection, of religious ideas and images. It is in jail, in conversation with Reverend Slocum, who is treated respectfully by all, that the Black Panther program crystalizes. And the Panthers' activities begin when Newton is depicted as saying in response to Reverend Slocum, "God helps those who help themselves." Indeed, the religious and theological background of the historical Black Panthers is even deeper.[2] Father Earl Neil of Oakland asserted that "the only difference between Jesus and the Black Panther Party is that Jesus fed 5,000 and the Black Panther Party feeds 10,000."[3] In California and beyond, the Panthers cultivated close relationships with individual churches, which more often than not provided the facilities to house the Panthers' free breakfast programs as well as other social services that formed the core of the Panthers' activities. Churches also provided spaces of sanctuary in the face of virulent police persecution. Beyond institutional sympathies, the Panthers drew on a range of Christian theological images, stories, and styles. If we take religion to be more about practices than beliefs, if we take theology to be more about tradition than proposition, and if we take secularism more often than not to mark false consciousness, the politics of the Black Panthers can be read as political theology. Doing so has the salutary effect of grounding discussions of political theology in real politics, in the concrete struggles of communities to build and retain power. In a field of scholarly inquiry that often loses itself in abstractions—of ontology and becoming, or of love and justice, or of community and intersectionality—reading the Panthers binds our reflections to the practices, norms, and powers of ordinary life.

"Huey P. Newton followed Malcolm X like Jesus Christ followed John the Baptist."[4] What does it mean to take this assertion, made by Panther leader Bobby Seale, at face value? How can such seemingly hyperbolic iconology be held together with statements such as, "Faith is not a mythical bullshit thing. Faith is where you directly relate yourself to reality"?[5] To address these questions this chapter will first explore what "real politics" might mean, then it will narrate Huey Newton's ascendance with the Panthers, and finally it will offer a series of suggestions as to how Newton can be read as exemplifying a theology of real politics. Black theology must be concerned with real politics; too often, it has not been.

Real Politics

The proverbial woman or man on the street is suspicious of abstractions. Abstractions don't point to anything real, anything concrete. They obfuscate. Technical terms might be necessary—they denote precisely, filling specialized roles that aren't encountered in everyday life—but abstractions ought to be abandoned. This conventional wisdom meets with the rejoinder, from academics, that abstractions make visible what is not immediately obvious, providing tools to better understand, critique, and transform the world around us. But framing a contest between the abstract and the concrete in these terms overlooks the particular challenges of politics (and, in a different way, of theology). For there is a temptation to imagine, in the abstract, how people could best live together and then to apply this vision to a specific group of people living together, here, now. In one sense, it seems quite reasonable to imagine lands of milk and honey and to strive to make them real here, now. But this is not politics. It is ethics, and perhaps it is prophecy. Politics involves how we do live together: the institutions and practices and values that allow us to live together, here, now. When the distinction between these two topics is collapsed—that is, when the vision of the world we want inflects our perception of the world as it is—both are contaminated. The world as it is blurs, and our aspirations are compromised. Abstractions are often the means by which this contamination takes place. Abstract ideals like justice, equality, and rights are imagined to be operative in political institutions and practices, but this obscures the workings of power and mystification. In other words, abstract ideals obscure the workings of real politics.

Put another way, and drawing on the formulation of Raymond Geuss, what actual politics looks like is quite different from what political philosophy talks about.[6] The "moralized tone" of political actors conceals this difference. Political actors use some of the same words employed by political philosophers (justice, equality, rights, and so on), yet for political actors this vocabulary is mere rhetoric: it is language used to persuade and to gain power. Political philosophers take this rhetoric too seriously, as substantive claims that can be put in conversation with systematic theories. Further, because of the resemblance between the vocabularies of political actors and political philosophers, political philosophers operate with the false consciousness that their systematic work could have an effect in the world, ignoring the actual mechanisms of persuasion and authority in real politics.

Geuss diagnoses the problem with contemporary political philosophy as rooted in a mistaken anthropology, a mistaken view of human nature. This anthropology is necessary because contemporary political philosophy sees its task as systematizing ethical intuitions, which requires humans to be the sort of creatures who have sets of intuitions that exist independent of context. But Geuss argues that "people are rarely more than locally consistent in action, thought, and desire, and in many domains of human life this does not matter at all, or might even be taken to have positive value."[7] Humans can love and hate at once. If we could not, we would not be human. Further, when intuitions can be discerned, it is more helpful to ask where these intuitions "come from, how they are maintained, and what interests they might serve" rather than to try to organize them into a system.[8] Historical and anthropological work may be more important than philosophy for understanding real politics. Even if the political philosopher could succeed in discerning intuitions, systematizing them, and extrapolating prescriptive rules, rules do not seem to be the sort of thing that matter in politics. As Geuss puts it, fairness in applying rules "may be the supreme virtue of the bureaucrat, the administrator, or the umpire, but, then, is all politics administration? Can there even be administration without power?"[9] If an umpire notices that he is officiating at a match between a team of adults and a team of children, what counts as a fair judgment may be quite different than if it were a match between all adults. In other words, even in the most apparently rule-governed aspects of politics, we should attend to differences in power.

When political philosophy conceives itself as applied ethics, it is making an intervention in real politics, but not the intervention it thinks. The intervention political philosophy makes is on the side of ideology, on the side of the powerful, because the powerful rely on mystifications that conceal the workings of power in order to keep themselves in power. If people realized that the status quo benefited a particular group at the expense of others, they wouldn't stand for it. The language of the political philosopher, like that of the political actor, conceals the interests of particular groups in the guise of the universal. The prescriptions offered by the political philosopher are presented as though they are discerned from systematizing intuitions that everyone has, and so they ought to garner the assent of all. In fact, these prescriptions, no matter how much they may appear to differ in their substance, have the same effect because of their shared form: they all support the interests of the powerful.

Geuss makes two constructive proposals, one about real politics and the other about political philosophy. Real politics, he argues, is about better and worse, not about good and bad. It is "a craft or skill, and ought precisely *not* to be analysed as the mastery of a set of principles or theories."[10] Theories do have a role, but they are to be used instrumentally, and part of the craft of politics is knowing when and how to employ models or theories while keeping in mind their limitations. There is no meta-theory to determine when theories are to be employed, only the craft or skill—the skill of political judgment. Geuss further proposes that there is, indeed, a role for political philosophy. Informed by close attention to history, anthropology, and economics, political philosophers can strive to understand what actually motivates people and how institutions actually operate.[11] This is the work of philosophers, and not just historians, anthropologists, and economists, because it involves ideology critique: rigorous interrogation of the concepts in use to discern in what ways they are being employed to advance the interests of the powerful. For ideology critique to be successful, it must be aware of an array of factors that are not discipline-specific. In other words, the role of political philosophy has inverted. Instead of securing its autonomy by authorizing the use of certain concepts in certain ways, political philosophy secures its autonomy by its capacity to question the authority of concepts used in other disciplines and by political actors, with the ultimate purpose of better exposing the actual workings of real politics.

Does political theology, or more specifically black theology, suffer from the same problem that Geuss diagnoses for political philosophy? If so, might it benefit from the same remedies?[12] There is an obvious dissimilarity in that political theology most often does not begin with, and certainly does not treat as ultimately authoritative, human intuitions. Rather, it often starts with the sorts of things Geuss commends: beliefs, experiences, and practices, all wrapped up together in tradition. Yet Geuss's queries about intuition still seem relevant: where do those beliefs, experiences, and practices come from, how are they maintained, and what interests do they serve? Moreover, if political theology discerns principles from tradition and then applies them to political practice, it faces the same objections concerning the insufficiency of principle-application as a way of understanding political practice.

Some political theologians who privilege virtue might see themselves aligned with Geuss's account of politics as a craft or skill, as most essentially the exercise of the virtue of political judgment. But it is not entirely clear that virtue in general, or particular virtues, translate into the skill of political judgment. Indeed, it seems plausible that the opposite may be the case: certain virtues may have to be suppressed in order to more accurately perceive and participate in the rough-and-tumble world of real politics. Even if they did translate perfectly, identifying virtues is a messy business, one that is also distorted by the interests of the powerful, particularly when those virtues have direct political consequences. Other political theologians, whose work flows from contextual theology, may see their scholarship as evading Geuss's critique because of their attentiveness to the rich textures of communities, to history, anthropology, and economics. These form the inescapable starting point through which tradition is engaged for contextual theologians. But this seems like politics as applied ethics in another guise, privileging the ethical values of a community while eliding the need to develop political judgment and skills for negotiating political institutions and practices that may not respect the epistemic privilege accorded by contextual theologians to their communities. Finally, political theologians who take community organizing as their starting point would find affinities with Geuss's realism and his emphasis on power analysis. But these political theologians often leave underdetermined the theological dimension of political theology—which often translates to a de-emphasis on ideology critique.

Geuss's challenge to political philosophy may seem irrelevant for political theology because political theology would seem necessarily committed to naming the impartial universal, the bête noire of Geuss's account. Yet political theology shares Geuss's suspicion of elevating the interests of certain groups in the name of the universal: that is idolatry. Political theology can avoid Geuss's critique of political philosophy if it conceives of its task first and foremost as that of the critique of ideology, understood interchangeably with the critique of idolatry. Rather than prescribing certain political stances or appealing to abstractions, political theology must root out the way religious ideas and practices are used to conceal the interests of the powerful, clearing space for the exercise of political judgment. But to describe political theology as focused solely on the political misappropriation of religious ideas and practices is to submit to secularist supremacy. Political theology, rather than focusing on the religious, refuses the repression of the religious; more precisely, since repression cannot be simply refused, political theology offers therapy to loosen that repression. Examining Huey P. Newton is part of that therapeutic practice, for Newton's life and image intensely intertwine the purportedly secular and the theological, and Newton's political practice exemplifies political theology at its best—as black theology.

Huey P. Newton

Born in 1942, Huey P. Newton was the seventh of seven children.[13] When he was a child, his family moved from Louisiana to California, where he was an unhappy student, often fighting with his classmates. As an adolescent he taught himself to read and began devouring political books. In 1966 he formed the Black Panther Party with Bobby Seale. The first activity of the Panthers was to organize police monitoring patrols: groups of black people who would follow police officers through black neighborhoods in order to witness abuses and to decrease the frequency of abuses. Newton led the drafting of a ten-point list of demands adopted by the Panthers, including demands for full employment, for housing, for education, and for an end to economic exploitation and police brutality. The first demand on this list asserts that power is the prerequisite for freedom: "We want freedom. We want power to determine the destiny of our Black Community. We believe that black people will not be free until we are able to determine our destiny." The tenth demand, calling for a United Nations plebiscite to determine the future of the "black colony" in America, is notable for quoting, verbatim, the first two paragraphs of the Declaration of Independence in its explication ("When, in the course of human events, it becomes necessary for one people to dissolve the political bonds which have connected them with another, and to assume, among the powers of the earth, the separate and equal station to which the laws of nature and nature's God entitle them . . . ").[14] As the Declaration of Independence citation suggests, the Panthers were particularly, and somewhat paradoxically, concerned with framing their work within the context of an American legal framework. Newton thought it important to be able to cite specific laws in confrontations with police. The iconic image of the Panthers bringing their guns into the California state capitol often overshadows the legal framework in which the event occurred. Openly carrying guns was legal, and the state legislature was debating a bill to restrict gun rights.

In 1967, Newton was involved in a violent confrontation with police. He was shot and injured, and he was put on trial for the murder of a police officer. The Panthers used this incident to mobilize support for the organization, making Newton into an icon (if not a deity, as we will see). Newton was freed in 1970 and treated as the natural successor to Malcolm X and Martin Luther King Jr., even if he lacked their oratorical abilities. However, it was difficult for Newton to reintegrate into the leadership of the Panthers, now populated with many new, younger members who had never met him in person and with his image having been magnified so greatly while he was in jail. Leadership difficulties ensued, particularly as Eldridge Cleaver and Bobby Seale were in and out of jail, and Cleaver drifted away from the Panthers' founders. These problems were compounded by FBI efforts to infiltrate, confuse, and divide the Panthers. There were discussions of a possible merger with the Student Nonviolent Coordinating Committee (SNCC), which had turned toward black power from the mid-1960s. By the early 1970s, despite swelling membership, the Panthers were in disarray, and Newton withdrew into insular philosophical meditations and esoterica. He was killed by an Oakland drug dealer in 1989.

The particular interest of this chapter is Huey P. Newton, and it is important to disentangle him from the Panthers in general, as well as from broader currents of black power and black nationalism. Black nationalism is a longstanding tradition of envisioning black Americans as a nation within a nation, affirming the distinctiveness of black culture, and often emphasizing the connection of black Americans with Africa. At times, black nationalists promote shopping at black-owned businesses, wearing distinctively "African" clothing, and participating in distinctive rituals, such as the celebration of Kwanzaa. The black power movement emerged in the mid-1960s as a response to the limitations of the civil rights movement. Not only do black people need rights, the argument went, they also need power—power to claim and maintain those rights, and power to ensure equitable treatment more broadly. The *black* in black power is significant, as it marked a shift from the earlier term, "Negro," as discussed in the previous chapter. Where black nationalism is a broad cultural, economic, and political current, in black power the political has priority. The Black Panthers were an organization that represented one manifestation of black power, and they explicitly opposed currents of black nationalism that privileged the cultural over the political. Within the Panthers, I take Huey P. Newton's voice as paradigmatic, with figures who joined later, such as Eldridge Cleaver, Elaine Brown, and Assata Shakur, as variations on Newton's paradigm—although of course these figures are significant in their own right.[15]

There are three main approaches to studying religion in the black power movement, emanating from early black theology, black pragmatism, and black humanism, respectively. Black theology emerged contemporaneously with the black power movement, and it was similarly (though implicitly) positioned as a step beyond the religious thought of the civil rights movement, as exemplified by figures such as Martin Luther King Jr. and Howard Thurman. James Cone famously wrote that black theology *is* black power, and black theologians more generally crafted their theological reflections in a way that would support the political conclusions of the black power movement.[16] As for the Black Panthers in particular, at times they sound strikingly similar to black theologians. As Newton put it, "The Black Panthers have never intended to turn Black people away from religion. We want to encourage them to change their consciousness of themselves and to be less accepting of the white man's version of God—the God of the downtrodden, the weak, and the undeserving."[17] Like SNCC in the late '60s and its iconic leader, Stokely Carmichael, black theology as a movement often leaned on fiery rhetoric and celebrity rather than on grassroots organizing.

In the academic study of black religion and politics today, black pragmatism is hegemonic. In large part this is due to the charisma and intellect of Cornel West, the African American religious thinker who positions himself in a trajectory of American pragmatists stretching from William James and John Dewey through Reinhold Neibuhr and Richard Rorty to himself. West's former colleagues at the Princeton Religion Department, Eddie Glaude and Jeffrey Stout, have analyzed black nationalism through the lens of black pragmatism, concluding that black nationalism is a form of piety.[18] Understood as a naturalized religious concept, piety connotes loyalty to one's forebears. But black pragmatists take issue with black nationalism for its excessive piety, which they suggest turns into patriarchy and the worship of power. Black nationalists need to recognize the "multiple traditions of American life" and to situate black culture among those multiple traditions.[19] When this approach is applied to Huey P. Newton, it does not seem particularly productive. The Black Panthers were explicitly opposed to uncritical piety directed at African heritage, although they also did not embrace the "multiple traditions of American life." The black pragmatist's suspicion of robust religious ideas and practices prevents her from encountering the religious ideas of Newton and the Panthers on their own terms.

Black humanism is the third major current of African American religious thought in the academy, and some black humanists have embraced Newton as one of their own. Anthony Pinn has included Newton in his canon of black humanist thought because Newton affirms the inherent worth and dignity of every human being and because Newton locates ultimate worth in the human, rather than in the divine.[20] Indeed, Newton does seem to embrace such a Feuerbachian reversal, inverting an all-powerful God with his embrace of "power to the people." As Newton writes, "My opinion is that the term 'God' belongs to the realm of concepts, that it is dependent upon man for its existence."[21] Elsewhere, Newton adds, "The greater man becomes, the less his God will be."[22] In his later, more speculative writings, Newton is even more explicit, describing a progression of mankind toward a "higher state": "'godliness,' where man will know the secrets of the beginning and the end and will have full control of the universe."[23] The Panthers' criticism of Christian churches could be pointed, even crude. When Panther leader David Hilliard addressed the National Committee of Black Churchmen in 1970, he angrily called them "a bunch of bootlicking pimps and motherfuckers," and he threatened that the Panthers would "off" some of the preachers if they disagreed with the Panthers.[24] On the black humanists' reading, the culmination of the Panthers' relationship with religion was their establishment of the Son of Man Temple in Oakland in the mid-1970s. It featured lectures and arts events on Sundays, at which it took collection; there were Temple committees to organize its work and bake sales and car washes for fundraising; and there were other familiar accoutrements of a religious organization. The Temple described itself as a "place in which we come together to express our humanity," not a place to "honor one God or one reverend." "This does not mean that we negate any religion; we all have different philosophies and views of our world. We are all part of everything and it is part of each of us.... We want our belief in the beauty of life to spread to freedom-loving people everywhere."[25] Over time, the Son of Man Temple's resemblance to a religious institution faded, and it became a more conventional cultural center.

While the black humanist's approach to Newton seems plausible, it misses the opportunity to more deeply engage with the religious ideas and practices employed by Newton. The black humanist's Feuerbachian premises commit her to religion as viewed through the eyes of the secularist: religion as the errant belief of an individual. But religious ideas and practices cannot be so easily reduced to repression, distortion, and fantasy. The early black theologians' approach fares little better, ignoring the Panthers' focus on community organizing, while the black pragmatist conflates several flavors of black nationalism, boiling them all down to a flaccid account of piety. What follows is an alternative approach, reading together narrative, aesthetics, political struggles, and political practice—a *new* approach to black theology. Although Newton and the early Panthers sometimes present seemingly discordant approaches to religion, this is an indication of a rich theological imagination closely tied with engagement in real politics,

politics that critiques ideology (as idolatry) while exalting the skill of political judgment.

Newton's political self-identity was constituted through struggle that cultivated political judgment. The founding of the Panthers was propelled by Newton's dissatisfaction with, on the one hand, black nationalist organizations, because their ideas were too detached from the black community, and, on the other hand, nonprofits intended to serve the black community. Because of their funding sources and structure, these nonprofits created a class of program administrators more interested in preserving their jobs and careers than in the well-being of the communities they ostensibly served. Newton's intuition was that political organizations ought to be by and for a community, not created by outsiders to serve a community, and not propelled by ideas distant from lived realities. Newton's political struggles continued within the Panthers. He sought to tack away from Carmichael's turn to "African ideology," with its concomitant rejection of everything associated with Marxism (the Panthers would critically appropriate Marxist ideas). He also distanced himself from SNCC's reliance on college students as its core; college students were prima facie distanced from the mainstream black community. At the same time, Newton sought to tack away from fellow Panther Eldridge Cleaver's focus on violent struggle and the hyperbolically proletarian ethos he cultivated. Cleaver's salty language and distaste for religion also created distance from the mainstream black community, and when Newton was released from prison he attempted to pull back the Panthers who had drifted in Cleaver's direction.

Refusing the prepackaged ideologies of both black nationalists and Marxists and refusing to privilege either the authority of higher education or the authority of street culture, Newton took attunement to concrete realities as the essential component of his own political perspective. As his collaborator Seale describes their shared position, "Our ideology is to be constantly moving, doing, solving, and attacking the real problems and the oppressive conditions we live under, while educating the masses of the people. This is what we try to do, and this is how we move to make the basic political desires and needs of the people realized."[26] Furthermore, rather than fetishizing revolution as messianic or deflating it to everyday political progress, Newton discerns an alternative. He writes that "revolution is a process rather than a conclusion or a set of principles," but he also refuses to associate revolution with any particular aspect of a process that could be named. "Any conclusion or particular action that we think is revolution is really reaction."[27] According to Newton, revolution gives the subject ("man") agency as he understands more about the world and "gains more control over himself." Paradoxically, this control over oneself is also what Newton names, significantly, "revolutionary suicide." This is also the title of his autobiography, in which he associates himself with the figure of the revolutionary suicide. Newton asserts that black people in America are already condemned to death, and the only way to reclaim agency is through struggle. Struggle gives life, gives freedom, even if it inevitably results in death. The Christological resonance is obvious. According to Newton, the only alternative is reactionary suicide: death without struggle, death without life, death without freedom.

Revolutionary Suicide opens with a dedication to Newton's parents, "who have given me strength and made me unafraid of death and therefore unafraid of life."[28] His father, we learn, was a pastor, and the whole family was very involved in church life. Newton sang in the choir, attended Sunday school, and served as a youth deacon. Participating in church life "gave us a feeling of importance unequaled anywhere else in our lives."[29] In the face of humiliations he endured at school, church life opened an alternative:

> Even though I did not want to spend my life there, I enjoyed a good sermon and shouting session. I even experienced sensations of holiness, of security, and of deliverance. They were strange feelings, hard to describe, but involving a tremendous emotional release. Though I never shouted, the emotion of others was contagious. One person stimulated another, and together we shared an ecstasy and believed our problems would be solved, although we never knew how. . . . Once you experience this feeling, it never leaves you.[30]

Newton reflects, "One of the most long-lasting influences on my life was religion."[31] Indeed, Newton contemplated becoming a minister until he took philosophy classes in college. Despite the apparent significance of this religious upbringing, and of his father in particular, Newton follows the dedication of *Revolutionary Suicide* with an epigraph, authored by "Huey P. Newton," seemingly disclaiming his parentage. "By having no family,/I inherited the family of humanity./By having no possessions,/I have possessed all./By rejecting the love of one,/I received the love of all./By surrendering my life to the revolution,/I found eternal life. Revolutionary Suicide."[32] The religion of his childhood has clearly transformed, but it has not been abandoned. Both author and symbol, whose wisdom is worthy of citation as epigraph, Newton demonstrates a self-awareness of his political-theological status as simultaneously earthly body and divine.

The Christomorphic form that Newton's autobiography sometimes takes echoes the sanctification, and sometimes deification, of Newton as part of an orchestrated campaign to both have Newton freed from jail and to use the struggle for Newton's freedom as an organization-building opportunity. In the last years of the 1960s there were "Free Huey" rallies held around the country, including one that brought more than five thousand people to Oakland Auditorium to hear from movement superstars Stokely Carmichael, James Forman, and H. Rap Brown. Images of a Newton speaking or preaching to the masses were widely disseminated. So, too, was the most famous image of Newton, seated in a wicker chair, wearing the Panther uniform of black leather jacket and black beret. In his left hand is a spear, and in his right hand is a rifle; to his side are two African shields. The chair forms a giant circular halo around Newton's head. Newton became Huey P. Newton, with the middle initial always included, elevating his name beyond the merely human. Panther cofounder Bobby Seale published his hagiography of Newton in 1970 using Newton's full name frequently throughout, as the words and wisdom of the founder are conveyed to Seale's readers. For example, "Huey P. Newton wanted that light there on the corner, and worked to see that the light was there"; "The cultural nationalists . . . wanted to sit down and articulate bullshit, while Huey P. Newton wanted to go out and implement stuff"; "For that reason Huey P. Newton wrote Executive Mandate Number Three, concerning Gestapo cops busting down our doors." In fact, the enterprise of writing a Huey P. Newton biography, according to Seale, was prompted by the explicitly Christomorphic remark by Eldridge Cleaver, cited previously: "Eldridge said that Huey P. Newton followed Malcolm X like Jesus Christ followed John the Baptist. That made a heck of a lot of sense to me. So Eldridge got some tapes and a recorder and a typewriter and took me down to Carmel to a little cabin to work on the book."[33]

In the lore of the Black Panthers, recorded by Seale, Newton himself, and others, religious parables are retold with new meaning. For example, after a discussion of "how brainwashed the society was," a white liberal friend of the Panthers asked his girlfriend to get him an apple. Eldridge Cleaver noted:

> [Y]ou let the omnipotent administrator send down a pig angel. His name was Chief Gain or any chief of police in the country. You let him come down with a flaming sword. With a weapon, you let him drive you out of the Garden of Eden. And you didn't defend it, you and your woman. . . . But if it had been Huey Newton in the middle of the

Garden of Eden and the pig angel came down after the omnipotent administrator had told Huey to go forth and exercise his constitutional rights and replenish the earth—if it had been Huey P. Newton and this pig had been swinging the flaming sword at him, Huey would have jumped back and said, "No, I'm defending myself. If you swing that sword at me, I'm shooting back."[34]

In this riff, retold by Bobby Seale, the book of Genesis is understood as a shared point of reference, and it is renarrated for the Black Panther context. The black humanist would understand Cleaver's renarration as Feuerbachian, showing that the human—Newton being the greatest of humans—is capable of asserting his own will and ultimately replacing God. (Note how Newton ascends in the narration from "Huey Newton" to the pure icon, "Huey P. Newton," when he asserts himself). But in light of the Christomorphic imagery so often used to describe Newton—this story is told one paragraph after Newton is explicitly described as Christ—it seems more reasonable to read Cleaver's new narration as a New Testament: the Christ-Newton, armed with gun instead of sword, capable of retaining his place in the Garden, overcoming the Fall. It is, after all, Huey P. Newton who can defeat the angel, not just any ordinary man. By following Newton, it is possible to challenge those who would hold the wisdom of the world for themselves, prohibiting access by others—those who would set themselves up as gods.

While love is largely absent from Bobby Seale's writings, love is a natural part of Newton's vocabulary. The Panthers, following Malcolm X, were highly critical of Martin Luther King's love language, and Newton's usage is quite distinct from King's. For Newton, love is not universal but particular: directed at a specific person or group of people. At the funeral of George Jackson, that great symbol of prison injustice, Newton spoke of how Jackson "bequeathed us his spirit and his love."[35] By "us," Newton meant something quite specific: the Panthers, not humanity. Similarly, at the funeral of Bobby Hutton, an early Panther killed by police at age seventeen, Newton eulogized, "Like a bright ray of light moving across the sky, Li'l Bobby came into our lives and showed us the beauty of our people. He was a living example of infinite love for his people and for freedom."[36]

Newton describes his initial exposure to a (secular) conception of "nonpossessive love" before his days with the Black Panthers. A friend of his was an advocate of free love, arguing that "nonpossessive love did not enslave or constrain the love object" as does the possessive love of the bourgeoisie. According to this friend, "Nonpossessive love is based upon shared experiences and friendship; it is the kind of love we have for our bodies, for our thumb or foot."[37] For a time Newton attempted to put nonpossessive love into practice in his romantic life, but with poor results. Newton encountered another pathology of love when he was in prison. In his account, sex was used indirectly as a mechanism of control by the prison authorities. Once the prisoners "became addicted to sex," "love and vulnerability and tenderness were distorted into functions of power, competition, and control."[38] It was not homosexuality that Newton decried (in fact, he spoke in support of the gay rights movement);[39] rather, it was the way that power distorts love by relying on the wrong kind of vulnerability—forced vulnerability that precludes tenderness. In other words, Newton refused both love that was ostensibly nonpossessive and love that was excessively possessive: both, he concludes, are at the service of the powerful. What remains is the difficult work of navigating what might be in between—work that involves cultivating virtue, not following rules.

What Huey P. Newton presents is less black humanism than black political theology grounded in real politics, black political theology as critique of idolatry. Newton explicitly refuses the reduction of his religious views to humanism, writing, "I'm a very religious person. I have my own definition of what religion is about, and what I think of God."[40] On the other hand, when an interviewer asks Newton about his religion, he responds that in all religions (Judaism, Christianity, and Islam) God is "the unknown, the unknowable."[41] But this God of Newton's is not hidden; this God's erasure is what animates the political-theological vision of Newton and the Panthers. Their commitment is to achieve the unknown, to struggle against those who would name it—who would name God, or who would name revolution. They struggle together: they organize. And they learn the law. Understanding the normative landscape is the prerequisite for political intervention. In organizing and learning law they gain agency. Agency is lost when actions are dictated by ideology or idolatry; it is gained in the struggle against ideology, against idolatry—a struggle without end. It is a struggle complemented by virtue and especially by love.

But what of Newton's Christomorphic presentation—sometimes self-presentation? Is Newton not dangerously close to becoming the God he refuses to name? Huey P. Newton had a stutter, was perpetually nervous, and was a remarkably poor public speaker. Unlike the smoother-talking King or Carmichael, or Bob Moses, who went so far as to change his name so as to dis-identify with his charismatic alter ego, Newton did not fit the part. And that, perhaps, is precisely why the Christomorphic imagery is appropriate: because it is so clearly a performative contradiction. As such, the critique of idolatry is located right at the center of Black Panther theology. The very body of the redemptive man continually refuses the authority that is thrust upon it, dramatizing the shortcomings of all ideology, the dangers of all idolatry. Reflection on the haloed image of Huey P. Newton is preparation for critique, training in virtue—training in love. As Newton says of himself, "I'm not a leader, I'm an organizer."[42]

CHAPTER 11

The Postracial Saint: On Barack Obama

There is no such thing as a racial saint. There are only postracial saints. Saints access the universal through the particular. Through a specific life, through a specific body, the saint participates in the transcendent, in the holy. Not just participates: makes accessible for the rest of us. This is precisely the meaning of the postracial as it is used today in the contemporary United States. A racially marked life, body, is seen to participate in a world transcending race—and so to make that world accessible to all of us. While the postracial seems to describe a state of affairs, a world where race no longer matters, in fact it describes a specific narrative, often with a protagonist. This protagonist is never white. He or she is always racially marked. Furthermore, the plot of the postracial narrative sanctifies its protagonist. The transcendence of racial divides is not merely a conceptual operation. Because of the richness of the world that race constructs—a world of bodies, myths, institutions, technologies, habits, and taboos—transcending race is a religious plot, and its protagonist is a religious figure. Its protagonist is the postracial saint.

Reading the postracial as a narrative, the continuing pull of race is the postracial's prerequisite. The postracial saint lives in a world chronically infected by race. Indeed, read as a religious narrative, a postracial world is eschatological, impossible to access from within our world. The postracial saint offers a glimpse of the eschaton. Devotion to the postracial saint means commitment to that other, impossible world. Emulation of the postracial saint means lifting our world closer to the world of our deepest desires. It is not only narrative structure that elicits this religious reading. St. Paul functions as the paradigmatic postracial saint, marked as a Jew but proclaiming an end to the distinction between Jew and Greek under the reign of Jesus Christ.

The postracial saint is no messiah (nor is she, I will argue, a prophet). In narratives of the postracial, the protagonist is incapable of single-handedly transforming the world. The protagonist proclaims and embodies the transcendence of racial difference. Such narratives are told by champions of the postracial world; sometimes they are told by postracial protagonists themselves. They can be read as hagiographies, sacred stories that confirm belief in the possibility of racial transcendence to a wavering public. They introduce readers or listeners who have never encountered the postracial before to its possibility.

Contemporary secularism forces postracial hagiographers to disclaim the theological dimension of their narratives. The attempt to disarticulate the religious and the racial results in idolatry; it results in transcendence, contra St. Paul, based on the false premise that the racial component of our worlds is an isolated problem, with an isolated solution. Peddlers of the postracial are selling late modern capitalism's story of transcendence, rooted in a simulacrum of hagiography, in the false appearance of the universal and the particular conjoined. To reach this critical conclusion, this chapter starts by considering the figures of the racial prophet, the racial messiah, and the (post)racial saint—this last is illusory. Then it examines the most famous postracial narratives of our moment: those surrounding Barack Obama, including those he tells, those told about him, and those somewhere in between. With these narratives in mind, the chapter concludes by reading Obama with St. Paul, reflecting on the antinomies produced in the dialectics of secularization—and the ideological, or idolatrous, figures of sainthood that result.

Obama the Saint

There is something religious about Barack Obama, but no one is sure quite what. Hortense Spillers refers to the "sacralization of the secular" found in images of the first Obama inauguration: images of prayer, reverence, and thanksgiving.[1] There was the rabid devotion of young people during his first campaign, volunteering because of their faith in candidate Obama. There were the excited commentaries hailing the momentous transition from one epoch to another in American history. There was the *Rolling Stone* cover with Obama's head against the background of the presidential seal, forming a halo.[2] There was Obama's invocation of the fullness of time, his refrain that "now is the time." There was his start: the speech at the 2004 Democratic National Convention where Obama's appeals to faith and hope promised to break the right's monopoly on religious language in politics. And of course there was the opposition: the demonization of Obama as Muslim, or Communist, or foreign-born, all with a fanaticism that cannot but evoke the religious.

The American presidency necessarily carries religious overtones. Scholarship on political theology reminds us that, as metonyms of sovereignty, leaders of nations, both subject to law and creators of law, occupy a space in the social imagination that can be traced back to the sacred kingship of the Middle Ages: sovereign ruler aligned with sovereign God.[3] American civil religion, too, sacralizes the presidency as it does the national spirit, with elections functioning as rituals of acclamation.[4] Moreover, Max Weber's characterization of the political change agent as necessarily charismatic, disrupting (before reinstating) bureaucratic rationality, and so necessarily tapping premodern, religious energies suggests that inhabiting at least a quasi-religious space is necessary for electability in a political culture with an insatiable appetite for change.[5]

In the case of Obama, these general religious overtones come together with the tropes of African American leadership. In the American cultural imaginary, the black leader, whether a preacher or politician, naturally blurs the sacred-secular divide. A charismatic speaker capable of mobilizing the masses, but also morally flawed and potentially misleading, this figure of the black leader held sway from Frederick Douglass and Sojourner Truth to Jesse Jackson and Cornel West.[6] This figure is the leader of a people, not of a nation. Because the people—the black community—is outside the realm of bureaucratic rationality, not descriptively but ideologically, always coded as premodern, the transformative potential Weber attributes to charismatic leadership is often absent. From the inside, from the perspective of the black community, such leaders fit the Weberian category of the traditional authority, articulating and reaffirming a community's values. From the outside, from the perspective of whites, such leaders appear charismatic, posing a challenge to modernity's status quo—to the reign of white supremacy. But they only *appear* charismatic: the black leader serves as a symbol of the sovereign exception, representing the outside of the rule of law that makes the rule of law itself possible—the racial exclusion that is the foundation of American national sovereignty. As Giorgio Agamben has shown, the sovereign exception, who can be killed without the act being considered murder, is *homo sacer*, sacred man—the obverse of the sacrality of the sovereign.[7] What seems to be disruptive charisma actually secures the status quo.

Focusing on the sacralization of Obama simply reinstates a post-Protestant mystification of the sacred. The religious aura of Obama need not be reduced to a knot of the inexplicable or irrational, alluring and dangerous and hinting at the transcendent. Rather, it follows norm-governed religious roles. Just as political and cultural leadership plays specific roles in American culture, inhabited and inflected in different ways in different contexts, the Christian religious context of modern Europe and the United States offers a finite set of possible roles for religious figures to fit or resist. The sociological and phenomenological studies of these roles once brought with them universalizing ambitions that have now been discredited, but the roles that they limned remain pragmatically useful because of their traction in our present cultural landscape. Most relevant here, to help us understand Obama's place in the American religious imaginary, are three such roles: the prophet, the messiah, and the saint.

The scholarship and advocacy of Cornel West has popularized the association of prophecy with African American leadership.[8] As he and others have explicated the office, prophecy involves appreciating tradition, discerning present social ills, underlining the seriousness of those ills, and pointing forward to a time when social harmony will be restored. In doing so, the prophet motivates others to do the concrete and burdensome labor of moving us from here to there, rectifying the social ills identified by the prophet. The prophet himself is merely a medium for a voice coming from the beyond, a god angered by the disobedience of his people but promising rewards for those who will change their ways. Martin Luther King Jr., for example, understood both white and black American social worlds, saw the injustice of segregation, used his rhetorical talents to underline this injustice, and pointed toward his dream of a day when his children "will not be judged by the color of their skin but by the content of their character." Indeed, the position of the race leader lends itself to the office of prophecy, for the very position entails a critique of social ills—particularly of racism.

Prophecy does not seem to be the right fit for the role Barack Obama occupies. The character and body of the prophet do not matter, just his message. In contrast, Obama's story is an essential part of his sacralized representation: his African father and mother from Kansas, his community organizing background, his wife from Chicago's South Side, his picture-perfect children, his thoughtfully written account of his journey of self-discovery. While it is Martin Luther King's children who, King hopes, will have the opportunity to transcend race prejudice, it is Obama himself who embodies the race-transcending world. While Obama on the campaign trail did use the word "hope" often, it was not part of a prophetic moral vision. Obama did not paint a picture of a world in which a certain grave ill, hitherto ignored, that threatened to destroy America would be repaired and in which the world would be made well. Most certainly Obama did not discern a particularly dangerous social ill concerning issues of race. He addressed issues of race as some among the many moral complexities of the contemporary American landscape, and he did not offer any novel approaches or vocabulary for discerning these issues. In one of his few public remarks on race, his much-vaunted speech on race after the Jeremiah Wright controversy, in March 2008, Obama proclaimed the message of his candidacy, "out of many, we are one," and he located racial animosity in an earlier generation, in his older black pastor and in his white grandmother. At most those problems of the past "haunt" the present.

Another religious vocation that might be brought to an analysis of Obama is that of the messiah. Where the prophet points to a better world ahead, the messiah announces the better world himself. The messiah not only represents but embodies divinity. Literally. His whole body is filled with divinity; every word and act is divine. He has unlimited capacities: unlimited knowledge, unlimited power. And he brings redemption. Humans can only be made right if they give their allegiance to him, setting aside all other worldly obligations. A racial messiah would have a body marked by race but would also, with the same body, transcend race. This is the account offered by Albert Cleage and James Cone of Jesus as black, accounts that utilize the racial messianic role.[9] Wallace Fard, founder of the Nation of Islam and considered an embodiment of God, reversed the American racial hierarchy, associating white America with sinners and redeeming, by their race, black Americans. Perhaps Jim Jones offered a variation on this messianic role, pastoring a multiracial community and evincing commitment to racial transcendence, though acknowledging the whiteness of his own redemptive body.

Shortly after Obama's election, Ta-Nehisi Coates worried in *Time Magazine* about those who think that Obama is "a God-child descending from the heavens to teacheth benighted African Americans." He concludes, missing the real power of metaphor, "Barack Obama is a black President, not black Jesus."[10] Cultural theorists have also found messianic overtones in Obama's peculiar location at the supposed change of racial epochs, announcing the significance of the present moment, as a time outside of time, leading crowds in chants proclaiming their own ability to take advantage of that moment—"yes we can."[11] But the role of messiah does not seem to fit Obama any better than that of prophet. Obama himself is not seen as racially transformative. It is his election that signifies an epochal shift. Further, it is not the entire character and body of Obama that are infused with divinity, with omnipotence and omniscience. His life story is powerful, but not because it is the life story that all should seek to reenact. Rather, his life story is powerful because of what it represents. Both the image of Obama "descending from the heavens to teacheth" and Obama conjuring the fullness of the present moment are suggestive of the prophet more than the messiah, as the former brings extra-worldly insights to worldly problems and demands response. The messiah does not need to bring something or demand something because he embodies all that is needed, and he demands total allegiance. Obama merely demanded a vote, a donation, and perhaps some volunteer work. (Note how, after the election, there were not legions of devotees volunteering their lives for government service.)

In our contemporary world, saturated with media and capital, there is a new variation on the messiah, and particularly on the racial messiah. This is a role that emerged before Obama and with which his media image often seems to resonate. The most admired black person in America, according to polls, is Oprah Winfrey. Her followers are devotees; she staged redemption on live television; and her own black body, having suffered racial and sexual abuse, is the instrument of salvific hugs and tears. Kathryn Lofton reads Oprah as a signal confluence of religion and consumerism: "It is Oprah's world. We're just buying in it, buying into it, and believing it."[12] Oprah elicits devotion, in the form of purchases, through her corporate media empire. She at once rejects the category of religion and performs religious authority, drawing her audience toward her with centripetal spiritual force. "Oprah is an instant of overflowing cultural iconography, providing stuffing for every nook and cranny of your psychological gaps and material needs," Lofton writes.[13] In other words, Oprah organizes the array of contemporary culture in a spiritually comforting manner. (This has always been the role of the messiah.) Race is just one piece of culture to be comfortably arranged.

The example of Oprah suggests that the role of the messiah today may look quite different than what we were expecting. Still embodied and still redemptive, the role of the messiah becomes that of transforming beliefs and desires that are now monetized. In a sense, this describes Obama well, as he sold himself to the market of voters. Like the modern capitalist messiah, he is immanent in, not orthogonal to, the plane of culture. His understanding of the policy issues of the day, his narration of his life, his self-presentation, and his conception of race all trade in contemporary cultural currency. None are particularly surprising. All would be publishable in the *New York Times*. The exception, Obama's relationship with Jeremiah Wright, whose racial views were out of bounds, was quickly neutralized with a heavy dose of eloquently arranged conventional wisdom. This is precisely Obama's modus operandi: reconfiguring the cultural landscape with magnetic performances so as to reorient the preferences of voters. But Obama lacks Oprah's complete immersion in the plane of popular culture. Obama's performances are more clearly *performances*. A remainder of inwardness remains, manifesting as what the commentariat has labeled his coldness. Obama's body is an integral part of his sacral performance, but it is not one with his public. An Obama hug always seems awkward, the polar opposite of an Oprah hug.

The body of a messiah is supersaturated with her religious role; there is no religious role beyond her overflowing person. In contrast, the specificity of the saint's body and story points to the universal, to the transcendent. It points rather than embodies: the saint is still human, and like all humans the saint struggles with obstacles and battles vice, but unlike other humans the saint does an exemplary job of seeking the good, the true, and the beautiful. In this way the saint, in the Christian tradition, models her life on the life of Christ, the paragon of goodness, truth, and beauty, but does so in a manner specific to her place, time, and circumstances. The saint actively shapes her life, restraining some of her desires and cultivating others, in light of her overarching desire to participate in the transcendent.[14] The transcendent shines through in the saint's life, visible to those she encounters, manifested in the miracles she causes, and recorded in hagiographic literature as well as in iconic representations for a broader community and for future generations to venerate.

All of these features remain with the role of the saint in the contemporary, post-Christian context. The saint's piety, once directed at Christ, now turns to some other worthy cause or some amorphous set of ideals. Gandhi fits the role of saint because of his selfless devotion to a certain set of values together with Indian self-rule. The physician Paul Farmer, founder of Partners in Health, works medical miracles in Haiti, lives ascetically to maximize his time in service to the poor, and was even the subject of a

New York Times bestselling hagiography.[15] Sometimes the word "saint" is used more loosely to include venerated celebrities such as Elvis Presley and Princess Diana.[16] But such figures do not fill the role of saint because they lack both the single-minded commitment and the rigorous self-fashioning entailed by that role. Single-minded commitment to worldly success does not a saint make. (Steve Jobs was no saint.)

A racial saint could mean a saint who happens to be racially marked, or it could mean a saint committed to something race-related. In the former case, race is merely one aspect among many of the saint's particularity, the particularity that provides a bridge to the universal. In the latter case, that to which the saint is devoted must be world-transcending race because any other object of devotion (such as one's own racial community) would suggest, like in the case of the celebrity, worldly rather than other-worldly commitment. In both cases, what seemed like a racial saint is actually a postracial saint, for race is not determinative. This is perhaps why the prophet and the messiah are much more familiar characters in the African American cultural-religious landscape. It has only been recently that a discourse in the United States that includes race, but where race is not determinative, has emerged.

There is one African American saintly figure that does turn up repeatedly, particularly in films. This figure was originally described by Anthony Appiah, who called it "the Saint" and took Whoopi Goldberg in *Ghost* as paradigmatic. Audrey Colombe added details to Appiah's account, describing a moment of proliferation of the "magical Black man" in films such as *The Legend of Bagger Vance* and *The Matrix*.[17] More recent scholarship and cultural criticism have settled on the term "Magic Negro" for this figure and have constructed a longer genealogy, from the unequivocally moral and nonthreatening characters of Sidney Poitier through *Six Degrees of Separation* and up to Gus Van Sant's *Elephant*.[18] In each case, the black character is articulate, asexual, and self-sacrificing, with supernatural powers used to help a film's white protagonist. Magic Negro characters have no history or future and no community, and they play merely instrumental roles in a film's plot. In short, these films seem to have overcome American racism by depicting likeable and helpful blacks, but actually they perpetuate racism by relegating blacks to subordinate roles in a white world, concealing black community and history.

The Magic Negro fulfills the first type of postracial saint role and shows the limits of this role. As portrayed on film, it just happens to be that the Magic Negro is black; it is one of her characteristics, part of her particularity that provides a bridge to the transcendent (think Morpheus in *The*

Matrix), but it does not seem essential to her sainthood. In fact, stepping back from the internal logic of the Magic Negro narrative to the way that it is deployed, race is essentially tied to sanctity in a very old-fashioned way: the racial other is depicted as a repository of authentic religious wisdom and practice.[19]

Early in Obama's first presidential campaign, David Ehrenstein argued in the *Los Angeles Times*, "Obama also is running for an equally important *unelected* office, in the province of the popular imagination—the 'Magic Negro.'"[20] According to Ehrenstein, Obama was seen, and perhaps aspired to be seen, as the essentially moral, unthreatening helpmate of the white man, complete with supernatural powers to overcome adversity and garner support. In this reading, Joseph Biden's infelicitous description of Obama as "clean and articulate" was not problematic because it suggested most African Americans are dirty and inarticulate, but because it cast Obama in the role of holy helper, as postracial saint. Ehrenstein concludes that, cast in this role, "Obama is there to help, out of the sheer goodness of a heart we need not understand. For as with all Magic Negroes, the less real he seems, the more desirable he becomes. If he were real, white America couldn't project all its fantasies of curative black benevolence on him."[21]

But the Magic Negro version of the postracial saint role does not quite fit Obama. He does have a history and a community, and they are essential to his perceived sanctity. They are key aspects of his particularity that allow transcendence to shine through. Further, self-sacrifice and asceticism are not essential aspects of Obama's image. Quite the opposite; his story is one of ambition fulfilled, the promise of America realized. Obama does not talk about long hours in the library studying or summer jobs in the factory. He describes a series of desires and opportunities. He does not talk about his own failings in moralistic terms. He recalls his encounters with drugs and lethargy as merely stages in his journey. If Obama exhibits self-discipline, often read equivocally as "coolness," it is because this is part of his nature, not achieved through effort. Moreover, the transcendence suggested by Obama is not a general holiness or otherworldliness but the specific transcendence of a racialized world. Obama's ascendance allows the promise of an alternative, postracial world to shine through to our world. In short, Obama seems to be the second type of postracial saint, not the saint who happens to be raced but the saint committed to a postracial world, with faith in that world. But as we will see, this narrative, just like the Magic Negro narrative, is not as redemptive as it seems.

Narrating Sanctity

A saint is created neither by the holy actions of a person nor by representing a person as holy. Sainthood involves a complex interaction between saintly actions and representation (or, more precisely, between various gradations of mediation) against the background of the norms governing the role of saint in a culture. Furthermore, if that to which the saint is committed is the transcendence of the racialized world, the saint must be particularly astute at predicting the ways her story and body will always already be racialized, and she must offer a personal performance of sanctity that is not overdetermined by the racialization of the culture in which she lives. The postracial saint will succeed only by living a life that allows the postracial world to shine through, offering a stark contrast with the racialized world that surrounds her. And she will succeed only if that life is legible to the media-savvy public and so capable of soliciting veneration and imitation.

Obama wrote a book, *Dreams from My Father*, before he was a political figure. It is hard not to read this book as a postracial auto-hagiography. His story is one of a humble, pensive young man coming of age in a world where race is determinative. The young man's biracial body and multicultural soul do not fit the racialized world, and he remains an outsider, an observer, wherever he finds himself. Because of his nonracial self-understanding, he is always in but not of the worlds he navigates: Muslim Indonesia, his white grandparents' home in Hawaii, black nationalists in California, an Ivy League university in Harlem, the South Side of Chicago, and, finally, his father's homeland, Kenya.

In this coming-of-age journey, the most pages are devoted to Obama's time in Chicago. He went to Chicago seeking redemption as an advocate for disempowered communities and seeking to find a racial community with which he could identify. Before he decided to go, he would lie in bed at night viewing, in his mind's eye, images of the civil rights movement, from lunch counter sit-ins to voter registration drives to jails filled with the songs of protest. "Such images became a form of prayer for me," he reflects.[22] Yet the images remain distant. They took place before his lifetime, and he does not feel connected to the world of African Americans. In his hyperreflective but also emotionally distant style, Obama recalls his thoughts at the time: "I saw the African-American community becoming more than just the place where you'd been born or the house where you'd been raised. Through organizing, through shared sacrifice, membership had been earned."²³ Obama moved to Chicago to become a community organizer: it held for him "the promise of redemption."²⁴

In *Dreams from My Father*, Obama recalls his own weakness and doubts, wondering at the time whether the community-building work he engaged in really was worthwhile. But in typical hagiographic style, humility and self-doubt ultimately function to confirm holiness. Obama's discerning eye points out the flaws of those around him, narratively positioning Obama himself as the only three-dimensional, self-aware, and so efficacious character. On the one hand, there are the male leaders of Chicago's black community, each of whom is tragically flawed. Harold Washington managed to achieve political victory with his election as Chicago's first black mayor, but his celebrity distorted his ability to help communities, and his death revealed that no lasting infrastructure was in place to permanently secure black political gains. Black male leaders in the neighborhoods coveted power, promoting their own interests to the detriment of those they supposedly represented. On the other hand, the ordinary women who were the leaders of the community organization with which Obama worked were versed in folk wisdom and exhibited virtue aplenty, but they needed an outsider's direction and motivation to get anything done. Although it remains unsaid in the narrative, the figure who takes the best from these two types is Obama himself. He is capable of identifying with the ordinary women but also capable of navigating the world of politics. He is thoughtful and articulate. (His prose and reported speech are unmarked; the reported speech of other blacks is often in dialect.) While Obama realizes that politics is based on assertively and sometimes cunningly advancing one's interests, Obama's interests are entirely identified with those of the ordinary black resident of Chicago's South Side.

The promise of redemption that motivated his Chicago sojourn turned out to be false. At this point in the narrative, Obama has not yet realized his own identity as an apostle of the postracial. He seeks a racial community, but he seeks to enter it as an outsider, as a paid worker helping the locals. Even if the community will embrace him, he does not fit comfortably into it. His identity is constantly being confused. One day he is thought to be Irish, the next day Muslim, the next day a black American. Unmoored, Obama reflects on what he was missing. He realizes that he had been brought to Chicago not just by a search for personal acceptance but by a "demanding impulse"—a religious impulse. What was needed to make the necessary "sacrifices," what was needed "to be right with yourself, to do right by others, to lend meaning to a community's suffering and take part in its healing," was "faith."²⁵ Obama had skills and talent, but he lacked faith in anything larger than himself. So he went out to find faith, and succeeded, in Jeremiah Wright's church. He went, and he listened, and he wept, and he left a convert. What he found was not the militant Afrocentrism that has more recently come to be associated with Wright and his congregation. Rather, what Obama found were stories of Ezekiel and David and Moses, stories "of survival and freedom, and hope" that "became our story, my story."[26] This was not the honorary blackness of the South Side. It was something more, something more universal. "Our trials and triumphs became at once unique and universal, black and more than black.... I also felt for the first time how that spirit carried within it, nascent, incomplete, the possibility of moving beyond our narrow dreams."[27] The spirit of the service, of Christian worship, could no longer be dismissed as merely provincial or as a symptom of false consciousness. Obama could now see how the religious spirit was aligned with the postracial and how the particularities of racial identity all opened up to the postracial horizon. He could now see how each step in his own personal journey was a step in a spiritual journey. Each racial affiliation he tried on, when understood rightly, offered a glimpse of that postracial eschaton. Obama had finally found faith in something more than himself, and he had realized that his life and body were already oriented by that faith.

Obama's piety was not pure as yet. A man, a mortal, stood in the way: Jeremiah Wright. While Obama understood Wright's church as offering a postracial message, that did not stop Wright from preaching in racial terms. When this came to the attention of the American public during the 2008 presidential campaign, Obama had to clarify to the world what his object of devotion really was. Obama explicated his object of faith in a much-heralded speech, "A More Perfect Union," that quoted at length from his postracial description of Wright's church in *Dreams from My Father*.[28] The speech's name, and its opening line's citation of the Declaration of Independence, mark Obama's political-theological object of faith. His is a commitment, despite the evidence, to a world without division—most significantly without racial division. Obama locates himself in a tradition of devotees of this idea, though past devotees all have their imperfections. The American founders promised equal citizenship and freedom for all, but left "the original sin of slavery" intact. Obama's faith "comes from my own American story," he tells his listeners, recounting his multiracial, multicultural heritage. His personal narrative "has seared into my genetic makeup the idea that this nation is more than the sum of its parts—that out of many, we are truly one." In other words, the saint's faith and story are inextricably bound together.

However, the fallen world wants us to see things in terms of black and white. Obama notes that he has been accused of being "too black" and of being "not black enough." Discussion of Obama's association with Wright had been "particularly divisive." The contrast between division and unity is the key theme of the speech. Wright's controversial statements "were not only wrong but divisive, divisive at a time when we need unity." Obama sets his own story and his own racially marked body as the site of unity, a site that can become one with America to overcome division. After discussing the racial hatred of both Wright and his own grandmother, Obama proclaims, "These people are a part of me. And they are a part of America, this country that I love." Obama is able to bring unity out of difference in his own life, incorporating and transcending the figure of Wright and the figure of his grandmother, foreshadowing a theological unity at the eschaton promised to America. Obama admits the impossibility of this promised world beyond race. He admits that the nation is mired in "a racial stalemate" that his candidacy will not solve. Yet there is work to do, for both blacks and whites, to achieve the postracial—by imitating the work that Obama himself has done. Obama asserts that he has "a firm conviction—a conviction rooted in my faith in God and my faith in the American people—that working together we can move beyond some of our old racial wounds, and that in fact we have no choice if we are to continue on the path of a more perfect union." The faith Obama has is the faith of "all the world's great religions" to treat others as we would have them treat us, which means, for Obama, an end to racial discrimination. Here again Obama's religious and racial (and national) faith blend, and Obama himself models the piety he extols.

In "A More Perfect Union," Obama proceeds to discuss the "division" around race, which he dismisses as a distraction fueled by the media. Obama proclaims that we should instead be talking about education, health care, the economy, and other pressing issues. We should begin to act in this world as if it were postracial, as if the actual existing divisions no longer mattered—a practice Obama himself will model. The speech closes with the tale of one of Obama's devotees, a young white woman, Ashley, who worked building support among blacks for the Obama campaign in a South Carolina town. Obama tells the story of Ashley telling her own story to a group of other volunteers. She speaks of her mother's illness and her struggle with the broken health care system. Then an "elderly black man who's been sitting there quietly the entire time" was asked why he was an Obama volunteer. According to Obama, he responded, "I am here because of Ashley." The presidential candidate concludes, "[T]hat single moment of recognition between the young white girl and the old black man" is the starting point in the quest for a more perfect union. The moment also represents proper devotion: the way to respond to the postracial saint is to participate in the postracial world, for a white woman to campaign for a black man in a black neighborhood—that is, to act as if the ills of racism are over, knowing that they are not.

The media coverage of Obama's speech focused on its postracial promise. Janny Scott's analysis for the *New York Times* states that Obama "confronted race head-on, then reached beyond it to talk sympathetically about the experiences of the white working class and the plight of workers stripped of jobs and pensions."[29] Commentators embraced Obama's narrative structure, describing the speech as even-handed, offering an account of both sides of the problem of race in America—and so offering a way forward. Andrew Sullivan called the speech "searing, nuanced, gut-wrenching, loyal, and deeply, deeply Christian." Jesse Jackson described the speech as "warm, filling, captive, reconciling, and comprehensive" and added that "it displayed real true grit."[30] These responses indicate that the speech served its political-theological purpose, not only distracting media attention from questions about the extent of Obama's association with Wright, but filling the hearts of listeners with a new vision of a postracial world, a vision where all of the components of the old world remain, but with our affective investment rearranged, and so with the world effectively reconfigured.

From Barack Obama to Paul of Tarsus

Alain Badiou's account of St. Paul closely matches this account of Obama.[31] For Badiou, St. Paul announces a transformation in the way things in the world fit together. St. Paul urges his audience to commit themselves to the new arrangement, even if what precisely it means remains obscure. In Badiou's account, we become subjects by having faith—faith in an event, in a transformative moment. Not only do we become subjects, we become equal. The previous status we held was secured by the old regime, the old way of organizing things, before the transformative event. All of that is up in the air with the event: the only thing that can be said for certain about subjects who accept the authority of the new regime is that they have faith. Thus, Badiou reads Paul's famous "neither Jew nor Greek" imperative as a refusal of two codependent discourses, Jewish and Greek, in favor of a third novel discourse that is Christian. Instead of accepting humanity divided in two, with two separate structures of authority, Badiou is committed to universality, to a "universal logic of salvation [that] cannot be tied to any law."[32]

While Badiou regrettably does not ponder Paul's status as saint, focusing instead on his status as disciple, we can observe the logic of the postracial in his account. Paul, as Jew, seeks to neither affirm nor reject his own Jewish affiliation. Rather, he seeks to render it obsolete through his own personal story (the road to Damascus) and bodily commitment to the new regime (his suffering and death). Obama, similarly, tells a story of two discourses, black and white rather than Jew and Greek, and seeks to overcome them with his own faith. Like Paul the Roman Jew, Obama the black American offers a path to the universal through his own particularity. Like Paul, Obama tells stories of followers rendered equal in their shared commitment to the project he announces: his presidential election campaign (Ashley and the unnamed old black volunteer, among others).

But this way of representing Paul leans on a history of Christian supersessionism, of the Christian effort to denigrate Judaism. This is a point made by Daniel Boyarin, who urges readers to pay attention to Paul's cultural context: "Pauline religion should be understood as a religio-cultural formation contiguous with other Hellenistic Judaisms."[33] Read in this context, Boyarin suggests that Paul is able to hold both literal and allegorical meanings together, in two registers. Ethnic and gender ("neither male nor female") identities remain in the literal register, but in the allegorical register, which is primary, identities are united in Christ. "By entering into the body of Christ in the spirit, people become one with the seed to which the promise was made and thus themselves heirs of Abraham and children of God according to the promise."[34] In other words, Paul was not rejecting his own Judaism but adding another dimension to it, opening the allegorical register. While differing with Paul philosophically and theologically, Boyarin finds that Paul raises certain important questions that Jews must address about ethnic particularity and nationalism, especially in light of the contemporary religious-national project of Israel. Instead of the choice between identity based on genealogy (the racial state) and identity based on claims of universality (the modern liberal state), Boyarin urges disaggregating "people, language, land, and culture" in a "diasporic" Jewish identity.[35]

If we are to jump again from the postracial Paul to the postracial Obama, and so from the supersession of Jewishness to the supersession of blackness, Boyarin's concerns seem well founded. As many commentators have noted, the "postracial" often is politically problematic, concealing the continuing force of American racism.[36] Moreover, holding racialized identity together with, but subordinate to, postracial identity, as Obama does seem to do, legitimates a liberal political discourse that relegates race to a matter of cultural difference and even personal taste, limiting the significance of race to little more than one among many identity boxes to check on forms. In light of Obama, it is unclear how the diasporic conception of identity that Boyarin proposes as an alternative to both Jewish and Greek conceptions (itself another supersession?) is less problematic. Obama would seem to be the paradigm of diasporic identity, with nation (his Indonesian and Hawaiian upbringing and Kenyan father) disaggregated from race (the blackness ascribed to him and the white institutions he navigates) disaggregated from culture (his Ivy League pedigree) disaggregated from language (his refusal, in *Dreams from My Father*, to write or represent his own speech in black dialect). Yet all of these features reinforce Obama's racial supersession. Indeed, they all add to his postracial sanctity. The more diverse the components of his identity, the more his own story and body allow the coming postracial world to shine through. Yet, at the end of the day, Obama is still read as black, as a black man aspiring to the postracial. Given the force of the American racial regime, no amount of identity disaggregation overrides racialization based on skin color. One wonders whether Boyarin's optimism about the potential effects of disaggregating Jewish identity is warranted, given the similarly intensive regimes of racialization that have been imposed on Jews.

Obama himself has some thoughts on Jewish identity, linked with black identity—thoughts that he shares in "A More Perfect Union." Immediately after reminding listeners that he has condemned Wright's controversial remarks, he describes just how troubling these remarks were:

> [T]he remarks that have caused this recent firestorm weren't simply controversial. They weren't simply a religious leader's effort to speak out against perceived injustice. Instead, they expressed a profoundly distorted view of this country—a view that sees white racism as endemic, and that elevates what is wrong with America above all that we know is right with America; a view that sees the conflicts in the Middle East as rooted primarily in the actions of stalwart allies like Israel, instead of emanating from the perverse and hateful ideologies of radical Islam.

Wright's comments on both whites and Palestinians caused controversy, and Obama's speech not only responds to these two separate controversies but also reveals a close connection between the promise of the postracial and the persistence of the racial state. The first wrongheaded, "divisive" view disclaimed here is a belief in the racism of most whites. While Obama labels slavery America's "original sin" and describes continuing racial problems, he positions whites as predominantly willing to convert to the postracial if only they are given the opportunity. Such conversion does not take rejection of the old (racism), just openness to the new (the postracial world illumined through Obama). This openness will inevitably lead the old to wither away. In the same line in his speech, the opportunity for conversion is foreclosed for those opponents of Israel, since their motivation is irrational—they are motivated by the hatred cultivated by "radical Islam." Similarly, while Obama's speech consistently questions the identification of America with the white race, he has no problem unequivocally affirming America's alliance with a state unabashedly committed to a particular racial identity: Israel. This antinomy points both to the specifically Christian nature of the postracial (excluding Islam) and to the way that not only domestic but also foreign racism is concealed through postracial narratives. Put another way, while Obama's role as postracial saint is distinct from the role of the Magic Negro, both roles simultaneously appear to further an antiracist agenda while in fact subtly perpetuating racism.

Is the postracial saint, then, just as much of a conceptual impossibility as the racial saint? Does the postracial saint function solely as a catalyst for interpellation, pacifying the grumbles of racialized subjects? Perhaps we made the jump from the first-century Mediterranean to the twenty-first-century United States too hastily. Perhaps we have played too fast and loose with the theological category of the saint in our secular age. Approached from the opposite direction: St. Paul himself, in that famous third book of Galatians, can be read as offering a forceful critique of secularism. He condemns those who would "rely on the works of the law." Those who do so are, St. Paul proclaims, "held in custody under law" and "under a curse," a curse removed by Christ. Now, under the authority of Christ, it is faith that makes humans right before God. St. Paul's opponents are committed secularists. They recognize only the authority of law, but law is simply the substitute for the authority of God. The role of the saint is to allow the authority of God to shine through, revealing secularism's dogmatic commitment to our worldly prison, its dogmatic refusal to be open to a higher authority.

St. Paul, then, trumpets his refusal of the plane of immanence, proclaiming a commitment to an authority orthogonal to the world. This is often lost when the concept of the saint is applied to secular contexts, to contexts where the religious is relegated to one among many domains of human interest. That to which the saint is committed, that which shines through in the life of the saint, is conceived in worldly, rather than other-worldly, terms. Even a smidgen of worldly content contaminates the transcendent. Badiou suggests that the Nazi commitment to a universal was contaminated by racial thinking, by the categories of Aryan and Jew, and a similar contamination is evident in the case of Obama's postracial transcendence.[37] The postracial seems to describe another world, totally different from our own, yet it is only different in one respect, with respect to race, with respect to a specific difference of our specific world. The postracial saint, then, is not a saint but a celebrity. She advances her own fame under the guise of a universal that conceals its particularity rather than with a particularity that points to a universal. Or, the postracial saint is a narrative device, deployed to advance the interests of some—at the expense of others.

CHAPTER 12

The Race of the Soul: On Gillian Rose

I thought I was interested in Gillian Rose because I was studying the philosophy of religion. Rose seemed like the perfect guide. She articulated frustrations I felt with analytic philosophy, with French theory, and with neopragmatism, yet she persisted in *doing* philosophy, not just writing about philosophy. She saw questions of religion as fundamental to all philosophy, and she did so by understanding religion as covering much more territory than questions about belief in God or the practice of rituals. For her, religion at its worst shuts down philosophy, taking certain commitments as given and immune from interrogation. Religion at its best animates philosophy, cultivating curiosity about our worlds and our selves that fuels continual, rigorous questioning. In a sense, the whole history of philosophy can be read as a history of the struggle of such religion, such theology, against heresy. For Rose, Hegel is the closest they come to an Angelic Doctor, with Derrida, Deleuze, and Foucault representing recent varieties of heterodoxy. By participating in this theological-philosophical tradition, championing its orthodoxy, and describing how intellectual work and life's work are one and the same, Rose offered a model to a college student trying to figure out how to think and how to live—and who I was.

Rose's enchanting effect was felt not only by twenty-year-olds but also by my teachers. Everywhere I went I kept encountering professors who loved Rose's work, who thought she was brilliant and right, but who had for one reason or another never mentioned her name in print. There were Jeffrey Stout and Cornel West at Princeton, both of whom taught Rose's books, Paul Mendes-Flohr at Chicago who knew her well, and Judith Butler and Daniel Boyarin at Berkeley, where I eventually wrote my dissertation on Rose. As a graduate student, she seemed like the right stock to put my money in: acknowledged as a great thinker but still under the radar, a penny stock whose value could explode. Moreover, Rose was interdisciplinary, and I wanted to be interdisciplinary. She brought together social theory, religion, philosophy, and literature, and she did so motivated by a desire for the true, the good, and the beautiful so often lacking in the academy.

The power of false consciousness is astounding. I never for a second considered the most obvious reason that Rose's thought was attractive to me. She was "too Jewish to be Christian and too Christian to be Jewish"; I was too white to be black and too black to be white.[1] Rose's work was about this "middle," and Rose made philosophy about this middle: philosophy was hers and mine. I threw myself into the study of Jewish and Christian thought and the philosophical tradition, carefully avoiding classes about race. This was sustainable when I was surrounded by communities that nurture false consciousness: elite universities and the ostensibly postracial San Francisco Bay area. When I tried to talk about Rose in Atlanta, a city where the essential American racial binary is undisguised, the first question I received was, "How does this relate to Martin Luther King Jr.?" I resisted, but only for a short time. Then the hard work began. That Rose's thought spoke to me was more than an example of psychic displacement. Somehow, the lessons from her struggle with identity were also lessons about race, but these lessons would not be obvious. Jewishness, after all, is not blackness, and psychic displacement seriously distorts.

What Rose has to say explicitly about race and ethnicity is not particularly promising. At best, these categories are presented as distractions from the real work of philosophy, and so (because it is for Rose subordinate to philosophy) the real work of politics. When Rose describes her Jewishness as ethnic, it is to demonstrate that she has transcended ethnic identity in her "return journeys between protestantism and Judaism."[2] Rose expresses frustration with authors who write "as a black" because such declarations assume identity is fixed, whereas Rose sees the task of writing as the task of probing and challenging identities.[3] Philosophy and writing and life are at their best when they are suspicious of the words and categories that make up our ordinary world. These words and categories mask the interests of the powers that be. To treat such language as if it really refers to the world is to advance those interests—it is, according to Rose, "fascist."[4] Understood in this way, race is simply one category among others, one way of marking identity along with religion and gender.

While Rose devotes a book to complicating Judaism as a religious identity, she only makes a few remarks about gender. Rose treats Judaism as a religious tradition and complicates it by engaging with that tradition—defending her theological-philosophical orthodoxy—but she treats gender, like race, as little more than a contemporary identity label mobilized politically. Her remarks on feminism are suggestive of her views on race politics. Rose has two primary complaints about feminism, explanations for why "feminism never offered me any help."[5] First, feminism's emphasis on women's oppression conceals women's power.[6] Power between men and women may be unequal, but this does not mean that women are powerless. Interpersonal relationships, just as social relations, are dynamic and depend on both parties continually acting in relation to each other. Those with less power are invested in relationships with those who have more power, resulting in ambivalence that must be acknowledged before injustices can be addressed. The second criticism Rose levels at feminism is that there are contexts in which women may actually have more power than men, or nearly equal power, where a woman challenges a man and is challenged by the man.[7] As desiring and desired, and as capable of withdrawal, in personal relationships women who take ownership of their desire can wield a mighty power. Yet these two worries about feminism address issues quite distinct from the realities of race. The asymmetry of power is so dramatic between whites and blacks, to take the archetypal case, that it is hard to seriously consider a space where black and white interact as equals; certainly not in the bedroom. Particularly given the vivid illustrations of the enduring power of anti-blackness in U.S. culture—police brutality, mass incarceration, economic inequality—it would seem as though Rose's insights have to be reworked or abandoned. Before making that decision, it is important to examine just how she comes to the conclusions she does about identity and so, by extension, race.

The Violence of Identity

Rose's philosophical writings, her autobiographical writings, and her reflections on religion all work together, making the same points in different registers. This is one of Rose's core commitments: we ought to grapple with abstract theoretical problems in the same way we grapple with problems in our personal relationships. Rose is critical of philosophical accounts of identity as static (and as purely fluid); she also offers a provocative example of how such accounts affect her. Diagnosed with terminal cancer, Rose finds that the popular discourse about cancer overdetermines her identity as "patient or victim, somebody who can be looked after, patronized, put in a category, seen to be ailing."[8] Family members, medical professionals, coworkers, and some friends take cancer as determinative of who Rose is. Yet Rose resists: "I refuse to identify with cancer as a generality."[9] The cancer victim is supposed to be passive, afflicted by the disease, but Rose describes herself as active, learning about and deciding between possible treatments, suspicious of some of the advice she receives, and deeply curious. Moreover, much of the time Rose does not feel sick even as she is identified with illness. By resisting this identification, Rose is able to accept her feeling of wellness rather than understanding it merely as an oasis in the desert of terminal illness.

Rose does not let even the loss of her hair in chemotherapy, the most obvious visual marker of the cancer victim, force her into that role. Rather, she sees it as an opportunity to "find a better way . . . to remain hidden."[10] To be hidden is to evade the grasp of identity markers. Having such distance from identity markers is the prerequisite to interrogating them, negotiating them, and reimagining them. Accepting an identity ascription results in the expected performances—saying, feeling, and thinking the right things—but it also results in existential angst, for we ultimately know that what we are is not who we are, that our thoughts and feelings are more complex than those prescribed by any identity category. It takes work to tap into these subterranean reserves of feeling and thought—to tap into what Rose calls "the soul." This is philosophical and personal work, and the social world discourages it. Such discouragement is part of the violence of the social that Rose so often describes: it makes us forget our souls, makes us adopt a set of identity categories that exhausts who we are.

In the philosophical terms that Rose draws from Hegel, identity categories are imposed on us by abstract legality. As she puts it:

> The boundary stake of abstract legality not only pierces the individual soul but renders invisible the actuality of others, their work, desire, and otherness, as well as oneself as other, and it is this anguish which makes phantasy projections of community, secured by an idealised outer boundary of religion, nation, so compelling. To arrest one's

self-understanding in a classification is to prevent the development of mutual recognition—it is to aestheticize politics.[11]

When we take identity to be described in the terms circulating in the social world—race, gender, religion, and so forth—the complexity of individual lives, of souls, is erased. All the more so when these identity categories are not only part of social discourse but are formalized in law and government: when there are boxes to check on official forms for gender, race, and religion. This gives us the illusion of fully understanding others and fully understanding ourselves, a confidence that often has destructive, violent consequences. Not only does accepting identity categories distort our view of individuals, Rose is arguing here, but the unexpressed anger caused by those distortions finds expression in fantasy, with affective investment in further abstractions such as the nation (or a racial or gendered community). Such abstractions are aesthetic in the sense that they correspond to collective imagining, absorbing otherwise inexpressible affect; they do not correspond to the way a community actually lives. Indeed, our perceptions of communities—racial, gendered, national, or otherwise—are mangled when they are the product of abstract legality's psychic remainder in this way.

Abstract legality was characteristic of modernity; postmodernity moves beyond its conception of identity in two ways—each operating in both the philosophical and the personal registers. On the one hand, according to Rose, there is a postmodern fetishization of the self. In other words, identity is not just socially ascribed. It is embraced and embellished. Each individual is understood to be "special," with talents to be discovered and cultivated. Even though such cultivation involves discipline and apparent work on the self, Rose sees it as ultimately directed at attracting the praise of others.[12] Rather than the ascesis of standing back from and interrogating socially ascribed identities, this fetishization of the self takes ascribed identities as given and goes further with them, enlarging the self but in the terms prescribed by society—and so suffering from an even subtler form of false consciousness, believing that socially ascribed identities do fully capture who an individual is.

On the other hand, Rose sees the deconstruction of identity as another postmodern move beyond modernity's abstract legality. No identity is taken too seriously, in this view. They are all contingent, shifting, and they ought to be denaturalized. Identity markers are signifiers at play; modernity tried to hold them in place. Rose diagnoses this view as resulting from unfinished mourning for the lost wholeness promised by modernity. This mourning without end fuels a suspicion of identity claims as part of (ironically) a desire for an impossible wholeness, an impossible perfect fit between socially ascribed identity and the individual to whom it is ascribed. In other words, this deconstructive trend is so intent on demystifying identity that it refuses to carefully examine and negotiate the complications of identity—the ways that socially ascribed identity both does not fit and, in some ways, does fit. Melancholically, deconstruction simply repeats over and over the banal fact that identity ascriptions fail.

As these views suggest, Rose is highly suspicious of identity politics. For her, politics should be approached in the same way as philosophy and personal life, exploring difficulties as well as the violence done in the attempt to conceal those difficulties. Mobilizing politically based on socially ascribed identities lends legitimacy to those identities, further solidifying the power (and so violence) of abstract legality. Moreover, giving power to communities that have been disempowered risks perpetuating a cycle of abuse, as the newly empowered community turns its resentment into political action.[13] Meanwhile, the discursive landscape (the categories created by the once-powerful) remains intact. Those categories are still doing violence, still misfitting those to whom they are ascribed and concealing souls.

Rose's essential concern about identity politics is that it distracts from the primary goal of politics: "Politics begins not when you organize to defend an individual or particular or local interest, but when you organize to further the 'general' interest within which your particular interest may be represented."[14] This general interest is not simply pragmatic. It is, in Rose's account, a "universal or shared notion of justice and the good."[15] Justice is not for me or for us but for everyone. It must be viewed clearly, and to achieve that right perception one must first distance oneself from the identities that one is ascribed in order to understand their limitations and the way they distort. Understanding justice or the common good rightly is a task at which we all will necessarily fail, but politics involves trying. Politics involves, as Rose puts it, "the risk of the universal interest."[16] At the end of the day, politics is animated by the same force that animates philosophy, and life, when they are rightly understood: the pursuit of the good, the true, and the beautiful.

From Identity to Soul

Instead of identity politics, Rose advocates soul politics, politics that acknowledges the soul is never captured by any socially ascribed identity. This is not a commitment to human rights or human dignity (which ascribes the identity "human"). It is not a commitment to any specific characteristics that would make up the human but rather a commitment to a fundamental desire for the good, the true, and the beautiful, and to a characteristically human capacity to pursue the good, the true, and the beautiful. This pursuit involves the critical interrogation of the world and the self, calling into question those labels that purport to fit perfectly. The words and concepts that we use to describe the world are tools of the soul, but too often we take them as constraints of the soul—or we forget about the soul altogether. The soul is not a site of pure freedom; it is a capacity to *practice* freedom by self-consciously negotiating the practices and norms of our social world. Before we can engage in politics, we must have a proper conception of the soul; otherwise we are likely to make the world much worse.

When questions of identity replace questions of soul, we ignore what life in the world really involves. We become overconfident, repressing the complications and difficulties of life in the world, which then express themselves in unhealthy ways. Life in the world consists in "being bounded and unbounded, selved and unselved, 'sure' only of this untiring exercise."[17] The world's concepts apply to us and change us, but we also resist them, refusing some and embracing others. Unlike theorists of ideology who would see the ideas of the ruling class entirely shaping who we are, Rose's account of the individual subject on whom these ideas are imposed shows the negotiation, resistance, and intellectual work that we all perform, even the meekest among us—for even the meekest have souls.

Rose recommends several practices for care for the soul, practices that remind us how we are more than our identities. Such practices take courage because they require leaving behind the security that identity provides: "We need to venture again the courage of suspense, not knowing who we are, in order to rediscover our infinite capacity for self-creation and response to our fellow self-creators."[18] Sometimes, such suspense is forced upon us—for example, in disaster or illness or death. In such circumstances, we see that we are not who we thought ourselves to be; we are not exhausted by the labels the world applies to us. It is tempting to conceal this insight from ourselves, finding people or objects to blame or to love as a way of calming the terror at not knowing who we are—tempting for those who lack the courage of suspense. If such courage has been mustered:

> My soul is naked: it has lost its scaffolding of regret and remorse or even repentance: it is turned: and the unexpected result is the sensation and the envelope of invisible and visible beauty. This does not make me ecstatic, unreal, unworldly: it returns me to the vocation of the every-

day—to Miss Marple's sense of quotidian justice—but it needed some response, some way of singing its mystery so that I can concentrate as ever on any fellowship or fickleness which presents itself.[19]

In other words, suspense does not necessarily lead to dramatic transformation or revelation. Rather, it leads to increased attunement. More of the means by which the world distorts our perception are wiped away. We can see better what is good, and true, and beautiful, and we can participate in the good, the true, and the beautiful.

Among the activities that cultivate the soul, the most important, for Rose, is love.[20] In the intimacy between two romantic partners, socially ascribed identities are set aside. Each partner sees that the other is not that which identity marks him or her, and each partner realizes the same about himself or herself. It is tempting to love momentarily, for a night, and then be gone, but that shows a lack of courage. To love for longer builds the courage that is needed, not just in love but in life, to interrogate who we are beyond what we are, to understand the world in ways that are not reducible to the preestablished categories of statistics and spreadsheets. Love requires vulnerability and necessarily brings with it pain, but so does life if it is to be lived soulfully, as Rose recommends. Love has nothing to do with gender, in Rose's account, and the specifics of the sexual encounter are irrelevant to its philosophical force, as it were. Indeed, the paradigmatic love act for Rose is kissing: "The embrace of face by face is the true carnival of sex beyond gender."[21] Gender identity is taken away along with all identity when love opens the soul.

What Rose describes with examples from her personal life she also describes philosophically, in her reading of Hegel. According to Rose, Hegel offers a new way of understanding identity that begins by stripping a concept of its familiar associations. From there Hegel portrays "an empty name, uncertain and problematic, gradually acquiring meaning as the result of a series of contradictory experiences."[22] Our concepts, like our selves, are not captured by any given set of necessary and sufficient conditions. Meaning comes about through relationships with other concepts, through a worldly history. Just as an individual's gender is suspended in love and certain other practices, according to Rose, the very meaning of gender or any other identity category is not fixed but dynamic, developing in time, in context. To understand the meaning of gender—or race, it would seem—our ordinary connotations must be suspended. Those connotations have accrued and been naturalized in a way that advances the interests of the powers that be and the powers that have been, distorting the actual experiences of those to whom the category is applied. (Rose and Judith Butler read Hegel to the same effect.)

Foregrounding the soul is not just a personal and philosophical issue for Rose; it is also a political issue. Rose defines politics as "the risk of action arising out of the negotiation of the law," clearly paralleling her account of the risk and courage involved in life in the world and in philosophy.[23] What does this mean in concrete terms? Politics does not involve dreaming of utopias, for this avoids "the negotiation of the law" in the actual existing world. Just as Rose rejects social theories that insulate a certain transcendental register from empirical testing and transformation, Rose rejects political theories that likewise make claims based on first principles or fixed definitions of concepts.[24] Instead, political theorists must examine actual political practices, institutions, and norms, must examine their histories, their limitations, and their possibilities. Such study, such theorizing, then challenges conventional political wisdom, destabilizing the political concepts that seem so natural to us. This process of critical interrogation and destabilization, Rose thinks, brings us closer to justice. It does not involve marching in the streets or running for office, though it is important to note that these concrete practices are neither commended nor condemned in Rose's view. Her account of politics is really an account of our stance toward politics. She remains agnostic on the concrete content, just as she remains agnostic on the content of how one ought to live one's life. From Rose's perspective it simply is not the role of the philosopher (or political theorist, or friend) to make such first-order normative judgments.

The Race of the Soul

In Rose's view, the soul is something all of us humans share, whether we are white or black, male or female, straight or queer. Such identities certainly affect us, but they do not determine who we are. It is in the excess of who we are beyond our socially ascribed identities that the soul comes alive and that philosophy and politics start. While Rose avoids first-order normative judgments, certain implications clearly follow from her thought. In her opposition to abstract legality, Rose would oppose policies and laws that excessively naturalize identities, although she would also oppose policies and laws that entirely ignore identities. Segregation in the U.S. South would seem to fit the former category; laws mandating race-blind admissions policies at universities would seem to fit the latter. Even though segregation might not seem to excessively naturalize identities from the perspective of a certain group at a certain moment, and even though race-blind admissions might seem similarly reasonable from some perspectives, Rose (with Hegel) urges us to step back from the logic of the present moment and look historically at how a concept develops. With such an investigation, it is clear that segregation involves forcefully ossifying racial identities, and race-blind admissions ignore the longstanding and continuing effects of racism.

The language that Rose uses to describe the effects of identities captures the force involved. She writes that "re-presentation is always misrepresentation, lack of identity."[25] Every attempt to classify an individual or a group gets them wrong. More importantly, in Rose's view misrepresentation is violent. Representation is integral to normativity—so-and-so ought to do this or that—so continual misrepresentation means continually being wrong, being unable to do what one is supposed to do. At the individual level, this means, for example, men who are considered too effeminate being reprimanded with words or blows. At the social level it means, for example, indigenous communities expected to live out a Hollywood stereotype and facing disparagement when they fall short. The language of violence that Rose embraces is particularly helpful in showing the continuity between the seemingly mild smarts of, say, race-blind admissions policies and the unmistakable brutality of racial lynching or the genocide of indigenous communities.

Rose further expresses a commitment to justice as a commitment to mitigate all such violence, but she is careful to distinguish mitigation from elimination. The aspiration to eliminate violence necessarily results in more violence, in her account. What she calls the "dream of a New Jerusalem," in philosophy, personal life, or politics, takes our attention away from the complications—the attempted representations that are actually misrepresentations—of the present and so allows their violence to go unchecked as we are toiling away at our plans for an entirely different world. Moreover, if we attempt to implement these plans, if we attempt to build a New Jerusalem in a fallen world, the result will be even greater misrepresentation and even greater violence, for the architectural plans do not correspond in the least to the reality of the terrain and the building materials available. These realities have been bracketed while the architect was cloistered in her studio, and now the architect must deform the terrain and improvise quarries—deforming and improvising with the lives of human beings.

In short, Rose recognizes the historical power of identity categories and the violence that they continue to inflict, but she suspects that the desire for peaceful coexistence would only compound this violence. Instead of envisioning various groups each having a seat at the social or political table—implying each is represented properly—Rose sees a dynamic forum, with participants standing rather than sitting, talking with each other, moving around, learning, arguing, occasionally getting hurt, but continuing to engage. Each participant in the forum has a race, a gender, and many other identity markers, and participants may talk in a cluster with those who share their race or gender, but then new clusters form, new conversations, reminding participants that they have no permanent allies and no permanent enemies. While each participant is not entirely free to choose with whom she or he speaks (the barriers to entry of some conversations are higher than to others), each is free to step back, to find other conversation partners for a while, and to decide whether to reenter an earlier conversation.

This vision of pluralism—not cultural pluralism but what might be called "soul pluralism"—avoids the pitfalls of many alternatives. It acknowledges both the power and the limitations of identity categories and communities. It emphasizes the need to appreciate the specific histories of communities. It accepts that political and social efforts to speak to identities do more than mirror the identities of a society, and it also accepts that the misrepresentation of the political and the social are integral to those identities, constitutive of them from the start rather than external impositions. Yet a major worry remains. While in Rose's account different communities and identities have different histories, it is not clear how her account would handle different amounts of power. The dynamic of representation and misrepresentation may be appealing if everyone (or every social group) is undergoing it in different ways, but if certain groups have more power to set the terms of representation and others perpetually suffer the violence of misrepresentation with little recourse, this picture seems rather less appealing. Certainly, even the group (or person) that wields disproportionate power is itself misrepresented, but the violence of such a misrepresentation—as stronger than others, for example—seems importantly softer than the violence of misrepresenting a minority group as, say, subhuman.

The limitations of Rose's thought along these lines start to become clear in her remarks on feminism. While the power of women and the active participation of both abuser and abused in the dynamic of abuse are certainly worth remembering, they also shift emphasis away from an overwhelming history of power inequality that has molded gender identities. Defying her own precept to fully appreciate the history of identity formation, Rose comments, "The model that one grows up in a patriarchal culture where women are oppressed certainly doesn't correspond to my experience. I've been encouraged at every stage by men in my family, by teachers, by tutors."[26] This quick dismissal of systematically pervasive power inequality (patriarchy) would at first seem to be unphilosophical in Rose's understanding of the task of philosophy. But perhaps this statement points rather to a tension within Rose's account of philosophy. What she seems to be referring to is the level of souls: her soul, with its capacity for critical engagement with self and world, is equal to every other soul. Neither privilege nor poverty automatically leads to this conclusion. It takes the right conditions to reach this conclusion: supportive family and teachers, but also, as Rose repeatedly describes, experiences that suspend her normal place in the world. She describes struggling as a child with dyslexia, as a young adult with the alienating style of Oxford philosophy, and as a middle-aged woman with terminal illness. In each case, she had support that allowed her to deal with the challenges in a soul-affirming rather than soul-repressing manner. Yet patriarchy, like racism, entails the likelihood that such support is unavailable. Without family or teachers or books that can transform an encounter with the violence of the world's contradictions into renewed engagement with the world, such encounters simply devastate. Rose often implies that this possibility of devastation would be a personal failing; it is a sin of which she accuses her mother. But this overlooks the material conditions required for the philosophical life Rose commends; patriarchy, racism, and other forms of systematic inequality determine those material conditions.

Another way of putting this worry has to do with racial melancholia. Anne Cheng has persuasively described the ways in which the gripping power of American racism results in a psychic loss, both for the objects of this racism who can never be fully incorporated into social and political life and for the beneficiaries of this racism who depend on a racial other to secure their own privileged status.[27] What Americans need to do, Cheng argues, is grapple with grief for these losses, but this grief is concealed when it is transformed into specific grievances, specific requests aimed at advancing racial justice. Cheng is clearly at odds with Rose; the latter argues for the refusal of melancholia, for the transformation of injury into action in social and political life. Rose writes, "Mourning draws on transcendent but representable justice, which makes the suffering of immediate experiences visible and speakable. When completed, mourning returns the soul to the city, renewed and reinvigorated for participation, ready to take on the difficulties and injustices of the existing city."[28] What seems like a debate about the psyche is actually a debate about the depths of racism (or patriarchy, or homophobia). While Rose would agree that the history of blackness is important and unavoidable, she would see it as of local importance, concerning only those affected. For Cheng, in contrast, anti-black and anti-immigrant racism is intertwined with the history of American society as a whole. Any specific articulation of racial grievance would overlook that broader history.

It is not obvious that the dynamic Cheng describes is at work for all identity groups or in all contexts, but it is plausible that it is at work in some. If so, Rose's model of a soul on top of which contingent, changing identities pause is misleading. Cheng suggests in a sense that it is the soul itself that is damaged by racism. Racial identity is not just one more predicate ascribed to us as subjects, not just one more community of which we are a part. Race fundamentally shapes our capacity to pursue the good, the true, and the beautiful. All of the concepts and norms with which we engage are tainted by race, so the process of engagement itself is tainted by race—and that process is what Rose calls "the soul." Race characterizes not only what we are but who we are. Rose is suspicious of melancholia and of accounts of philosophy or politics motivated by loss because they prevent clearheaded engagement with the world as it really is. But Cheng's claim is that there is no way to access the world as it really is unless we first account for the distortions of race. A similar claim has been advanced powerfully by both philosophers and theologians who contend that anti-blackness has been central to the metaphysics of the West—in some accounts a continuation of anti-Semitism.[29] Similar stories have been told about patriarchy, though there does seem to be an important difference. Where the practice of love offers Rose a glimpse of gender equality as it marks a path from social identities to souls, it is hard to imagine an analogous practice with regard to race. Love certainly does not function in this way, as James Baldwin's writings dramatically illustrate.[30]

If there is a racial practice that comes closest to the kind of training that Rose finds in love, it may be the practice of organizing against racism. In struggling against the defenders of racism (racist policing, racist prisons, racist housing practices, racist economic systems), the contingency of racial identities becomes clear, as it is increasingly obvious that the self-interest of the wealthy and powerful lies behind the purportedly natural, biological definition of race. The practice of organizing puts participants at risk: their time may be spent in vain, their reputations may be tainted, or their bodies may be injured. Organizing means working together with those who have very different life stories, it requires listening to those stories, and it requires restraining our own instincts in favor of those of the collective or those with more experience.[31] While whites and blacks (and others) may bring to anti-racist organizing different experiences and different privileges, confrontation with the stubborn and ruthless defenders of racism certainly has an equalizing effect, demystifying race for both whites and blacks while also showing the power and difficulty of collective action. And anti-racist organizing requires a commitment to a project despite obstacles and hardships, motivated by a desire for justice. Viewed in this way, anti-racist organizing does the kind of work on the race-distorted soul that Rose attributes to love. Yet Rose would likely be skeptical of anti-racist organizing because, from her perspective, it represents politics motivated by particular interests rather than general interests. However, if the claim that racism is so pervasive and deep-seated that it distorts all souls is persuasive, then racial justice is a question of the general interest, not particular interest.

Rose presents her own stance between Judaism and Christianity, at once religious and ethnic categories in her view, as allowing easier awareness of the contingency and fluidity of identity and of the souls that lie beneath. Yet this valorization of "the middle" is plausible when the distribution of power between the identities in question is more or less equal; otherwise, it risks false consciousness. National Socialism certainly did not recognize a middle space between Judaism and Christianity in any sense. Efforts to establish a "biracial" identity category in the United States do little to counteract the binary through which race is viewed. As Jared Sexton has persuasively shown, such efforts ultimately distract from the underlying dynamic animating American racism: anti-blackness.[32] The same might be said, in certain contexts, for anti-Semitism or Islamophobia.

Indeed, Rose's relationship to Judaism hints at an awareness of this dynamic. In the opening pages of *Judaism and Modernity*, she describes her process of writing about Judaism as a struggle with identity starting from a position of uncertainty. She writes that it was her philosophical commitment to a view "which persists in acknowledging the predicament of identity and lack of identity, independence and dependence, power and powerlessness, that has led me to Judaism."[33] Even standing between identities, Rose has a special relationship with one, with the identity of the minority, with the identity that is in a sense oppositional. While she certainly is interested, personally and philosophically, in Christianity, for Rose Judaism changed from identity to tradition. In *Judaism and Modernity* she explored the contestations and limitations within that tradition. But it is important to remember that, in Rose's telling, her original interest in Judaism was prompted by the words of a Jew she met at a dinner party: "An Orthodox Jew doesn't have to worry about whether he believes in God or not. As long as he observes the law."[34] In a sense, Rose's writings on Judaism are an attempt to understand what the law means and so how to be faithful to it. Despite her protestations to the contrary, this seems an essentially Jewish project, and perhaps Rose's writings may even be read, counterintuitively, as an attempt to read the philosophical tradition from a Jewish perspective. After all, for her, philosophy, like life, is essentially about law. If this is Rose's project, then it implicitly offers a model that moves one step beyond her explicit embrace of liminal identity. It treats a minority community not only as a socially ascribed identity label, not only as a tradition, but as a tradition through which the world as a whole can be understood.

Rose is hostile to identity politics, but by that she really means something more like identity ethics. She does not want identity to determine how one ought to live. In her view, one ought to live soulfully, grappling with the complications of identity, committed to the pursuit of goodness, truth, and beauty. Rose is purposefully agnostic on first-order questions of what ought to be done, deferring perhaps to the Jewish commitment to following the law (in the broadest sense). Rose supplements this commitment with her account of how one ought to relate to the law. She leaves open space for others to explicate the law, and particularly the law from the perspective of minority communities. In other words, it may be most productive to understand Rose as writing about ethics rather than politics, even if her ambition is to speak to both. Politics requires telling stories, making deals, and imagining new possibilities. Politics draws on a repertoire of practices and commitments held by a tradition but does not allow for the time to fully interrogate them as decisions need to be made, as the wheels of institutional machinery turn. The ethics Rose describes seems best understood as a kind of training for politics and a check on politics, a reminder that, in everyday life and in philosophical life, we need to step back from the political view of the world. When the relationship between ethics and politics is understood in this way, minority political organizing that confronts majority power becomes a unique point of intersection between ethics and politics, at once an ethical and political practice.

After having my dissertation on Gillian Rose signed by my committee members, I went to my advisor's office to obtain the final signature. A luminary of the Jewish Studies world, he chatted with me for a few minutes, signed the paperwork, and wished me well. As I was walking out the door, he added, "I just realized that you are African American!" I was not sure what the proper response was, or how this realization had come to him after five years of working with me. I had imagined myself too white to be black and too black to be white studying a woman too Christian to be Jewish and too Jewish to be Christian—I was existing in a world where identities were forever interrogated, rarely owned. It would be a lie to claim that I had, at that moment, a flash of insight about Rose's views of race, but it marked the start of a series of worries that continue to trouble me.

Coda: The Birth of the Black Church

The black church is dead. So it was proclaimed in the *Huffington Post* by black religion scholar Eddie Glaude. He did not mean that black people have stopped going to church, or that black belief in God has waned. Rather, he meant that "the idea of this venerable institution as central to black life and as a repository for the social and moral conscience of the nation has all but disappeared."[1] Why is this? Glaude offers a number of explanations, including the increasing variety of black religious practice, the increasing differentiation of the black community itself, and the routinization of once-prophetic preaching. The result is that black Christians no longer have a voice on the national stage, despite the dire conditions still facing black Americans today. Glaude argues that, to have a national voice, black Christians must appreciate the complex racial landscape in America today, and they must individually embrace "prophetic energies" rather than relying on the prophetic aura passed down from earlier generations.

Glaude is ostensibly responding to secularization, but he writes as an advocate of black secularism. In his essay, theological ideas are carefully excluded or managed. For him, religion is an essentially individual practice, and its terms must be chosen by the individual once she properly understands her place in the world. Church is reduced from the theological to the sociological, a collection of increasingly diverse institutions and individuals. Belief in God becomes "fullness of meaning." The normativity of tradition becomes vestigial "prophetic energies." The task of black Christians becomes that of advocating for the public policy proposals of white liberals, advocating for health care reform, job creation, and poverty alleviation. In Glaude's view, black churches ought to speak out in public, together, on issues of shared concern, but these issues are determined through a secular lens, and public advocacy is imagined in secular terms as institutions and individuals with shared interests making the pragmatic choice to speak out together.

What about the church conceived in theological terms, not merely as a collection of individuals and institutions but as a shared body, the Body of Christ, by definition irreducible to worldly terms? Understood in this way, empirical facts about individual Christians or religious institutions are not determinative, and histories are not burdens to be set aside to free up new ways of life. To the contrary, individuals, institutions, and histories, together with ways of seeing, reasoning, feeling, and imagining, are woven together in the tradition. It is easy to forget that tradition is dynamic, responsive to changing and complex circumstances, yet still constitutive and normative. We cannot understand who we are without understanding ourselves as participants in tradition, and our attempts at ethical or political intervention will always misfire unless we first acknowledge tradition. The ideas of the wealthy and powerful can masquerade as tradition, but this rings hollow when tradition is considered from below, from the perspective of the least of these. Even from this perspective, in the tradition of blackness, hubris remains a temptation. We forget that we cannot comprehend blackness, but blackness nonetheless constitutes us and imposes norms on us. This is the power of paradox, represented as the person of Jesus Christ in Christianity: to remind us that tradition is both essential and ultimately inaccessible. Tradition conceived in this way, blackness conceived in this way, is named "church."

The institutions that are named by the world "black churches" do not define the black church, but they participate in the black church. Institutions and shared practices are necessary to cultivate the virtues that gird us against the ideas of the wealthy and powerful, ideas that pervade the institutions and practices of the world, even seeping into church walls. Necessary, too, are religious authorities, the bane of the secularist's existence. There are some who are gifted with the ability to resist the wisdom of the world, to see otherwise, and there are some who are vested with the responsibility of interpreting the world otherwise in a way that is normative for others. It may be frustrating to subject oneself to the decisions of a religious authority, to the bishop, but the fallen world is a frustrating, maddening place. We must humble ourselves: while cultivating our own capacity to judge, we must remind ourselves that we are always far from understanding the world rightly, even on those issues with which we have the most confidence. From our perspective, it may seem perfectly clear that the religious authority, the bishop, is wrong, acting for self-interested or secularist or plainly pathological reasons, yet obedience reminds us that we cannot trust our own perception and that to live in community we must learn the virtue of obedience. It is ultimately obedience to individuals and to the traditions they imperfectly embody that gives us the capacity to see the world rightly and to act rightly—and to advance justice.

The black church, understood theologically rather than empirically, is the seat of black theology. This means that we find the black church where there are people seeing the world differently, from the perspective of blackness as tradition and blackness as paradox. Once the secularist divisions are refused, the divisions that delimit the bounds of the religious and the racial, black theology is to be found implicit in every corner of the world. It is the task of the black theologian and the black church to make the implicit explicit. Doing so involves seeing and reading against the grain, uncovering how that which is ostensibly value neutral is actually oriented toward the true, the good, and the beautiful. It similarly involves looking at the world and discerning blackness, not as conceived from the perspective of whiteness or from an ostensibly race-neutral perspective, but as that which exists orthogonal to the world of white supremacy. The claim of black theology is that these two activities are one and the same, that where we find blackness we find an orientation toward the true, the good, and the beautiful, and where we find such an orientation, we find blackness. The further claim of black theology is that such a process of discernment is not confined to one day of the week or one class in school; rather, it inheres in life itself—in the good life—and it is made possible by supporting communities, authorities, and institutions (the black church).

We are all called to this task, regardless of which identity labels the world ascribes to us. Yet those identity labels may not be ignored. Conversion is necessary, and conversion necessarily involves renunciation. For whites, and for those most invested in secularism, renunciation is particularly challenging. It is not as simple as checking white privilege or reading religious texts. Whiteness and secularism, conjoined, thoroughly shape reasoning, feeling, and imagining. These ideologies have powerful immune systems, with well-established means of encountering and neutralizing the racial or religious other. The ideas of the ruling class, of which whiteness and secularism are preeminent, manifest in social practices and institutions, and it is these that must be renounced. Encountering blackness and religion is not enough—it's the equivalent of pointing to that one black friend. A purge of affective investments can only be accomplished by severing relationships and divesting capital, most importantly social capital. Only then can one hope and pray that participation in the black church—participation in God—may be a possibility.

That the black church ought to be understood in theological terms is not a new idea. In 1898, W. E. B. Du Bois offered what at first seems like a sociological description of black religious institutions. The church is the primary institution of black social life, according to Du Bois, and individual congregations serve as "the real units of race life."[2] Yet Du Bois's description also transcends the empirical. He argues that the "Negro Church" has existed continuously from "the African forest" to the present, and he asserts that the "Christian pastor" is a direct descendent of the African "priest or medicine man." In making these claims, Du Bois is stepping back from his role as social scientist. While he speaks of congregations as empirical entities, he also locates them as manifestations of a rich and continuous tradition, one that stretches back to time immemorial. Indeed, it is by appealing to this sense of tradition outside the bounds of the secular that Du Bois is able to counter the denigration of black experience by white social scientists and critics who, on the basis of supposed empirical evidence, conclude that black culture and capacities are lacking.[3]

A *New York Times* advertisement purchased in 1966 by the National Committee of Negro Churchmen, in support of the black power movement, was even more explicit in its political understanding of church. "The Negro Church was created as a result of the refusal to submit to the indignities of a false kind of 'integration' in which all power was in the hands of white people," they wrote.[4] With this statement, the church leaders are reminding their readers of the origins of the black Protestant denominations in the United States. They were formed when blacks who had been denied access to full participation in worship services in predominantly white denominations joined together to form their own churches. Just allowing blacks in a white-owned and white-run church building was not enough; the deep-seated social norms around race had to first transform before a church could become a place for genuine Christian community rather than an organ of white supremacy. Until that transformation happened,

Christian community would only be found in black-controlled religious spaces, in the black church.

The rapidly developing black power movement pushed black church leaders to think further about the role that the church might play in the movement. In addition to preserving a tradition of creating spaces for religious worship minimally contaminated by white supremacy, these leaders argued that the black church must embrace its status as the leading social institution in the black community—and use that status to catalyze political mobilization. While acknowledging the continuing import of the specifically Christian mission of the church, they called for the church to become "a community organization, in the technical sense of the term, which uses its resources, influence, and manpower to address the problems of estrangement, resignation, and powerlessness in the political, cultural, and economic life of the black community."[5] Indeed, the religious mission of the church and the secular project of community organizing did not need to be understood separately: they were fused in the mission of the black church as it at once removed images of a white God and supported freedom schools, financial literacy classes, and organizer trainings.

Very much in the spirit of this moment of political-theological ferment, C. Eric Lincoln wrote an obituary forty years before Glaude's of a quite different nature:

> The "Negro Church"... no longer exists. It died an agonized death in the harsh turmoil which tried the faith so rigorously in the decade of the "Savage Sixties."... With sadness and reluctance, trepidation and confidence, the Negro Church accepted death in order to be reborn. Out of the ashes of its funeral pyre there sprang the bold, strident, self-conscious phoenix that is the contemporary Black Church.[6]

Lincoln reminds us that secularism has not always governed how we understand the black church. Indeed, he points us to how the specifically theological and the specifically racial entwine: the black church was coined as a means of refusing both whiteness and secularism, creating the space for imagining what the theological and the black might mean when understood on their own terms—and so necessarily conjoined. Lincoln's move is precisely the opposite of Glaude's. Rather than reducing the theological to the empirical, Lincoln discerns the theological amid the empirical. Furthermore, Lincoln situates his claim in a very specific historical moment, and he frames the black church as soliciting conversion most acutely at that moment. Both Lincoln and Glaude write at moments of racial tumult, but Glaude resists the opportunity, leaning back on and so securing the way of seeing the world advanced by the powers that be, whereas Lincoln takes the opportunity to turn away from the powers that be.

If the black church is dead, it was killed by secularism and by whiteness masquerading as multiculturalism. But it is not dead. Ideologies are powerful, but their power is never total. The wealthy and the powerful try to tell a story about the world that keeps everyone in place, securing their wealth and power, but the world will not stay in place. There are rumblings from the depths. The poor and, particularly in the United States today, black folks see through the charade. We refuse to let our lives and our bodies be captured in ideological shackles. We will join together to assure that the black church is continuously reborn in a spiritual struggle against the logics of white supremacy.

NOTES

INTRODUCTION

1. See the transcript in Malcolm X, "Message to the Grass Roots," in *Malcolm X Speaks: Selected Speeches and Statements* (New York: Grove Press, 1965), 3–17. Manning Marable notes that the audio recording and transcript both are edited to remove references to Elijah Muhammad; see Marable, *Malcolm X: A Life of Reinvention* (New York: Viking, 2011), 265. This speech was before Malcolm's break with the Nation of Islam, but strains were showing.

2. See Angela D. Dillard, *Faith in the City: Preaching Radical Social Change in Detroit* (Ann Arbor: University of Michigan Press, 2007), 273–74.

3. "Revolution is based on land. Land is the basis of all independence. Land is the basis of freedom, justice, and equality"; Malcolm X, "Message to the Grass Roots," 9.

4. G. Barry Golson, ed., *The Playboy Interview* (New York: Playboy Press, 1981), 41.

5. Ibid., 44; Albert B. Cleage, *The Black Messiah* (New York: Sheed & Ward, 1968).

6. See especially Talal Asad, *Formations of the Secular: Christianity, Islam, Modernity* (Stanford, Calif.: Stanford University Press, 2003); Saba Mahmood, *Politics of Piety: The Islamic Revival and the Feminist Subject* (Princeton, N.J.: Princeton University Press, 2005); and Hussein Ali Agrama, *Questioning Secularism: Islam, Sovereignty, and the Rule of Law in Modern Egypt* (Chicago: University of Chicago Press, 2012). Critics of secularism from the right rarely interrogate the way secularism and white supremacy are entangled, turning instead to a romanticized version of Judeo-Christian community that never existed.

1. CONE

Material from this chapter previously appeared in Vincent Lloyd, "Paradox and Tradition in Black Theology," *Black Theology* 9, no. 3 (2011): 265–86, used courtesy of Taylor and Francis Group, www.tandfonline.com.

1. Most notably Charles Taylor, *A Secular Age* (Cambridge, Mass.: Belknap Press, 2007), and John Milbank, *Theology and Social Theory: Beyond Secular Reason* (Oxford: Blackwell, 1993).

2. Ivan Petrella, *Beyond Liberation Theology: A Polemic* (London: SCM Press, 2008); see also Alistair Kee, *The Rise and Demise of Black Theology* (London: SCM Press, 2008).

3. This argument is made by J. Kameron Carter, *Race: A Theological Account* (Oxford: Oxford University Press, 2008); Willie James Jennings, *The Christian Imagination: Theology and the Origins of Race* (New Haven, Conn.: Yale University Press, 2010); and Brian Bantum, *Redeeming Mulatto: A Theology of Race and Christian Hybridity* (Waco, Tex.: Baylor University Press, 2010).

4. In addition to Carter, *Race*, see Carter, "Black Theology: A Review Essay," *Modern Theology* 19, no. 1 (2003): 117–38, and "Christology, Or Redeeming Whiteness: A Response to James Perkinson's Appropriation of Black Theology," *Theology Today* 60, no. 4 (2004): 525–39.

5. Among other places, this criticism is made forcefully in a book by Cone's brother, Cecil Wayne Cone, *The Identity Crisis in Black Theology* (Nashville, Tenn.: AMEC, 1975). James Cone describes how he grappled with these critics in his *My Soul Looks Back* (Nashville, Tenn.: Abington, 1982), 61. (Further writings of James Cone will be listed under "Cone.")

6. Cone, *A Black Theology of Liberation*, 20th anniv. ed. (1970; Maryknoll, N.Y.: Orbis, 1990), 10.

7. For example, Cone, *The Spirituals and the Blues: An Interpretation* (1972; Maryknoll, N.Y.: Orbis, 1991), 5, and *God of the Oppressed* (1975; Maryknoll, N.Y.: Orbis, 1997), 2.

8. I mean "secular reason" in an expansive sense. Giving an account of affect, the emotions, or the psyche to explain moments of perplexity or incongruity is also participating in secular reason.

9. Cornel West, *Prophesy Deliverance! An Afro-American Revolutionary Christianity* (Philadelphia: Westminster, 1982), 98; cf. Cone, *Black Theology and Black Power* (1969; Maryknoll, N.Y.: Orbis, 1997), ix: "Since theology is *human* speech and *not* God speaking, I recognize . . . that *all* attempts to speak about ultimate reality are limited by the social history of the speaker."

10. Cone, *Black Theology of Liberation*, 7; see also 203–4, nn. 4, 5. Compare Cone's earlier *Black Theology and Black Power*, where he writes, "Being black in America has very little to do with skin color. To be black means that your heart, your soul, your mind, and your body are where the dispossessed are" (151). In *God of the Oppressed*, Cone writes of "Christ's blackness" as "both literal and symbolic" (125).

11. Cone, *Black Theology of Liberation*, 66.

12. Cone, *God of the Oppressed*, 33.

13. Cone, *Risks of Faith: The Emergence of a Black Theology of Liberation, 1968–1998* (Boston: Beacon Press, 1999), xxi.

14. I have found the discussion of this sort of move by Jacques Rancière and, in the context of prophecy, George Shulman, especially helpful: Rancière, *Dis-Agreement: Politics and Philosophy*, trans. Julie Rose (Minneapolis: University of Minnesota Press, 1999); Shulman, *American Prophecy: Race and Redemption in American Political Culture* (Minneapolis: University of Minnesota Press, 2008).

15. Eddie Glaude Jr., "The Black Church Is Dead," *Huffington Post*, February 24, 2010, http://www.huffingtonpost.com/eddie-glaude-jr-phd/the-black-church-is-dead_b_473815.html; see also Cone, *Speaking the Truth: Ecumenism, Liberation, and Black Theology* (Grand Rapids, Mich.: Eerdmans, 1986), 112, 121–22.

16. Cone, *Risks of Faith*, xx, xxvi.

17. For example, ibid., 4. Cone presents dignity in a similar way in *Black Theology of Liberation*, 16.

18. Cone, *Risks of Faith*, 4. While critics, and to some extent Cone himself, dismiss some of these early remarks as overly influenced by white thinkers (especially French existentialists), Cone critically appropriates the ideas of his intellectual interlocutors in the service of his novel theological endeavor. In the paragraph containing this quotation he turns to both Albert Camus and the words of a black spiritual for support.

19. Ibid., 5.

20. Ibid., 4, 5.

21. Ibid., 6, where Cone closely links freedom and human dignity.

22. Cone, *Black Theology and Black Power*, 27: "What he fails to realize is that there is no place for him in this war of survival."

23. Cone, *Risks of Faith*, 48.

24. Ibid., 129.

25. Cone, *Black Theology and Black Power*, 42.

26. Alain Badiou, also drawing on the existentialist tradition, helpfully develops this point in his *Saint Paul: The Foundation of Universalism*, trans. Ray Brassier (Stanford, Calif.: Stanford University Press, 2003).

27. Cone, *Risks of Faith*, 8.

28. See Cone, *God of the Oppressed*, 134: "The image of God . . . [is that] which makes all people struggle against captivity. It is the ground of rebellion and revolution among slaves." I have found David Bentley Hart's mirror imagery particularly evocative; see his "The Mirror of the Infinite: Gregory of Nyssa on the *Vestigia Trinitatis*," *Modern Theology* 18, no. 4 (2002): 541–61, and *Beauty of the Infinite: The Aesthetics of Christian Truth* (Grand Rapids, Mich.: Eerdmans, 2003).

29. Cone, *Risks of Faith*, 10.
30. Cone, *Black Theology and Black Power*, 60.
31. Ibid., 120.
32. Ibid., 42.
33. This point is explored in detail by Carter, *Race*, Chap. 4.
34. Cone, *Risks of Faith*, 81; see also Cone, *Spirituals and the Blues*, Chap. 5.
35. Cone, *Black Theology and Black Power*, 102.
36. Cone, *Risks of Faith*, 36–37.
37. Cone, *Risks of Faith*, 37; Cone, *Black Theology of Liberation*, 94. This point is reminiscent of the existential demarcation of friends and enemies proposed by Carl Schmitt as the foundation of politics; see Schmitt, *The Concept of the Political*, trans. George Schwab (Chicago: University of Chicago Press, 2007).
38. In contrast, Cone writes of the contradictions of black life and his own childhood experience: "I do not remember any black church person in Bearden using religion to cover up oppression or as an escape from the harsh realities of life"; Cone, *My Soul Looks Back*, 22.
39. Cone, *Black Theology of Liberation*, 108.
40. Ibid., 11.
41. Ibid., 8.
42. Ibid., 107.
43. Cone, *Risks of Faith*, 48; emphasis in the original.
44. Cone, *Black Theology of Liberation*, 87.
45. Cone, *Risks of Faith*, x.
46. See, for example, Cone, *Black Theology of Liberation*, 78.
47. Cone, *Black Theology and Black Power*, 8.
48. Cone, *Risks of Faith*, 23.
49. One might even say that the object of faith—the descriptions of God—is a projection of that commitment.
50. See the Introduction to Cone, *Risks of Faith*, as well as *My Soul Looks Back*.
51. A point made forcefully in a different context by Diana Taylor, *The Archive and the Repertoire: Performing Cultural Memory in the Americas* (Durham, N.C.: Duke University Press, 2003).
52. See Cone, *Spirituals and the Blues*, as well as the Introduction to *Risks of Faith*.
53. Cone suggests that paradox is ubiquitous in blues lyrics: from "I love the blues, they hurt so nice" to "I can't stand you, Baby, but I need you,/You're bad, but you're oh so good"; Cone, *Spirituals and the Blues*, 5.
54. Cone, *Black Theology of Liberation*, xi; *God of the Oppressed*, 14. However, in *God of the Oppressed*, Cone is still committed to Jesus Christ being the transcendent reality expressed in the songs and stories of black people.

This, he writes, "prevents Black Theology from being reduced merely to the cultural history of black people" (29). Later he invokes "the divine One" as distinguishing black theology from secular black politics (77). One wonders whether the increasing focus on God's transcendence foretells the later slip into a more extreme contextualism.

55. Cone, *Spirituals and the Blues*, 106: "Black people accepted the dictum: Truth is experience, and experience is the Truth. If it is lived and encountered, then it is real."

56. Cone, *God of the Oppressed*, xi (where Cone seems to use "black experience" and "black tradition of struggle" interchangeably), xiv.

57. See, for example, Judith Butler, *Gender Trouble: Feminism and the Subversion of Identity* (New York: Routledge, 1990). Cone also writes of the sins of the oppressed and suggests that all are sinful—it is just that oppressors have the deadly combination of sin plus power; Cone, *Speaking the Truth*, 9; Cone, *Risks of Faith*, xxvi.

58. Moreover, at the root of patriarchy is the desire for identity to be unparadoxical, for the tension created by my origins elsewhere, in others, to be resolved by ascribing ultimate power to the father and to men.

59. Cone, *Black Theology and Black Power*, xii: "Life-giving power for the poor and the oppressed is the primary criterion that we must use to judge the adequacy of our theology, not abstract concepts"; Cone, *Speaking the Truth*, 14: "The truth of the black faith-claim is found in whether the people receive that extra strength to fight until freedom comes."

60. Cone, *Black Theology and Black Power*, 127 (drawing on Nietzsche); Cone, *God of the Oppressed*, 191 (where Cone sees this taking place in the lives of slaves), 199.

61. Cone, *Black Theology and Black Power*, 60; see also *Black Theology of Liberation*, 17: "What could the concept of 'winning' possibly mean? Blacks do what they do because and only because they can do no other; and black theology says simply that such action is in harmony with divine revelation."

2. Baldwin

Material from this chapter will appear in "The Negative Political Theology of James Baldwin," in *A Political Companion to James Baldwin*, ed. Susan McWilliams (Lexington: University Press of Kentucky, forthcoming).

1. See Clarence E. Hardy, *James Baldwin's God: Sex, Hope, and the Crisis in Black Holiness Culture* (Knoxville: University of Tennessee Press, 2003).

2. On this view of the prophet, see Michael Walzer, *Interpretation and Social Criticism* (Cambridge, Mass.: Harvard University Press, 1987).

3. George Shulman, *American Prophecy: Race and Redemption in American Political Culture* (Minneapolis: University of Minnesota Press, 2008).

4. Baldwin's writings are cited as: B: *If Beale Street Could Talk* (New York: Dial, 1974); C: *The Cross of Redemption* (New York: Pantheon, 2010); E: *Collected Essays* (New York: Library of America, 1998); ET: *The Evidence of Things Not Seen* (New York: Holt, Rinehart and Winston, 1985); N: *Early Novels and Stories* (New York: Library of America, 1998).

5. Compare René Girard, *Violence and the Sacred* (Baltimore: Johns Hopkins University Press, 1977).

6. Simone Weil, *Gravity and Grace* (London: Ark, 1987); Iris Murdoch, *The Sovereignty of Good* (London: Routledge & Kegan Paul, 1970).

7. See Eric Gregory, *Politics and the Order of Love: An Augustinian Ethic of Democratic Citizenship* (Chicago: University of Chicago Press, 2008).

8. Martin Luther King Jr., *A Testament of Hope: The Essential Writings of Martin Luther King, Jr.* (San Francisco: Harper & Row, 1986), 247.

3. MBEMBE

Material from this chapter appears in Vincent Lloyd, "Achille Mbembe as Black Theologian," *Modern Believing* 57, no. 3 (2016): 241–51, reproduced with permission of Liverpool University Press via PLSclear.

1. Rosalind Hackett, Review of *Afriques indociles*, *Journal of Religion in Africa* 20, no. 3 (1990): 306.

2. Achille Mbembe, "Africa and the Night of Language: An Interview with Achille Mbembe," Johannesburg Workshop in Theory and Criticism, *Salon* 2, http://jwtc.org.za/the_salon/volume_2/annalisa_oboe_africa_the_night_of_language.htm.

3. Ibid; see also the autobiographical first chapter of Mbembe, *Sortir de la grande nuit: Essai sur l'Afrique décolonisée* (Paris: La Découverte, 2010), as well as Shipley, "Africa in Theory: A Conversation between Jean Comaroff and Achille Mbembe," *Anthropological Quarterly* 83, no. 3 (2010).

4. See Mbembe, *Critique de la raison nègre* (Paris: La Découverte, 2013), 20, where Mbembe projects a fourth and final volume on "l'afropolitanisme."

5. Mbembe, "Religion, Politics, Theology: A Conversation with Achille Mbembe," *boundary 2* 34, no. 2 (2007): 168.

6. See Talal Asad, Wendy Brown, Judith Butler, and Saba Mahmood, *Is Critique Secular? Blasphemy, Injury, and Free Speech* (Berkeley: University of California Press, 2009).

7. Mbembe, "Religion, Politics, Theology," 168.

8. Mbembe, "Africa and the Night of Language."

9. Ibid.; see also Mbembe, *Critique de la raison nègre*, 252.

10. John Milbank, *Theology and Social Theory: Beyond Secular Reason* (Oxford: Blackwell, 1993); Catherine Pickstock, *After Writing: On the Liturgical Consummation of Philosophy* (Oxford: Blackwell, 1998); William T. Cavanaugh, *Theopolitical Imagination* (London: T & T Clark, 2002).

11. This theme is especially developed in Mbembe, "Necropolitics," *Public Culture* 15, no. 1 (2003): 11–40.

12. Giorgio Agamben, *Homo Sacer: Sovereign Power and Bare Life* (Stanford, Calif.: Stanford University Press, 1998); *State of Exception* (Chicago: University of Chicago Press, 2005).

13. See the suggestive comments of Slavoj Žižek in *The Puppet and the Dwarf: The Perverse Core of Christianity* (Cambridge, Mass.: MIT Press, 2003).

14. Mbembe, "Africa and the Night of Language."

15. See, for example, Mbembe, *Sortir de la grande nuit*, Chap. 6.

16. See Judith Butler, *Precarious Life: The Powers of Mourning and Violence* (London: Verso, 2004), 144.

17. A similar point is made by Alistair Kee in *The Rise and Demise of Black Theology* (London: SCM Press, 2008), as discussed in Chap. 1.

18. See Slavoj Žižek, *Violence: Six Sideways Reflections* (New York: Picador, 2008).

19. Mbembe, "Africa and the Night of Language."

20. Gillian Rose makes a similar critique of postmodern theology in *The Broken Middle: Out of Our Ancient Society* (Oxford: Blackwell, 1992), Chap. 6.

21. See especially Jared Hickman, "Globalization and the Gods, or the Political Theology of Race," *Early American Literature* 45, no. 1 (2010): 145–82; Jonathon S. Kahn and Vincent W. Lloyd, eds., *Race and Secularism in America* (New York: Columbia University Press, 2016).

22. René Lemarchand, review of *Afriques indociles*, *African Studies Review* 32, no. 3 (1989): 154; Jeremy Weate, "Achille Mbembe and the Postcolony: Going Beyond the Text," *Research in African Literatures* 34, no. 4 (2003): 27–41. See also Judith Butler's defense of Mbembe's method as mirroring the bricolage of the postcolonial subject in "Mbembe's Extravagant Power," *Public Culture* 5, no. 1 (1992): 67–74.

23. Mbembe, "*On the Postcolony*: A Brief Response to Critics," *Qui Parle* 15, no. 2 (2005): 13.

24. It also precludes judgment, seemingly one of the characteristically human capacities Mbembe would want to embrace; see Linda M. G. Zerilli, "The Turn to Affect and the Problem of Judgment," *New Literary History* 46, no. 2 (2015): 261–86.

25. Mbembe, "Africa and the Night of Language."

4. Derrida, Agamben, Wynter

Material from this chapter will be included in Vincent Lloyd, "Race and the Philosophy of Religion," in *Philosophy of Religion after "Religion,"* ed. Michael Ch. Rodgers and Richard Amesbury (Tübingen: Mohr Siebeck, forthcoming); used with permission of Mohr Siebeck.

1. Wilfred Cantwell Smith, *The Meaning and End of Religion: A New Approach to the Religious Traditions of Mankind* (New York: Macmillan, 1963). For influential accounts of religion emerging from within Christianity, see Jonathan Z. Smith, "Religion, Religions, Religious," in *Critical Terms in Religious Studies*, ed. Mark C. Taylor (Chicago: University of Chicago Press, 1998); Talal Asad, *Genealogies of Religion: Discipline and Reasons of Power in Christianity and Islam* (Baltimore: Johns Hopkins University Press, 1993).

2. This point is made persuasively in Denise Buell's introduction to her *Why This New Race: Ethnic Reasoning in Early Christianity* (New York: Columbia University Press, 2005).

3. Daniel Boyarin, "Semantic Differences; or, 'Judaism'/'Christianity,'" in *The Ways That Never Parted*, ed. Adam H. Becker and Annette Yoshiko Reed (Minneapolis: Fortress, 2007); *Border Lines: The Partition of Judaeo-Christianity* (Philadelphia: University of Pennsylvania Press, 2004).

4. See especially Jonathan Z. Smith, "Religion, Religions, Religious," and Jared Hickman, "Globalization and the Gods, or the Political Theology of Race," *Early American Literature* 45, no. 1 (2010): 145–82.

5. Hickman, "Globalization and the Gods," 155.

6. For example, David Chidester, *Savage Systems: Colonialism and Comparative Religion in Southern Africa* (Charlottesville: University Press of Virginia, 1996); Richard King, *Orientalism and Religion: Postcolonial Theory, India, and "the Mystical East"* (London: Routledge, 1999).

7. See Tomoko Masuzawa, *The Invention of World Religions, Or, How European Universalism Was Preserved in the Language of Pluralism* (Chicago: University of Chicago Press, 2005).

8. The reason that the curse, as depicted in Genesis, skips a generation remains obscure.

9. Stephen R. Haynes, *Noah's Curse: The Biblical Justification of American Slavery* (Oxford: Oxford University Press, 2007), and, more generally, Colin Kidd, *The Forging of Races: Race and Scripture in the Protestant Atlantic World, 1600–2000* (Cambridge: Cambridge University Press, 2006).

10. Kidd, *Forging of Races*, 25; italics in original.

11. I develop this point more fully in Lloyd, "Race and Religion," *Critical Research on Religion* 1, no. 1 (2013): 80–86.

12. Martin Luther King Jr., *The Papers of Martin Luther King, Jr.* (Berkeley: University of California Press, 2000), 4:321; James Baldwin, *Collected Essays* (New York: Library of America, 1998), 342.

13. Henry Goldschmidt, "Introduction: Race, Nation, and Religion," in *Race, Nation, and Religion in the Americas*, ed. Henry Goldschmidt and Elizabeth McAlister (Oxford: Oxford University Press, 2004). See also Hickman's criticism of Goldschmidt in "Globalization and the Gods," 161.

14. For helpful discussions of Derrida's reflections on race, see Christopher Wise, *Derrida, Africa, and the Middle East* (New York: Palgrave Macmillan, 2009); Grant Farred, "'Nostalgeria': Derrida, before and after Fanon," *South Atlantic Quarterly* 112, no. 1 (2013): 145–62; Pal Ahluwalia, *Out of Africa: Post-Structuralism's Colonial Roots* (New York: Routledge, 2010); and Agnes Czajka and Bora Isyar, eds., *Europe after Derrida: Crisis and Potentiality* (Edinburgh: Edinburgh University Press, 2014).

15. Geoffrey Bennington and Jacques Derrida, *Jacques Derrida* (Chicago: University of Chicago Press, 1993), 58.

16. Barnor Hesse very productively develops this point in his "Racialized Modernity: An Analytics of White Mythologies," *Ethnic and Racial Studies* 30, no. 4 (2007): 643–63.

17. Derrida, "White Mythology: Metaphor in the Text of Philosophy," *New Literary History* 6, no. 1 (1974): 11.

18. Derrida, "Plato's Pharmacy," in *Dissemination* (Chicago: University of Chicago Press, 1981), 61–119.

19. Derrida, "Admiration of Nelson Mandela, or The Laws of Reflection," *Law and Literature* 26, no. 1 (2014): 9–30; see also Derrida, "Racism's Last Word," *Critical Inquiry* 12 (1985): 290–99.

20. See also Derrida, "The Force of Law: The 'Mystical Foundation of Authority,'" in *Deconstruction and the Possibility of Justice*, ed. Drucilla Cornell, Michel Rosenfeld, and David Carlson (New York: Routledge, 1992).

21. Merold Westphal, "Derrida as Natural Law Theorist," in *Overcoming Onto-Theology* (New York: Fordham University Press, 2001), 219–28.

22. Edward Baring, "Liberalism and the Algerian War: The Case of Jacques Derrida," *Critical Inquiry* 36, no. 2 (2010): 239–61; *The Young Derrida and French Philosophy, 1945–1968* (Cambridge: Cambridge University Press, 2011).

23. For discussion of race in Agamben's writings, see especially Ewa Plonowska Ziarek, "Bare Life on Strike: Notes on the Biopolitics of Race and Gender," *South Atlantic Quarterly* 107, no. 1 (2008): 89–105; Andrew Benjamin, "Particularity and Exceptions: On Jews and Animals," *South Atlantic Quarterly* 107, no. 1 (2008): 71–87; and Utz McKnight, *Race and the Politics of the Exception: Equality, Sovereignty, and American Democracy* (New York: Routledge, 2013). See also Achille Mbembe and Alexander G. Weheliye's explorations of the limits of Agamben's thought for discussing race in Mbembe, "Necropolitics," *Public Culture* 15, no. 1 (2003): 11–40, and Weheliye, *Habeas Viscus: Racializing Assemblages, Biopolitcs, and Black Feminist Theories of the Human* (Durham, N.C.: Duke University Press, 2014). Mark Rifkin presents a fascinating assessment and development of Agamben's thought from an indigenous perspective in "Indigenizing Agamben: Rethinking Sovereignty in

Light of the 'Peculiar' Status of Native Peoples," *Culture Critique* 73 (2009): 88–124.

24. Giorgio Agamben, *Homo Sacer: Sovereign Power and Bare Life* (Stanford, Calif.: Stanford University Press, 1998). For Agamben's own reflections on his method, see his *The Signature of All Things: On Method* (New York: Zone, 2009).

25. Agamben does not qualify his theorizing with "in the West," but this may be taken as implicit in his choice of examples.

26. Agamben, *Homo Sacer*, 15.

27. Ibid., 77.

28. The latter is explored in Agamben, *State of Exception* (Chicago: University of Chicago Press, 2005).

29. Agamben, *The Open: Man and Animal* (Stanford, Calif.: Stanford University Press, 2004), 16.

30. For a similar worry, focused on Christianity today, see Luke Bretherton, *Christianity and Contemporary Politics: The Conditions and Possibilities of Faithful Witness* (Chichester: Wiley-Blackwell, 2010), Chap. 1.

31. Jonathon S. Kahn and Vincent W. Lloyd, eds., *Race and Secularism in America* (New York: Columbia University Press, 2016).

32. For a related point in postcolonial theory, see Dipesh Chakrabarty, *Provincializing Europe: Postcolonial Thought and Historical Difference* (Princeton, N.J.: Princeton University Press, 2000).

33. Theological efforts to address these issues, along with the entangled genealogies of race and religion, include most notably J. Kameron Carter, *Race: A Theological Account* (Oxford: Oxford University Press, 2008), and Willie James Jennings, *The Christian Imagination: Theology and the Origins of Race* (New Haven, Conn.: Yale University Press, 2010); see also Theodore Vial, *Modern Religion, Modern Race* (New York: Oxford University Press, 2016).

34. Sylvia Wynter, "1492: A New World View," in *Race, Discourse, and the Origin of the Americas: A New World View*, ed. Vera Lawrence Hyatt and Rex Nettleford (Washington, D.C.: Smithsonian Institution Press, 1995).

35. Wynter, "Beyond the Word of Man: Glissant and the New Discourse of the Antilles," *World Literature Today* 63, no. 4 (1989): 642.

36. Ibid., 643.

37. See, for example, Wynter, "On Disenchanting Discourse: 'Minority' Literary Criticism and Beyond," *Cultural Critique* 7 (1987): 207–44.

38. Wynter, "Unsettling the Coloniality of Being/Power/Truth/Freedom: Towards the Human, After Man, Its Overrepresentation—An Argument," *CR: The New Centennial Review* 3, no. 3 (2003): 257–337.

39. Wynter, "1492," 16.

5. What Is Black Tradition?

Material in this chapter was included in Vincent Lloyd, "Of Fathers and Sons, Prophets and Messiahs," *Souls* 16, nos. 3–4 (2014): 209–26; reprinted by permission of the University of Illinois-Chicago, www.uic.edu.

1. The publishing world had more ambitious hopes for the book, seeing Obama as a potential successor to James Baldwin; David Remnick, *The Bridge: The Life and Rise of Barack Obama* (New York: Alfred A. Knopf, 2010), 227.

2. Barack Obama, *Dreams from My Father: A Story of Race and Inheritance* (New York: Three Rivers Press, 2004), xiv.

3. I develop this point further in Lloyd, "From the Theopaternal to the Theopolitical: On Barack Obama," in *Common Goods: Economy, Ecology, and Political Theology* (New York: Fordham University Press, 2015), 326–43.

4. For example, in his description of "the comfort offered by the strict constructionist" and the critical legal theorist who enjoys "the freedom of the relativist, the rule breaker, the teenager who has discovered his parents are imperfect"; Obama, *The Audacity of Hope: Thoughts on Reclaiming the American Dream* (New York: Three Rivers, 2006), 92.

5. While my use of "transmission," taking "generational transmission" as paradigmatic, may seem narrower than its ordinary usage, "transmission" always implies a temporal aspect, from somewhere at one time to somewhere else at a later time.

6. Stephen Best, "On Failing to Make the Past Present," *Modern Language Quarterly* 73, no. 3 (2012): 453–74.

7. Cornel West, *Race Matters* (Boston: Beacon, 1993), Chap. 1.

8. W. E. B. Du Bois, *Writings* (New York: Literary Classics of the United States, 1986), 370.

9. The chapter before these two is, significantly, "Of the Sons of Master and Man"; Du Bois's *Souls of Black Folk* is included in his *Writings*.

10. Du Bois, *Writings*, 493, 494.

11. Ibid., 505.

12. For example, Wilson Jeremiah Moses considers the prophetic one example of the messianic in his *Black Messiahs and Uncle Toms: Social and Literary Manipulations of a Religious Myth* (University Park, Pa.: Pennsylvania State University Press, 1993). See also Ross Posnock's interchangeable use of the terms in his discussion of Du Bois in *Color and Culture: Black Writers and the Making of the Modern Intellectual* (Cambridge, Mass.: Harvard University Press, 1998), 182.

13. West, *The American Evasion of Philosophy: A Genealogy of Pragmatism* (Madison: University of Wisconsin Press, 1989), 228.

14. This idea is developed by Walter Benjamin, for example, in his "Theologico-Political Fragment," in *Walter Benjamin: Selected Writings*

(Cambridge, Mass.: Harvard University Press, 2002), 3:305–6. For an application in political theory, see Wendy Brown, *Politics Out of History* (Princeton, N.J.: Princeton University Press, 2001).

15. Du Bois, *Writings*, 823.
16. Ibid., 822.
17. Ibid., 832.
18. Ibid.
19. Ibid., 506.
20. Ibid., 506, 507.
21. Ibid., 507, 510.
22. Ibid., 507.
23. David Levering Lewis, *W. E. B. Du Bois, 1868–1919: Biography of a Race* (New York: H. Holt, 1993).
24. Richard Iton, "Still Life," *Small Axe* 17, no. 1 (March 2013): 37.
25. Ibid., 39. Iton continues, "I am thinking here, for example, of the use of space and silence in the musical works of Shirley Horn, Ahmad Jamal, and Miles Davis, and in Erykah Badu's video for 'Window Seat' and Charles Lane's 1989 silent film Sidewalk Stories; and the suspension of coloration in Toni Morrison's most recent novel *Home*."
26. Iton, *In Search of the Black Fantastic* (Oxford: Oxford University Press, 2008), 289–90.
27. Iton, *Solidarity Blues: Race, Culture, and the American Left* (Chapel Hill: University of North Carolina Press, 2000), 183.
28. Ibid., 224.
29. Iton, *In Search of the Black Fantastic*, 17.
30. Ibid., 16.
31. Ibid., 57.
32. Ibid., 289–90.
33. Walter Benjamin, "On the Concept of History," trans. H. Zohn, in *Walter Benjamin: Selected Writings 1938–1940*, ed. H. Eiland and M. W. Jennings (Cambridge, Mass.: Belknap Press, 2003), 4:391.
34. Iton, *In Search of the Black Fantastic*, 301, n. 46, assenting to a view Iton attributes to Barnor Hesse.
35. Frank B. Wilderson III, *Red, White, and Black: Cinema and the Structure of U.S. Antagonisms* (Durham, N.C.: Duke University Press, 2010).
36. Fred Moten, *In the Break: The Aesthetics of the Black Radical Tradition* (Minneapolis: University of Minnesota Press, 2003); "The Case of Blackness," *Criticism* 50, no. 2 (Spring 2008): 177–218; "Blackness and Nothingness (Mysticism in the Flesh)," *South Atlantic Quarterly* 112, no. 4 (Fall 2013): 737–80.
37. To go even more theological: Iton's black fantastic opposes transmission to gracious gift, to a gift that cannot be returned. As Derrida points

out, the gift always brings with it an obligation when it is passed on, yet this obligation cannot be quantified or localized; see Jacques Derrida, *Given Time*, vol. 1, *Counterfeit Money* (Chicago: University of Chicago Press, 1992); Jean-Luc Marion, *Being Given: Toward a Phenomenology of Givenness*, trans. Jeffrey L. Kosky (Stanford, Calif.: Stanford University Press, 2002).

38. "My President Is Black," YouTube, http://www.youtube.com/watch?v=V27fPhjBtjo.

39. "Young Jeezy—My President ft. Nas," YouTube, http://www.youtube.com/watch?v=O9sABRosdNg.

6. What Is Black Organizing?

Material from this chapter appeared in Vincent Lloyd, "Organizing Race: Taking Race Seriously in Faith-Based Community Organizing," *Journal of Religious Ethics* 42, no. 4 (2014): 640–60; reprinted with permission of John Wiley and Sons, Inc.

1. Barack Obama, "Why Organize? Problems and Promise in the Inner City," *Illinois Issues* 42 (1988), http://www.lib.niu.edu/1988/ii880840.html.

2. Obama, *Dreams from My Father: A Story of Race and Inheritance* (New York: Three Rivers, 2004), 132.

3. See especially C. Melissa Snarr, *All You That Labor: Religion and Ethics in the Living Wage Movement* (New York: New York University Press, 2011); Luke Bretherton, *Resurrecting Democracy: Faith, Citizenship, and the Politics of a Common Life* (New York: Cambridge University Press, 2015); Jeffrey Stout, *Blessed are the Organized: Grassroots Democracy in America* (Princeton, N.J.: Princeton University Press, 2010); Mary McClintock Fulkerson, "Receiving from the Other: Theology and Grass-Roots Organizing," *International Journal of Public Theology* 6, no. 4 (2012): 421–34; and Stanley Hauerwas and Romand Coles, *Christianity, Democracy, and the Radical Ordinary: Conversations between a Radical Democrat and a Christian* (Eugene, Ore.: Cascade, 2008).

4. Saul Alinsky, *Rules for Radicals: A Practical Primer for Realistic Radicals* (New York: Vintage, 1971), 12.

5. Jodi Melamed, *Represent and Destroy: Rationalizing Violence in the New Racial Capitalism* (Minneapolis: University of Minnesota Press, 2011).

6. Aldon D. Morris, *Origins of the Civil Rights Movement: Black Communities Organizing for Change* (New York: Free Press, 1984).

7. Charles Payne, *I've Got the Light of Freedom: The Organizing Tradition and the Mississippi Freedom Struggle* (Berkeley: University of California Press, 1996); Barbara Ransby, *Ella Baker and the Black Freedom Movement: A Radical Democratic Vision* (Chapel Hill: University of North Carolina Press, 2003).

8. Joshua Bloom and Waldo E. Martin Jr., *Black against Empire: The*

History and Politics of the Black Panther Party (Berkeley: University of California Press, 2013).

9. Devin Fergus, *Liberalism, Black Power, and the Making of American Politics, 1965–1980* (Athens: University of Georgia Press, 2009).

10. Lisa Duggan, *The Twilight of Equality? Neoliberalism, Cultural Politics, and the Attack on Democracy* (Boston: Beacon, 2003); Melamed, *Represent and Destroy*.

11. John Ernest, *A Nation within a Nation: Organizing African-American Communities before the Civil War* (Chicago: Ivan R. Dee, 2011); Corey D. B. Walker, *A Noble Fight: African American Freemasonry and the Struggle for Democracy in America* (Urbana: University of Illinois Press, 2008); and Theda Skocpol, Ariane Liazos, and Marshall Ganz, *What a Mighty Power We Can Be: African American Fraternal Groups and the Struggle for Racial Equality* (Princeton, N.J.: Princeton University Press, 2006); Evelyn Brooks Higginbotham, *Righteous Discontent: The Women's Movement in the Black Baptist Church, 1880–1920* (Cambridge, Mass.: Harvard University Press, 1993).

12. Cornel West, *Race Matters* (Boston: Beacon, 1993).

13. Alinsky, *Rules for Radicals*; Sanford D. Horwitt, *Let Them Call Me Rebel: Saul Alinsky, His Life and Legacy* (New York: Knopf, 1989).

14. Alinsky, *Reveille for Radicals* (Chicago: University of Chicago Press, 1946), 17.

15. Ibid., 110–11.

16. Alinsky, *Rules for Radicals*, 102.

17. Ibid., 61.

18. Ernesto Cortes, "Reweaving the Social Fabric," *Boston Review* 19 (1994): 12–14, is the source of quotations in this paragraph.

19. Richard L. Wood and Brad R. Fulton, *A Shared Future: Faith-Based Organizing for Racial Equity and Ethical Democracy* (Chicago: University of Chicago Press, 2015), Chap. 3.

20. Mark R. Warren, *Dry Bones Rattling: Community Building to Revitalize American Democracy* (Princeton, N.J.: Princeton University Press, 2001).

21. Ibid., 117.

22. Ibid., 119.

23. Wood and Fulton, *Shared Future*.

24. Stout, *Blessed are the Organized*, 5; see also Heidi J. Swarts, *Organizing Urban America: Secular and Faith-Based Progressive Movements* (Minneapolis: University of Minnesota Press, 2007), 55.

25. Swarts, *Organizing Urban America*, 55.

26. William T. Cavanaugh, *Theopolitical Imagination* (London: T & T Clark, 2002); John Milbank, *Theology and Social Theory: Beyond Secular Reason* (Oxford: Blackwell, 1993).

27. Snarr, *All You That Labor*, 60.

28. Bretherton, *Christianity and Contemporary Politics: The Conditions and Possibilities of Faithful Witness* (Chichester: Wiley-Blackwell, 2010), Chap. 2.

29. Ibid., 87.

30. Susan Stall and Randy Stoecker, "Community Organizing or Organizing Community? Gender and the Crafts of Empowerment," *Gender and Society* 12, no. 6 (1998): 729–56; Deborah G. Martin, "Constructing the 'Neighborhood Sphere': Gender and Community Organizing," *Gender, Place and Culture* 9, no. 4 (2002): 333–50; Verta Taylor, "Gender and Social Movements: Gender Processes in Women's Self-Help Movements," *Gender and Society* 13, no. 1 (1999): 8–33.

31. Snarr, *All You That Labor*, Chap. 4.

32. Tera Hunter's account of black women's organizing after the Civil War in *To 'Joy My Freedom: Southern Black Women's Lives and Labors after the Civil War* (Cambridge, Mass.: Harvard University Press, 1997) shows these convergences particularly well, though the scarcity of evidence preserved from the period limits our view of the concrete practices involved, and Hunter pays only limited attention to religion.

33. Payne, *I've Got the Light of Freedom*, 243.

34. West, *Race Matters*, 66.

35. Ibid., 70.

36. Richard L. Wood, *Faith in Action: Religion, Race, and Democratic Organizing in America* (Chicago: University of Chicago Press, 2011).

37. Ibid., 116.

38. Ibid., 114.

39. Ibid., 148.

40. For a related point, see Frank B. Wilderson III, *Red, White, and Black: Cinema and the Structure of U.S. Antagonisms* (Durham, N.C.: Duke University Press, 2010). See also Jared Sexton's critique of multiracialism, in *Amalgamation Schemes: Antiblackness and the Critique of Multiracialism* (Minneapolis: University of Minnesota Press, 2008), and Barnor Hesse's critique of the postracial, in "Self-Fulfilling Prophecy: The Postracial Horizon," *South Atlantic Quarterly* 110, no. 1 (2011): 155–78.

41. Warren, *Dry Bones Rattling*, 200.

42. Ibid. Alinsky offers a discussion of Moses as organizer in *Rules for Radicals*.

43. Warren, *Dry Bones Rattling*, 202.

44. James Cone, *Risks of Faith: The Emergence of a Black Theology of Liberation, 1968–1998* (Boston: Beacon, 1999), 7.

45. Cone, *Martin and Malcolm and America: A Dream or a Nightmare?* (Maryknoll, N.Y.: Orbis, 1991), 299.

46. Cone, *A Black Theology of Liberation*, 20th anniv. ed. (1970; Maryknoll, N.Y.: Orbis, 1990), 47.

47. Ironically, in the final days of the primary campaign, remarks Lumumba made indicating his agnosticism on the question of Christ's resurrection were used against him by his opponent.

48. Warren, *Dry Bones Rattling*, 125.

49. Wilderson, *Red, White, and Black*, 9.

7. FOR WHAT ARE BLACKS TO HOPE?

Material from this chapter appeared in Vincent W. Lloyd, "Afro-Pessimism and Christian Hope," in *Grace, Governance, and Globalization*, ed. Lieven Boeve, Stephan van Erp, and Martin G. Poulsom (T & T Clark, 2017). Used with permission of Bloomsbury T & T Clark, an imprint of Bloomsbury Publishing Plc.

1. On the distinction between hope and optimism, see Christopher Lasch, *The True and Only Heaven: Progress and Its Critics* (New York: Norton, 1991).

2. Lauren Berlant, *Cruel Optimism* (Durham, N.C.: Duke University Press, 2011).

3. See Chap. 1 of this volume.

4. James Cone, *A Black Theology of Liberation*, 20th anniv. ed. (1970; Maryknoll, N.Y.: Orbis, 1990), 7; see also Chap. 1 of this volume.

5. See, for example, Cone, *The Spirituals and the Blues: An Interpretation* (1972; Maryknoll, N.Y.: Orbis, 1991); Arthur C. Jones, *Wade in the Water: The Wisdom of the Spirituals* (Maryknoll, N.Y.: Orbis, 1993).

6. Frank B. Wilderson III coined the term and offers a powerful, synthetic account of the issues involved in the introduction to his *Red, White, and Black: Cinema and the Structure of U.S. Antagonisms* (Durham, N.C.: Duke University Press, 2010).

7. See, for example, Emmanuel Eze, ed., *Race and the Enlightenment: A Reader* (Cambridge, Mass.: Blackwell, 1997).

8. J. Kameron Carter, *Race: A Theological Account* (Oxford: Oxford University Press, 2008).

9. Sylvia Wynter, "Unsettling the Coloniality of Being/Power/Truth/Freedom: Towards the Human, After Man, Its Overrepresentation—An Argument," *CR: The New Centennial Review* 3, no. 3 (2003): 257–337.

10. See Jonathon S. Kahn and Vincent W. Lloyd, eds., *Race and Secularism in America* (New York: Columbia University Press, 2016).

11. On this issue, see especially Fred Moten, "Blackness and Nothingness (Mysticism in the Flesh)," *South Atlantic Quarterly* 112, no. 4 (Fall 2013): 737–80.

12. For an exception, concluding that Afro-pessimism must reject hope

and embrace nihilism, see Calvin L. Warren, "Black Nihilism and the Politics of Hope," *CR: The New Centennial Review* 15, no. 1 (2015): 215–48.

13. Jonathan Lear, *Radical Hope: Ethics in the Face of Cultural Devastation* (Cambridge, Mass.: Harvard University Press, 2006).

14. Lee Edelman, *No Future: Queer Theory and the Death Drive* (Durham, N.C.: Duke University Press, 2004).

15. Carter, "Paratheological Blackness," *South Atlantic Quarterly* 112, no. 4 (2013): 589–611; my formulation here differs somewhat from his.

16. Stefano Harney and Fred Moten, *The Undercommons: Fugitive Planning and Black Study* (Wivenhoe, UK: Minor Compositions, 2013).

17. Edward Schillebeeckx, *God the Future of Man* (New York: Sheed & Ward, 1968). Johann Baptist Metz offers similar reflections on secularization in his *Theology of the World* (New York: Seabury Press, 1973).

18. Schillebeeckx, *God the Future of Man*, 193–94.

19. See Stephen Best, "On Failing to Make the Past Present," *Modern Language Quarterly* 73, no. 3 (2012): 453–74.

20. See Chap. 5 of this volume as well as Lloyd, "From the Theopaternal to the Theopolitical: On Barack Obama," in *Common Goods: Economy, Ecology, and Political Theology* (New York: Fordham University Press, 2015), 326–43.

8. For What Are Whites to Hope?

Material from this chapter previously appeared in Vincent Lloyd, "For What Are Whites to Hope?," *Political Theology* 17, no. 2 (2016): 168–81, used courtesy of Taylor and Francis, www.tandfonline.com.

1. James Cone, *Risks of Faith: The Emergence of a Black Theology of Liberation, 1968–1998* (Boston: Beacon, 1999).

2. See especially Jodi Melamed, *Represent and Destroy: Rationalizing Violence in the New Racial Capitalism* (Minneapolis: University of Minnesota Press, 2011).

3. Clayborne Carson, "Martin Luther King, Jr.: Charismatic Leadership in a Mass Struggle," *Journal of American History* 74, no. 2 (1987): 448–54; Erica R. Edwards, *Charisma and the Fictions of Black Leadership* (Minneapolis: University of Minnesota Press, 2012).

4. I develop an argument against hope as a theological virtue—without particular focus on race—in Lloyd, *The Problem with Grace: Reconfiguring Political Theology* (Stanford, Calif.: Stanford University Press, 2011).

5. For an elaboration on this definition, see Adrienne Martin, *Hope We Hope: A Moral Psychology* (Princeton, N.J.: Princeton University Press, 2013). For a clear account of the relationship between reasons and desires understood along these lines, see Derek Parfit, *On What Matters* (Oxford: Oxford University Press, 2011).

6. See especially Teresa Brennan, *The Transmission of Affect* (Ithaca, N.Y.: Cornell University Press, 2004).

7. Lauren Berlant, *Cruel Optimism* (Durham, N.C.: Duke University Press, 2011).

8. See also Robert Adams, "Moral Faith," *Journal of Philosophy* 92, no. 2 (1995): 75–95.

9. Linda M. G. Zerilli, "The Turn to Affect and the Problem of Judgment," *New Literary History* 46, no. 2 (2015): 261–86.

10. Christopher Lasch, *The True and Only Heaven: Progress and Its Critics* (New York: Norton, 1991).

11. See Bryan Garsten, *Saving Persuasion: A Defense of Rhetoric and Judgment* (Cambridge, Mass.: Harvard University Press, 2006).

12. See particularly Ernst Bloch, *Atheism in Christianity: The Religion of the Exodus and the Kingdom* (New York: Herder and Herder, 1972); Jürgen Moltmann, *A Theology of Hope: On the Ground and the Implications of a Christian Eschatology* (New York: Harper & Row, 1967).

13. Moltmann, *Religion, Revolution, and the Future* (New York: Scribner, 1969).

14. Moltmann, *Experiences in Theology: Ways and Forms of Christian Theology* (Minneapolis: Fortress, 2000), 215.

15. See José Míguez Bonino, *Doing Theology in a Revolutionary Situation* (Philadelphia: Fortress, 1975).

16. See especially James W. Perkinson, *White Theology: Outing Supremacy in Modernity* (New York: Palgrave Macmillan, 2004); Frederick Herzog, *Liberation Theology: Liberation in the Light of the Fourth Gospel* (New York: Seabury, 1972); and James Cone, *A Black Theology of Liberation*, 20th anniv. ed. (1970; Maryknoll, N.Y.: Orbis, 1990).

17. This point is developed in a philosophical register by José Medina, *The Epistemology of Resistance: Gender and Racial Oppression, Epistemic Injustice, and Resistant Imaginations* (Oxford: Oxford University Press, 2013).

18. Pierre Bourdieu, *Distinction: A Social Critique of the Judgement of Taste* (Cambridge, Mass.: Harvard University Press, 1984).

19. Søren Kierkegaard, *The Sickness Unto Death: A Christian Psychological Exposition for Upbuilding and Awakening* (Princeton, N.J.: Princeton University Press, 1980). For a thorough discussion of Kierkegaard on despair and hope, see Mark Bernier, *The Task of Hope in Kierkegaard* (Oxford: Oxford University Press, 2015).

20. For philosophical accounts of such community, see, for example, Jean-Luc Nancy, *The Inoperative Community* (Minneapolis: University of Minnesota Press, 1991); Giorgio Agamben, *The Coming Community* (Minneapolis: University of Minnesota Press, 1993).

9. THE REVELATION OF RACE: ON STEVE BIKO

Material from this chapter first appeared in V. W. Lloyd, "Steve Biko and the Subversion of Race," *Philosophia Africana* 6, no. 2 (2003): 19–35.

1. The account that follows is based on Lindy Wilson, "Bantu Stephen Biko: A Life," in *Bounds of Possibility: The Legacy of Steve Biko and Black Consciousness*, ed. N. Barney Pityana, Mamphela Ramphele, Malusi Mpumlwana, and Lindy Wilson (Cape Town: David Philip, 1991); Anthony W. Marx, *Lessons of Struggle: South African Internal Opposition, 1960–1990* (New York: Oxford University Press, 1992); Steve Biko, *Black Consciousness in South Africa*, ed. M. Arnold (New York: Random House, 1978); and Biko, *I Write What I Like: Selected Writings*, ed. A. Stubbs (Chicago: University of Chicago Press, 2002).

2. Biko, *I Write What I Like*, 4–5.

3. Ibid., 23–24.

4. Biko, *Black Consciousness in South Africa*, 293. South Africa's Truth and Reconciliation Commission (TRC) denied applications for amnesty submitted by five policemen involved in the interrogation and death of Biko. The TRC determined this because "None of the Applicants [for amnesty] alleged that they were actuated by a political motive in participating in the scuffle with Biko," and the scuffle was "not directly linked to the wider objective of extracting information or admissions . . . from Biko." Moreover, the TRC was not satisfied that the police officers had fully disclosed their knowledge of the situation; Truth and Reconciliation Commission, "Application in Terms of Section 18 of the Promotion of National Unity and Reconciliation Act No. 34 of 1995," 1999, http://www.justice.gov.za/trc/decisions%5C1999/99_snyman.html.

5. In poststructuralist appropriations of Lacan such as Žižek's, "symbolic" means all systems of signification in an ideology.

6. Slavoj Žižek, *Tarrying with the Negative: Kant, Hegel, and the Critique of Ideology* (Durham, N.C.: Duke University Press, 1993), 148.

7. Žižek, *Sublime Object of Ideology* (London: Verso, 1989), 100–102.

8. Saul Kripke, *Naming and Necessity* (Cambridge, Mass.: Harvard University Press, 1980), 119.

9. Žižek, *Sublime Object of Ideology*, 88.

10. Ibid., 94–95.

11. Žižek, *Tarrying with the Negative*, 149.

12. Ibid.

13. Žižek, *Sublime Object of Ideology*, 96–97.

14. Ibid., 127.

15. Judith Butler, *Gender Trouble: Feminism and the Subversion of Identity* (New York: Routledge, 1990), 183.

16. Ibid., 185.

17. Butler, *Bodies that Matter: On the Discursive Limits of "Sex"* (New York: Routledge, 1993), 214.

18. Ernesto Laclau develops a closely related point in *On Populist Reason* (London: Verso, 2005).

19. Biko, *I Write What I Like*, 70.

20. Marx, *Making Race and Nation: A Comparison of the United States, South Africa, and Brazil* (Cambridge: Cambridge University Press, 1999), 105.

21. Biko, *I Write What I Like*, 69.

22. Ibid., 48.

23. Ibid., 48–49.

24. Biko, *Black Consciousness in South Africa*, 120.

25. Ibid., 121.

26. I use "symbolic" and "discourse" basically interchangeably, though "discourse" of course has a broader scope than "symbolic." In contrast to psychoanalytic accounts, I take the symbolic to be infused with the ideas of the ruling class—that is, ideology. On these points I am in agreement with Žižek.

27. Sharon Marcus, "Fighting Bodies, Fighting Words: A Theory and Politics of Rape Prevention," in *Feminists Theorize the Political*, ed. Judith Butler and Joan Scott (New York: Routledge, 1992), 390.

28. Ibid., 392.

29. Ibid., 395.

30. Ibid., 396.

31. Ibid., 400.

32. Biko, *I Write What I Like*, 18.

33. Ibid., 15–16.

34. Alain Badiou makes a similar point about the need for radical novelty in his *Ethics: An Essay on the Understanding of Evil* (London: Verso, 2001).

35. Biko, *Black Consciousness in South Africa*, 117.

36. Biko, *I Write What I Like*, 22–23.

37. Geoff Budlender, "Black Consciousness and the Liberal Tradition: Then and Now," in *Bounds of Possibility: The Legacy of Steve Biko and Black Consciousness*, ed. N. Barney Pityana, Mamphela Ramphele, Malusi Mpumlwana, and Lindy Wilson, 228–37. Cape Town: David Philip, 1991.

38. Tom W. Smith, "Changing Racial Labels: From 'Colored' to 'Negro' to 'Black' to 'African American,'" *Public Opinion Quarterly* 56 (1992): 299.

39. Ibid., 501.

40. Ben L. Martin, "From Negro to Black to African American: The Power of Names and Naming," *Political Science Quarterly* 106 (1991): 92.

41. Ibid., 91.

42. Robin D. G. Kelley, *Race Rebels: Culture, Politics, and the Black Working Class* (New York: Free Press, 1996), 210.

43. Ibid.

44. Tony N. Brown, "Predictors of Racial Label Preference in Detroit: Examining Trends from 1971 to 1992," *Sociological Spectrum* 19 (1999): 421–42; Smith, "Changing Racial Labels."

45. Smith, "Changing Racial Labels," 498.

46. See, for example, Noel Ignatiev, *How the Irish Became White* (New York: Routledge, 1995); Ignatiev and John Garvey, eds., *Race Traitor* (New York: Routledge, 1996).

10. The Racial Messiah: On Huey P. Newton

Material from this chapter was previously published in Vincent Lloyd, "Theology and Real Politics: On Huey P. Newton," in *Renegotiating Power, Theology, and Politics*, ed. Joshua Daniel and Rick Elgendy (Houndmills, Basingstoke: Palgrave Macmillan, 2015); reproduced with permission of Palgrave Macmillan.

1. *Panther*, directed by Mario Van Peebles, Gramercy Pictures, 1995; based on Melvin Van Peebles, *Panther: A Novel* (New York: Thunder's Mouth, 1995).

2. For the deep connections between black power and black religion in another context, in Detroit, see Angela D. Dillard, *Faith in the City: Preaching Radical Social Change in Detroit* (Ann Arbor: University of Michigan Press, 2007).

3. Jeffrey O. G. Ogbar, *Black Power: Radical Politics and African American Identity* (Baltimore: Johns Hopkins University Press, 2004), 155.

4. Bobby Seale, *Seize the Time: The Story of the Black Panther Party and Huey P. Newton* (New York: Random House, 1970), 264.

5. Ibid., 104.

6. Raymond Geuss, *Philosophy and Real Politics* (Princeton, N.J.: Princeton University Press, 2008).

7. Ibid., 3.

8. Ibid., 90.

9. Ibid., 93.

10. Ibid., 97.

11. Geuss has little to say about religion, other than the Nietzschean conflation of Christian ethics and modern moral philosophy. He does allow a place for "imaginative life" in these actual motivations. He opposes reality to illusion, which is always distorted; imagination, in contrast, is a part of reality and can lead to real motivations; see also Geuss, *Politics and the Imagination* (Princeton, N.J.: Princeton University Press, 2009).

12. "Two thousand (and more) years of moral preaching have not seemed to provide much evidence that this is an effective way to improve human behavior, and training children properly self-evidently does not require having the correct 'ideal theory'"; Geuss, *Philosophy and Real Politics*, 101.

13. Biographical details draw on Seale, *Seize the Time*, and Huey P. Newton, *Revolutionary Suicide* (New York: Penguin, 2009); see also Joshua Bloom and Waldo E. Martin Jr., *Black against Empire: The History and Politics of the Black Panther Party* (Berkeley: University of California Press, 2013).

14. Different versions of Point Ten appear in Bobby Seale's and Huey Newton's post facto accounts of the platform's drafting.

15. Notably, Cleaver converted to Christianity and wrote an ostensibly theological reflection on his Black Panther days: Eldridge Cleaver, *Soul on Fire* (Waco, Tex.: Word, 1978).

16. See especially James Cone, *Black Theology and Black Power* (Maryknoll, N.Y.: Orbis, 1997).

17. Newton, *Revolutionary Suicide*, 179.

18. Eddie Glaude Jr., ed., *Is It Nation Time? Contemporary Essays on Black Power and Black Nationalism* (Chicago: University of Chicago Press, 2002); Jeffrey Stout, *Democracy and Tradition* (Princeton, N.J.: Princeton University Press, 2005).

19. Stout, *Democracy and Tradition*, 52.

20. Anthony B. Pinn, ed., *By These Hands: A Documentary History of African American Humanism* (New York: New York University Press, 2001).

21. Newton, *Revolutionary Suicide*, 179.

22. Ibid., 180.

23. David Hilliard and Donald Weise, eds., *The Huey P. Newton Reader* (New York: Seven Stories, 2002), 189.

24. Ibid., 225.

25. Hilliard, ed., *The Black Panther Party: Service to the People Programs* (Albuquerque: University of New Mexico Press, 2008), 14–15.

26. Seale, *Seize the Time*, 426.

27. Hilliard and Weise, *Huey P. Newton Reader*, 214.

28. Newton, *Revolutionary Suicide*, v.

29. Ibid., 38.

30. Ibid.

31. Ibid., 35.

32. Ibid., xxi.

33. Seale, *Seize the Time*, 264.

34. Ibid., 265.

35. Hilliard and Weise, *Huey P. Newton Reader*, 243.

36. Newton, *Revolutionary Suicide*, xx.

37. Ibid., 61.
38. Ibid., 271.
39. Newton, "The Women's Liberation and Gay Liberation Movements," in Hilliard and Weise, *Huey P. Newton Reader*.
40. Hilliard and Weise, *Huey P. Newton Reader*, 280.
41. Ibid., 281.
42. Ibid., 276. I elaborate on this distinction between charismatic leadership that grows out of contradiction (like Newton's) and charismatic leadership that grows out of consistent self-presentation in Lloyd, *Is Charisma Moral?* (New York: Columbia University Press, 2018).

11. THE POSTRACIAL SAINT: ON BARACK OBAMA

Material from this chapter previously appeared as Vincent W. Lloyd, "The Post-Racial Saint? On Barack Obama," in *Sainthood and Race: Marked Flesh, Holy Flesh*, by Molly H. Bassett and Vincent W. Lloyd (Routledge, copyright 2014); reproduced by permission of Taylor and Francis Group, LLC, a division of Informa Plc.

1. Hortense Spillers, "Destiny's Child: Obama and Election '08," *boundary 2* 39, no. 2 (2012): 5.
2. The August 20, 2009, cover was designed by Shepard Fairey. The words that ring the presidential seal in the image are "Bold Action or Compromise?" *Time* also featured an evocatively haloed Obama on the cover of its March 10, 2008, issue. *Newsweek* featured Obama with a rainbow-colored halo, captioned "The First Gay President," May 21, 2012.
3. Carl Schmitt, *Political Theology: Four Chapters on the Concept of Sovereignty* (Cambridge, Mass.: MIT Press, 1985); Giorgio Agamben, *Homo Sacer: Sovereign Power and Bare Life* (Stanford, Calif.: Stanford University Press, 1998); Ernst H. Kantorowicz, *The King's Two Bodies: A Study in Mediaeval Political Theology* (Princeton, N.J.: Princeton University Press, 1957).
4. Robert N. Bellah, "Civil Religion in America," *Daedalus* 96, no. 1 (1967): 1–21; Agamben, *The Kingdom and the Glory: For a Theological Genealogy of Economy and Government* (Stanford, Calif.: Stanford University Press, 2011), Chap. 7.
5. Max Weber, *Economy and Society: An Outline of Interpretive Sociology* (Berkeley: University of California Press, 1978).
6. See Erica R. Edwards, *Charisma and the Fictions of Black Leadership* (Minneapolis: University of Minnesota Press, 2012).
7. Agamben, *Homo Sacer*; George Shulman, "White Supremacy and Black Insurgency as Political Theology," in *Race and Secularism in America*, ed. Jonathon S. Kahn and Vincent W. Lloyd (New York: Columbia University Press, 2016); see also Chap. 4 of this volume.

8. Cornel West, *Prophesy Deliverance! An Afro-American Revolutionary Christianity* (1982; Louisville, Ky.: Westminster John Knox Press, 2002); West, *The American Evasion of Philosophy: A Genealogy of Pragmatism* (Madison: University of Wisconsin Press, 1989); see also Shulman, *American Prophecy: Race and Redemption in American Political Culture* (Minneapolis: University of Minnesota Press, 2008); Christopher Z. Hobson, *Mount of Visions: African American Prophetic Tradition, 1800–1950* (Oxford: Oxford University Press, 2012). Compare Max Weber's much more general account of the prophet as one who has a calling to proclaim religious teaching in *The Sociology of Religion* (Boston: Beacon, 1963).

9. Albert B. Cleage, *The Black Messiah* (New York: Sheed & Ward, 1968); James Cone, *Black Theology and Black Power* (1969; Maryknoll, N.Y.: Orbis, 1997).

10. Ta-Nehisi Coates, "Obama and the Myth of the Black Messiah," *Time* Online (November 13, 2008), http://content.time.com/time/magazine/article/0,9171,1858897,00.html. But see Corey D. B. Walker's provocative suggestion that "Obama is the messiah without messianism"—for white Americans; Walker, "Barack Obama and the Crisis of the White Intellectual," *Counterpunch* (January 12–14, 2008), http://www.counterpunch.org/2008/01/12/barack-obama-and-the-crisis-of-the-white-intellectual/.

11. Spillers, "Destiny's Child"; Donald E. Pease, "Black Orpheus: Barack Obama's Governmentality," *REAL: Yearbook of Research in English and American Literature* 27 (2011): 57–72.

12. Kathryn Lofton, *Oprah: The Gospel of an Icon* (Berkeley: University of California Press, 2011), 19.

13. Ibid., 8.

14. Contra Susan Wolf, every choice the saint makes is not dictated by a normative program. Rather, the desire for the transcendent shapes the saint's life in broad strokes; Wolf, "Moral Saints," *Journal of Philosophy* 79, no. 8 (1982): 419–39.

15. Tracy Kidder, *Mountains beyond Mountains* (New York: Random House, 2003).

16. See the scope of chapters included in Françoise Meltzer and Jas Elsner, *Saints: Faith without Borders* (Chicago: University of Chicago Press, 2011).

17. K. Anthony Appiah, "'No Bad Nigger': Blacks as the Ethical Principles in the Movies," in *Media Spectacles*, ed. Marjorie Garber, Jann Matlock, and Rebecca L. Walkowitz, 77–90 (New York: Routledge, 1993); Audrey Colombe, "White Hollywood's New Black Boogeyman," *Jump Cut: A Review of Contemporary Media* 45 (2002), http://www.ejumpcut.org/archive/jc45.2002/colombe/index.html.

18. Forest Whitaker in Jim Jarmusch's *Ghost Dog* is a particularly rich and complex example, with the saintly black man as protagonist, explicitly committed to an other-worldly moral code.

19. See Curtis Evans, *The Burden of Black Religion* (Oxford: Oxford University Press, 2008).

20. David Ehrenstein, "Obama the 'Magic Negro,'" *Los Angeles Times* (March 19, 2007), http://www.latimes.com/news/opinion/commentary/la-oe-ehrenstein19mar19,0,3391015.story. Ehrenstein's comment resonated with conservative radio host Rush Limbaugh, who discussed it on air and then repeatedly during the campaign season aired a song called "Barack the Magic Negro," to the tune of "Puff the Magic Dragon." A singer mimicking the voice of Rev. Al Sharpton complains about Obama's appeal to white voters, attributed to his lack of racial authenticity. The song went largely unnoticed outside of the world of conservative talk radio until Chip Saltsman, a candidate for chairman of the Republican National Committee, distributed CDs containing the song. Competing candidates for the chairmanship criticized Saltsman, making the song a national issue.

21. Ibid.

22. Barack Obama, *Dreams from My Father: A Story of Race and Inheritance* (New York: Three Rivers, 2004), 134.

23. Ibid., 134–35.

24. Ibid., 135.

25. Ibid., 278–79.

26. Ibid., 294.

27. Ibid.

28. Obama, "A More Perfect Union," http://constitutioncenter.org/amoreperfectunion/.

29. Janny Scott, "Obama Chooses Reconciliation over Rancor," *New York Times* (March 19, 2008), A1.

30. Sam Stein, "Jesse Jackson: Obama Just Turned Crisis into Opportunity," *Huffington Post* (July 8, 2008), http://www.huffingtonpost.com/2008/03/18/jesse-jackson-obama-just-_n_92109.html?.

31. Alain Badiou, *Saint Paul: The Foundation of Universalism*, trans. Ray Brassier (Stanford, Calif.: Stanford University Press, 2003).

32. Ibid., 42.

33. Daniel Boyarin, *A Radical Jew: Paul and the Politics of Identity* (Berkeley: University of California Press, 1994), 13.

34. Ibid., 24.

35. Ibid., 243.

36. Touré, "No Such Place as 'Post-Racial' America," *New York Times*, November 8, 2011, http://campaignstops.blogs.nytimes.com/2011/11/08

/no-such-place-as-post-racial-america/; Coates, "Fear of a Black President," *Atlantic* (August 22, 2012), http://www.theatlantic.com/magazine/archive/2012/09/fear-of-a-black-president/309064/; Eduardo Bonilla-Silva, *Racism without Racists: Color-Blind Racism and the Persistence of Racial Inequality in America* (Lanham, Md.: Rowman & Littlefield, 2003).

37. Badiou, *Ethics: An Essay on the Understanding of Evil* (London: Verso, 2001).

12. THE RACE OF THE SOUL: ON GILLIAN ROSE

Material from this chapter first appeared in Vincent Lloyd, "Gillian Rose, Race, and Identity," *Telos* 173 (Winter 2015): 107–24.

1. A phrase attributed to Rose by George Carey; see Andrew Shanks, *Against Innocence: Gillian Rose's Reception and Gift of Faith* (London: SCM Press, 2008), 1.

2. Rose does not capitalize "protestantism," as she wishes to indicate something broader than the religion; Gillian Rose, *Love's Work* (New York: New York Review of Books, 2011), 57.

3. Lloyd, ed., "Interview with Gillian Rose," *Theory, Culture, and Society* 25, nos. 7–8 (2008): 210; see also Rose, *Judaism and Modernity: Philosophical Essays* (Oxford: Blackwell, 1993), ix.

4. Lloyd, "Interview with Gillian Rose," 210.

5. Rose, *Love's Work*, 140.

6. Lloyd, "Interview with Gillian Rose," 215.

7. Rose, *Love's Work*, 140.

8. Lloyd, "Interview with Gillian Rose," 213.

9. Rose, *Paradiso* (London: Menard, 1999), 46.

10. Ibid., 47.

11. Rose, *Mourning Becomes the Law: Philosophy and Representation* (Cambridge: Cambridge University Press, 1996), 98.

12. See, for example, Rose's account of Edna's dance career as exemplifying the wrong kind of self-mastery, in *Paradiso*, 29.

13. Rose, *Mourning Becomes the Law*, 5; see also Wendy Brown, *States of Injury: Power and Freedom in Late Modernity* (Princeton, N.J.: Princeton University Press, 1995).

14. Rose, *Mourning Becomes the Law*, 4.

15. Rose, *Paradiso*, 43.

16. Rose, *Mourning Becomes the Law*, 62.

17. Rose, *Love's Work*, 134.

18. Rose, *Paradiso*, 63.

19. Ibid., 21.

20. I develop this point in Lloyd, *The Problem with Grace: Reconfigur-*

ing Political Theology (Stanford, Calif.: Stanford University Press, 2011), Chap. 1.

21. Rose, *Love's Work*, 73.

22. Rose, *Hegel Contra Sociology* (London: Athlone, 1995), 29. Compare the account of Hegel on naming in Chap. 9 of this volume.

23. Rose, *Mourning Becomes the Law*, 85.

24. Raymond Geuss has more recently developed this point, as discussed in Chap. 10 of this volume. Like Rose, he identifies his opponents as exemplifying a neo-Kantian spirit. Rose's development of these issues is found in her *Dialectic of Nihilism: Post-Structuralism and Law* (Oxford: Blackwell, 1984).

25. Rose, *Hegel Contra Sociology*, 217.

26. Lloyd, "Interview with Gillian Rose," 215.

27. Anne Anlin Cheng, *Melancholy of Race: Psychoanalysis, Assimilation, and Hidden Grief* (Oxford: Oxford University Press, 2001); see also Chap. 7 of this volume.

28. Rose, *Mourning Becomes the Law*, 36.

29. J. Kameron Carter, *Race: A Theological Account* (Oxford: Oxford University Press, 2008); Frank B. Wilderson III, *Red, White, and Black: Cinema and the Structure of U.S. Antagonisms* (Durham, N.C.: Duke University Press, 2010); Sylvia Wynter, "Unsettling the Coloniality of Being/Power/Truth/Freedom: Towards the Human, After Man, Its Overrepresentation—An Argument," *CR: The New Centennial Review* 3, no. 3 (2003): 257–337.

30. E.g., "Going to Meet the Man," in James Baldwin, *Early Novels and Stories* (New York: Library of America, 1998).

31. C. Melissa Snarr, *All You That Labor: Religion and Ethics in the Living Wage Movement* (New York: New York University Press, 2011).

32. Jared Sexton, *Amalgamation Schemes: Antiblackness and the Critique of Multiracialism* (Minneapolis: University of Minnesota Press, 2008).

33. Rose, *Judaism and Modernity*, ix.

34. Rose, *Love's Work*, 23–24.

CODA: THE BIRTH OF THE BLACK CHURCH

1. Eddie Glaude Jr., "The Black Church Is Dead," *Huffington Post*, February 24, 2010, http://www.huffingtonpost.com/eddie-glaude-jr-phd/the-black-church-is-dead_b_473815.html.

2. W. E. B. Du Bois, ed., *Some Efforts of American Negroes for Their Own Social Betterment* (Atlanta: Atlanta University Press, 1898), 4; see also Du Bois, ed., *The Negro Church* (Atlanta: Atlanta University Press, 1903), where Du Bois places a set of social scientific studies within a quite unscientistic frame.

3. See Curtis Evans, *The Burden of Black Religion* (Oxford: Oxford University Press, 2008).

4. Gayraud S. Wilmore and and James H. Cone, eds., *Black Theology: A Documentary History* (Maryknoll, N.Y.: Orbis, 1979), 25. For an expansive history of black religious organizing for social justice during this "Negro Church" period, see Gary J. Dorrien, *The New Abolition: W. E. B. Du Bois and the Black Social Gospel* (New Haven, Conn.: Yale University Press, 2015).

5. Wilmore and Cone, *Black Theology*, 64.

6. E. Franklin Frazier and C. Eric Lincoln, *The Negro Church in America/The Black Church Since Frazier* (New York: Schocken, 1974), 105–6.

BIBLIOGRAPHY

Adams, Robert. "Moral Faith." *Journal of Philosophy* 92, no. 2 (1995): 75–95.
Agamben, Giorgio. *The Coming Community*. Minneapolis: University of Minnesota Press, 1993.
———. *Homo Sacer: Sovereign Power and Bare Life*. Stanford, Calif.: Stanford University Press, 1998.
———. *The Kingdom and the Glory: For a Theological Genealogy of Economy and Government*. Stanford, Calif.: Stanford University Press, 2011.
———. *The Open: Man and Animal*. Stanford, Calif.: Stanford University Press, 2004.
———. *The Signature of All Things: On Method*. New York: Zone, 2009.
———. *State of Exception*. Chicago: University of Chicago Press, 2005.
Agrama, Hussein Ali. *Questioning Secularism: Islam, Sovereignty, and the Rule of Law in Modern Egypt*. Chicago: University of Chicago Press, 2012.
Ahluwalia, Pal. *Out of Africa: Post-Structuralism's Colonial Roots*. New York: Routledge, 2010.
Alinsky, Saul. *Reveille for Radicals*. Chicago: University of Chicago Press, 1946.
———. *Rules for Radicals: A Practical Primer for Realistic Radicals*. New York: Vintage, 1971.
Appiah, K. Anthony. "'No Bad Nigger': Blacks as the Ethical Principles in the Movies." In *Media Spectacles*, edited by Marjorie Garber, Jann Matlock, and Rebecca L. Walkowitz, 77–90. New York: Routledge, 1993.
Asad, Talal. *Formations of the Secular: Christianity, Islam, Modernity*. Stanford, Calif.: Stanford University Press, 2003.
———. *Genealogies of Religion: Discipline and Reasons of Power in Christianity and Islam*. Baltimore: Johns Hopkins University Press, 1993.
Asad, Talal, Wendy Brown, Judith Butler, and Saba Mahmood. *Is Critique Secular? Blasphemy, Injury, and Free Speech*. Berkeley: University of California Press, 2009.
Badiou, Alain. *Ethics: An Essay on the Understanding of Evil*. London: Verso, 2001.
———. *Saint Paul: The Foundation of Universalism*. Translated by Ray Brassier. Stanford, Calif.: Stanford University Press, 2003.

Baldwin, James. *Collected Essays*. New York: Library of America, 1998.
———. *The Cross of Redemption: Uncollected Writings*. New York: Pantheon, 2010.
———. *Early Novels and Stories*. New York: Library of America, 1998.
———. *The Evidence of Things Not Seen*. New York: Holt, Rinehart and Winston, 1985.
———. *If Beale Street Could Talk*. New York: Dial Press, 1974.
Bantum, Brian. *Redeeming Mulatto: A Theology of Race and Christian Hybridity*. Waco, Tex.: Baylor University Press, 2010.
Baring, Edward. "Liberalism and the Algerian War: The Case of Jacques Derrida." *Critical Inquiry* 36, no. 2 (2010): 239–61.
———. *The Young Derrida and French Philosophy, 1945–1968*. Cambridge: Cambridge University Press, 2011.
Bellah, Robert N. "Civil Religion in America." *Daedalus* 96, no. 1 (1967): 1–21.
Benjamin, Andrew. "Particularity and Exceptions: On Jews and Animals." *South Atlantic Quarterly* 107, no. 1 (2008): 71–87.
Benjamin, Walter. "On the Concept of History." Translated by H. Zohn. In *Walter Benjamin: Selected Writings 1938–1940*, edited by H. Eiland and M. W. Jennings, 4:389–400. Cambridge, Mass.: Belknap Press, 2003.
———. "Theologico-Political Fragment." In *Walter Benjamin: Selected Writings*. Cambridge, Mass.: Harvard University Press, 2002, 3:305–6.
Bennington, Geoffrey, and Jacques Derrida. *Jacques Derrida*. Chicago: University of Chicago Press, 1993.
Berlant, Lauren. *Cruel Optimism*. Durham, N.C.: Duke University Press, 2011.
Bernier, Mark. *The Task of Hope in Kierkegaard*. Oxford: Oxford University Press, 2015.
Best, Stephen. "On Failing to Make the Past Present." *Modern Language Quarterly* 73, no. 3 (2012): 453–74.
Biko, Steve. *Black Consciousness in South Africa*. Edited by M. Arnold. New York: Random House, 1978.
———. *I Write What I Like: Selected Writings*. Edited by A. Stubbs. Chicago: University of Chicago Press, 2002.
Bloch, Ernst. *Atheism in Christianity: The Religion of the Exodus and the Kingdom*. New York: Herder and Herder, 1972.
Bloom, Joshua, and Waldo E. Martin Jr. *Black against Empire: The History and Politics of the Black Panther Party*. Berkeley: University of California Press, 2013.
Bonilla-Silva, Eduardo. *Racism without Racists: Color-Blind Racism and the Persistence of Racial Inequality in America*. Lanham, Md.: Rowman & Littlefield, 2003.

Bonino, José Míguez. *Doing Theology in a Revolutionary Situation*. Philadelphia: Fortress, 1975.
Bourdieu, Pierre. *Distinction: A Social Critique of the Judgement of Taste*. Cambridge, Mass.: Harvard University Press, 1984.
Boyarin, Daniel. *Border Lines: The Partition of Judaeo-Christianity*. Philadelphia: University of Pennsylvania Press, 2004.
———. *A Radical Jew: Paul and the Politics of Identity*. Berkeley: University of California Press, 1994.
———. "Semantic Differences; or, "Judaism"/"Christianity." In *The Ways That Never Parted*, edited by Adam H. Becker and Annette Yoshiko Reed, 65–85. Minneapolis: Fortress, 2007.
Brennan, Teresa. *The Transmission of Affect*. Ithaca, N.Y.: Cornell University Press, 2004.
Bretherton, Luke. *Christianity and Contemporary Politics: The Conditions and Possibilities of Faithful Witness*. Chichester: Wiley-Blackwell, 2010.
———. *Resurrecting Democracy: Faith, Citizenship, and the Politics of a Common Life*. New York: Cambridge University Press, 2015.
Brown, Tony N. "Predictors of Racial Label Preference in Detroit: Examining Trends from 1971 to 1992." *Sociological Spectrum* 19 (1999): 421–42.
Brown, Wendy. *Politics Out of History*. Princeton, N.J.: Princeton University Press, 2001.
———. *States of Injury: Power and Freedom in Late Modernity*. Princeton, N.J.: Princeton University Press, 1995.
Budlender, Geoff. "Black Consciousness and the Liberal Tradition: Then and Now." In *Bounds of Possibility: The Legacy of Steve Biko and Black Consciousness*, edited by N. Barney Pityana, Mamphela Ramphele, Malusi Mpumlwana, and Lindy Wilson, 228–37. Cape Town: David Philip, 1991.
Buell, Denise. *Why This New Race: Ethnic Reasoning in Early Christianity*. New York: Columbia University Press, 2005.
Butler, Judith. *Bodies That Matter: On the Discursive Limits of "Sex."* New York: Routledge, 1993.
———. *Gender Trouble: Feminism and the Subversion of Identity*. New York: Routledge, 1990.
———. "Mbembe's Extravagant Power." *Public Culture* 5, no. 1 (1992): 67–74.
———. *Precarious Life: The Powers of Mourning and Violence*. London: Verso, 2004.
Carson, Clayborne. "Martin Luther King, Jr.: Charismatic Leadership in a Mass Struggle." *Journal of American History* 74, no. 2 (1987): 448–54.
Carter, J. Kameron. "Black Theology: A Review Essay." *Modern Theology* 19, no. 1 (2003): 117–38.

———. "Christology, Or Redeeming Whiteness: A Response to James Perkinson's Appropriation of Black Theology." *Theology Today* 60, no. 4 (2004): 525–39.
———. "Paratheological Blackness." *South Atlantic Quarterly* 112, no. 4 (2013): 589–611.
———. *Race: A Theological Account*. Oxford: Oxford University Press, 2008.
Cavanaugh, William T. *Theopolitical Imagination*. London: T & T Clark, 2002.
Chakrabarty, Dipesh. *Provincializing Europe: Postcolonial Thought and Historical Difference*. Princeton, N.J.: Princeton University Press, 2000.
Cheng, Anne Anlin. *The Melancholy of Race: Psychoanalysis, Assimilation, and Hidden Grief*. Oxford: Oxford University Press, 2001.
Chidester, David. *Savage Systems: Colonialism and Comparative Religion in Southern Africa*. Charlottesville: University Press of Virginia, 1996.
Cleage, Albert B. *The Black Messiah*. New York: Sheed & Ward, 1968.
Cleaver, Eldridge. *Soul on Fire*. Waco, Tex.: Word, 1978.
Coates, Ta-Nehisi. "Fear of a Black President." *Atlantic* (August 22, 2012). http://www.theatlantic.com/magazine/archive/2012/09/fear-of-a-black-president/309064/.
———. "Obama and the Myth of the Black Messiah." *Time* Online (November 13, 2008). http://content.time.com/time/magazine/article/0,9171,1858897,00.html.
Colombe, Audrey. "White Hollywood's New Black Boogeyman." *Jump Cut: A Review of Contemporary Media* 45 (2002). http://www.ejumpcut.org/archive/jc45.2002/colombe/index.html.
Cone, Cecil Wayne. *The Identity Crisis in Black Theology*. Nashville, Tenn.: AMEC, 1975.
Cone, James. *Black Theology and Black Power*. Maryknoll, N.Y.: Orbis, 1997. Originally published in 1969.
———. *A Black Theology of Liberation*. 20th anniv. ed. Maryknoll, N.Y.: Orbis, 1990. Originally published in 1970.
———. *God of the Oppressed*. Maryknoll, N.Y.: Orbis, 1997. Originally published in 1975.
———. *Martin and Malcolm and America: A Dream or a Nightmare?* Maryknoll, N.Y.: Orbis, 1991.
———. *My Soul Looks Back*. Nashville, Tenn: Abington, 1982.
———. *Risks of Faith: The Emergence of a Black Theology of Liberation, 1968–1998*. Boston: Beacon, 1999.
———. *Speaking the Truth: Ecumenism, Liberation, and Black Theology*. Grand Rapids, Mich.: Eerdmans, 1986.
———. *The Spirituals and the Blues: An Interpretation*. Maryknoll, N.Y.: Orbis, 1991. Originally published in 1972.

Cortes, Ernesto. "Reweaving the Social Fabric." *Boston Review* 19 (1994): 12–14.
Czajka, Agnes, and Bora Isyar, eds. *Europe after Derrida: Crisis and Potentiality*. Edinburgh: Edinburgh University Press, 2014.
Derrida, Jacques. "Admiration of Nelson Mandela, or The Laws of Reflection." *Law and Literature* 26, no. 1 (2014): 9–30.
———. "The Force of Law: The 'Mystical Foundation of Authority.'" In *Deconstruction and the Possibility of Justice*, edited by Drucilla Cornell, Michel Rosenfeld, and David Carlson, 3–67. New York: Routledge, 1992.
———. *Given Time*. Vol. 1, *Counterfeit Money*. Chicago: University of Chicago Press, 1992.
———. "Plato's Pharmacy." In *Dissemination*. Chicago: University of Chicago Press, 1981, 61–119.
———. "Racism's Last Word." *Critical Inquiry* 12 (1985): 290–99.
———. "White Mythology: Metaphor in the Text of Philosophy." *New Literary History* 6, no. 1 (1974): 5–74.
———. *Writing and Difference*. Chicago: University of Chicago Press, 1978.
Dillard, Angela D. *Faith in the City: Preaching Radical Social Change in Detroit*. Ann Arbor: University of Michigan Press, 2007.
Dorrien, Gary J. *The New Abolition: W. E. B. Du Bois and the Black Social Gospel*. New Haven, Conn.: Yale University Press, 2015.
Du Bois, W. E. B. *Writings*. New York: Literary Classics of the United States, 1986.
Du Bois, W. E. B., ed. *The Negro Church*. Atlanta: Atlanta University Press, 1903.
———. *Some Efforts of American Negroes for Their Own Social Betterment*. Atlanta: Atlanta University Press, 1898.
Duggan, Lisa. *The Twilight of Equality? Neoliberalism, Cultural Politics, and the Attack on Democracy*. Boston: Beacon, 2003.
Edelman, Lee. *No Future: Queer Theory and the Death Drive*. Durham, N.C.: Duke University Press, 2004.
Edwards, Erica R. *Charisma and the Fictions of Black Leadership*. Minneapolis: University of Minnesota Press, 2012.
Ehrenstein, David. "Obama the 'Magic Negro.'" *Los Angeles Times*, March 19, 2007. http://www.latimes.com/news/opinion/commentary/la-oe-ehrenstein19mar19,0,3391015.story.
Ernest, John. *A Nation within a Nation: Organizing African-American Communities Before the Civil War*. Chicago: Ivan R. Dee, 2011.
Evans, Curtis. *The Burden of Black Religion*. Oxford: Oxford University Press, 2008.
Eze, Emmanuel, ed. *Race and the Enlightenment: A Reader*. Cambridge, Mass.: Blackwell, 1997.

Farred, Grant. "'Nostalgeria': Derrida, Before and After Fanon." *South Atlantic Quarterly* 112, no. 1 (2013): 145–62.
Fergus, Devin. *Liberalism, Black Power, and the Making of American Politics, 1965–1980*. Athens: University of Georgia Press, 2009.
Frazier, E. Franklin, and C. Eric Lincoln. *The Negro Church in America / The Black Church Since Frazier*. New York: Schocken, 1974.
Fulkerson, Mary McClintock. "Receiving from the Other: Theology and Grass-Roots Organizing." *International Journal of Public Theology* 6, no. 4 (2012): 421–34.
Garsten, Bryan. *Saving Persuasion: A Defense of Rhetoric and Judgment*. Cambridge, Mass.: Harvard University Press, 2006.
Geuss, Raymond. *Philosophy and Real Politics*. Princeton, N.J.: Princeton University Press, 2008.
———. *Politics and the Imagination*. Princeton, N.J.: Princeton University Press, 2009.
Girard, René. *Violence and the Sacred*. Baltimore: Johns Hopkins University Press, 1977.
Glaude, Eddie Jr. "The Black Church Is Dead." *Huffington Post*, February 24, 2010. http://www.huffingtonpost.com/eddie-glaude-jr-phd/the-black-church-is-dead_b_473815.html.
———, ed. *Is It Nation Time? Contemporary Essays on Black Power and Black Nationalism*. Chicago: University of Chicago Press, 2002.
Goldschmidt, Henry. "Introduction: Race, Nation, and Religion." In *Race, Nation, and Religion in the Americas*, edited by Henry Goldschmidt and Elizabeth McAlister, 3–31. Oxford: Oxford University Press, 2004.
Golson, G. Barry, ed. *The Playboy Interview*. New York: Playboy Press, 1981.
Gregory, Eric. *Politics and the Order of Love: An Augustinian Ethic of Democratic Citizenship*. Chicago: University of Chicago Press, 2008.
Hackett, Rosalind. Review of *Afriques indociles*. *Journal of Religion in Africa* 20, no. 3 (1990): 305–6.
Hardy, Clarence E. *James Baldwin's God: Sex, Hope, and the Crisis in Black Holiness Culture*. Knoxville: University of Tennessee Press, 2003.
Harney, Stefano, and Fred Moten. *The Undercommons: Fugitive Planning and Black Study*. Wivenhoe, UK: Minor Compositions, 2013.
Hart, David Bentley. *Beauty of the Infinite: The Aesthetics of Christian Truth*. Grand Rapids, Mich.: Eerdmans, 2003.
———. "The Mirror of the Infinite: Gregory of Nyssa on the *Vestigia Trinitatis*." *Modern Theology* 18, no. 4 (2002): 541–61.
Hauerwas, Stanley, and Romand Coles. *Christianity, Democracy, and the Radical Ordinary: Conversations between a Radical Democrat and a Christian*. Eugene, Ore.: Cascade, 2008.

Haynes, Stephen R. *Noah's Curse: The Biblical Justification of American Slavery.* Oxford: Oxford University Press, 2007.
Herzog, Frederick. *Liberation Theology: Liberation in the Light of the Fourth Gospel.* New York: Seabury Press, 1972.
Hesse, Barnor. "Racialized Modernity: An Analytics of White Mythologies." *Ethnic and Racial Studies* 30, no. 4 (2007): 643–63.
———. "Self-Fulfilling Prophecy: The Postracial Horizon." *South Atlantic Quarterly* 110, no. 1 (2011): 155–78.
Hickman, Jared. "Globalization and the Gods, or the Political Theology of Race." *Early American Literature* 45, no. 1 (2010): 145–82.
Higginbotham, Evelyn Brooks. *Righteous Discontent: The Women's Movement in the Black Baptist Church, 1880–1920.* Cambridge, Mass.: Harvard University Press, 1993.
Hilliard, David, ed., *The Black Panther Party: Service to the People Programs.* Albuquerque: University of New Mexico Press, 2008.
Hilliard, David, and Donald Weise, eds. *The Huey P. Newton Reader.* New York: Seven Stories, 2002.
Hobson, Christopher Z. *The Mount of Visions: African American Prophetic Tradition, 1800–1950.* Oxford: Oxford University Press, 2012.
Horwitt, Sanford D. *Let Them Call Me Rebel: Saul Alinsky, His Life and Legacy.* New York: Knopf, 1989.
Hunter, Tera. *To 'Joy My Freedom: Southern Black Women's Lives and Labors after the Civil War.* Cambridge, Mass.: Harvard University Press, 1997.
Ignatiev, Noel. *How the Irish Became White.* New York: Routledge, 1995.
Ignatiev, Noel, and John Garvey, eds. *Race Traitor.* New York: Routledge, 1996.
Iton, Richard. *In Search of the Black Fantastic.* Oxford: Oxford University Press, 2008.
———. *Solidarity Blues: Race, Culture, and the American Left.* Chapel Hill: University of North Carolina Press, 2000.
———. "Still Life." *Small Axe* 17, no. 1 (March 2013): 22–39.
Jennings, Willie James. *The Christian Imagination: Theology and the Origins of Race.* New Haven, Conn.: Yale University Press, 2010.
Jones, Arthur C. *Wade in the Water: The Wisdom of the Spirituals.* Maryknoll, N.Y.: Orbis, 1993.
Kahn, Jonathon S., and Vincent W. Lloyd, eds. *Race and Secularism in America.* New York: Columbia University Press, 2016.
Kantorowicz, Ernst H. *The King's Two Bodies: A Study in Mediaeval Political Theology.* Princeton, N.J.: Princeton University Press, 1957.
Kee, Alistair. *The Rise and Demise of Black Theology.* London: SCM Press, 2008.
Kelley, Robin D. G. *Race Rebels: Culture, Politics, and the Black Working Class.* New York: Free Press, 1996.

Kidd, Colin. *The Forging of Races: Race and Scripture in the Protestant Atlantic World, 1600–2000*. Cambridge: Cambridge University Press, 2006.
Kidder, Tracy. *Mountains beyond Mountains*. New York: Random House, 2003.
Kierkegaard, Søren. *The Sickness unto Death: A Christian Psychological Exposition for Upbuilding and Awakening*. Princeton, N.J.: Princeton University Press, 1980.
King, Martin Luther Jr. *The Papers of Martin Luther King, Jr*. Vol. 4. Berkeley: University of California Press, 2000.
———. *A Testament of Hope: The Essential Writings of Martin Luther King, Jr*. San Francisco: Harper & Row, 1986.
King, Richard. *Orientalism and Religion: Postcolonial Theory, India, and "the Mystical East."* London: Routledge, 1999.
Kripke, Saul. *Naming and Necessity*. Cambridge, Mass.: Harvard University Press, 1980.
Laclau, Ernesto. *On Populist Reason*. London: Verso, 2005.
Lasch, Christopher. *The True and Only Heaven: Progress and Its Critics*. New York: Norton, 1991.
Lear, Jonathan. *Radical Hope: Ethics in the Face of Cultural Devastation*. Cambridge, Mass.: Harvard University Press, 2006.
Lemarchand, René. Review of *Afriques indociles*. *African Studies Review* 32, no. 3 (1989): 153–54.
Lewis, David Levering. *W. E. B. Du Bois, 1868–1919: Biography of a Race*. New York: H. Holt, 1993.
Lloyd, Vincent. "From the Theopaternal to the Theopolitical: On Barack Obama." In *Common Goods: Economy, Ecology, and Political Theology*. New York: Fordham University Press, 2015, 326–43.
———, ed. "Interview with Gillian Rose." *Theory, Culture, and Society* 25, nos. 7–8 (2008): 201–18.
———. *Is Charisma Moral?* New York: Columbia University Press, 2018.
———. *The Problem with Grace: Reconfiguring Political Theology*. Stanford, Calif.: Stanford University Press, 2011.
———. "Race and Religion." *Critical Research on Religion* 1, no. 1 (2013): 80–86.
Lofton, Kathryn. *Oprah: The Gospel of an Icon*. Berkeley: University of California Press, 2011.
Mahmood, Saba. *Politics of Piety: The Islamic Revival and the Feminist Subject*. Princeton, N.J.: Princeton University Press, 2005.
Malcolm X. "Message to the Grass Roots." In *Malcolm X Speaks: Selected Speeches and Statements*. New York: Grove Press, 1965, 3–17.
Marcus, Sharon. "Fighting Bodies, Fighting Words: A Theory and Politics of Rape Prevention." In *Feminists Theorize the Political*, edited by Judith Butler and Joan Scott, 385–403. New York: Routledge, 1992.

Marion, Jean-Luc. *Being Given: Toward a Phenomenology of Givenness*. Translated by Jeffrey L. Kosky. Stanford, Calif.: Stanford University Press, 2002.
Marable, Manning. *Malcolm X: A Life of Reinvention*. New York: Viking, 2011.
Martin, Adrienne. *How We Hope: A Moral Psychology*. Princeton, N.J.: Princeton University Press, 2013.
Martin, Ben L. "From Negro to Black to African American: The Power of Names and Naming." *Political Science Quarterly* 106 (1991): 83–107.
Martin, Deborah G. "Constructing the 'Neighborhood Sphere': Gender and Community Organizing." *Gender, Place and Culture* 9, no. 4 (2002): 333–50.
Marx, Anthony W. *Lessons of Struggle: South African Internal Opposition, 1960–1990*. New York: Oxford University Press, 1992.
———. *Making Race and Nation: A Comparison of the United States, South Africa, and Brazil*. Cambridge: Cambridge University Press, 1999.
Masuzawa, Tomoko. *The Invention of World Religions, Or, How European Universalism Was Preserved in the Language of Pluralism*. Chicago: University of Chicago Press, 2005.
Mbembe, Achille. "Africa and the Night of Language: An Interview with Achille Mbembe." Johannesburg Workshop in Theory and Criticism. *Salon* 2. http://jwtc.org.za/the_salon/volume_2/annalisa_oboe_africa_the_night_of_language.htm.
———. *Afriques indociles: Christianisme, pouvoir et État en société postcoloniale*. Paris: Karthala, 1988.
———. *Critique de la raison nègre*. Paris: La Découverte, 2013.
———. *De la postcolonie: Essai sur l'imagination politique dans l'Afrique contemporaine*. Paris: Éditions Karthala, 2000.
———. *Les jeunes et l'ordre politique en Afrique noire*. Paris: Editions L'Harmattan, 1985.
———. *La Naissance du maquis dans le Sud-Cameroun, 1920–1960: Histoire des usages de la raison en colonie*. Paris: Karthala, 1996.
———. "Necropolitics." *Public Culture* 15, no. 1 (2003): 11–40.
———. *On the Postcolony*. Berkeley: University of California Press, 2001.
———. "*On the Postcolony*: A Brief Response to Critics." *Qui Parle* 15, no. 2 (2005): 1–49.
———. "Religion, Politics, Theology: A Conversation with Achille Mbembe." *boundary 2* 34, no. 2 (2007): 149–70.
———. *Sortir de la grande nuit: Essai sur l'Afrique décolonisée*. Paris: La Découverte, 2010.
McKnight, Utz. *Race and the Politics of the Exception: Equality, Sovereignty, and American Democracy*. New York: Routledge, 2013.
Medina, José. *The Epistemology of Resistance: Gender and Racial Oppression, Epistemic Injustice, and Resistant Imaginations*. Oxford: Oxford University Press, 2013.

Melamed, Jodi. *Represent and Destroy: Rationalizing Violence in the New Racial Capitalism*. Minneapolis: University of Minnesota Press, 2011.
Meltzer, Françoise, and Jaś Elsner, eds. *Saints: Faith without Borders*. Chicago: University of Chicago Press, 2011.
Metz, Johann Baptist. *Theology of the World*. New York: Seabury Press, 1973.
Milbank, John. *Theology and Social Theory: Beyond Secular Reason*. Oxford: Blackwell, 1993.
Moltmann, Jürgen. *Experiences in Theology: Ways and Forms of Christian Theology*. Minneapolis: Fortress, 2000.
———. *Religion, Revolution, and the Future*. New York: Scribner, 1969.
———. *A Theology of Hope: On the Ground and the Implications of a Christian Eschatology*. New York: Harper & Row, 1967.
Morris, Aldon D. *Origins of the Civil Rights Movement: Black Communities Organizing for Change*. New York: Free Press, 1984.
Moses, Wilson Jeremiah. *Black Messiahs and Uncle Toms: Social and Literary Manipulations of a Religious Myth*. University Park, Pa.: Pennsylvania State University Press, 1993.
Moten, Fred. "Blackness and Nothingness (Mysticism in the Flesh)." *South Atlantic Quarterly* 112, no. 4 (Fall 2013): 737–80.
———. "The Case of Blackness." *Criticism* 50, no. 2 (Spring 2008): 177–218.
———. *In the Break: The Aesthetics of the Black Radical Tradition*. Minneapolis: University of Minnesota Press, 2003.
Murdoch, Iris. *The Sovereignty of Good*. London: Routledge & Kegan Paul, 1970.
Nancy, Jean-Luc. *The Inoperative Community*. Minneapolis: University of Minnesota Press, 1991.
Newton, Huey P. *Revolutionary Suicide*. New York: Penguin, 2009.
Obama, Barack. *The Audacity of Hope: Thoughts on Reclaiming the American Dream*. New York: Three Rivers, 2006.
———. *Dreams from My Father: A Story of Race and Inheritance*. New York: Three Rivers, 2004.
———. "A More Perfect Union." http://constitutioncenter.org/amoreperfectunion/.
———. "Why Organize? Problems and Promise in the Inner City." *Illinois Issues* 42 (1988). http://www.lib.niu.edu/1988/ii880840.html.
Ogbar, Jeffrey O. G. *Black Power: Radical Politics and African American Identity*. Baltimore: Johns Hopkins University Press, 2004.
Parfit, Derek. *On What Matters*. Oxford: Oxford University Press, 2011.
Payne, Charles. *I've Got the Light of Freedom: The Organizing Tradition and the Mississippi Freedom Struggle*. Berkeley: University of California Press, 1996.

Pease, Donald E. "Black Orpheus: Barack Obama's Governmentality." *REAL: Yearbook of Research in English and American Literature* 27 (2011): 57–72.
Perkinson, James W. *White Theology: Outing Supremacy in Modernity*. New York: Palgrave Macmillan, 2004.
Petrella, Ivan. *Beyond Liberation Theology: A Polemic*. London: SCM Press, 2008.
Pickstock, Catherine. *After Writing: On the Liturgical Consummation of Philosophy*. Oxford: Blackwell, 1998.
Pinn, Anthony B., ed. *By These Hands: A Documentary History of African American Humanism*. New York: New York University Press, 2001.
Posnock, Ross. *Color and Culture: Black Writers and the Making of the Modern Intellectual*. Cambridge, Mass.: Harvard University Press, 1998.
Rancière, Jacques. *Dis-Agreement: Politics and Philosophy*. Translated by Julie Rose. Minneapolis: University of Minnesota Press, 1999.
Ransby, Barbara. *Ella Baker and the Black Freedom Movement: A Radical Democratic Vision*. Chapel Hill: University of North Carolina Press, 2003.
Remnick, David. *The Bridge: The Life and Rise of Barack Obama*. New York: Alfred A. Knopf, 2010.
Rifkin, Mark. "Indigenizing Agamben: Rethinking Sovereignty in Light of the 'Peculiar' Status of Native Peoples." *Culture Critique* 73 (2009): 88–124.
Rose, Gillian. *The Broken Middle: Out of Our Ancient Society*. Oxford: Blackwell, 1992.
———. *Dialectic of Nihilism: Post-Structuralism and Law*. Oxford: Blackwell, 1984.
———. *Hegel Contra Sociology*. London: Athlone, 1995.
———. *Judaism and Modernity: Philosophical Essays*. Oxford: Blackwell, 1993.
———. *Love's Work*. New York: New York Review of Books, 2011.
———. *Mourning Becomes the Law: Philosophy and Representation*. Cambridge: Cambridge University Press, 1996.
———. *Paradiso*. London: Menard, 1999.
Schillebeeckx, Edward. *God the Future of Man*. New York: Sheed & Ward, 1968.
Schmitt, Carl. *The Concept of the Political*. Translated by George Schwab. Chicago: University of Chicago Press, 2007.
———. *Political Theology: Four Chapters on the Concept of Sovereignty*. Cambridge, Mass.: MIT Press, 1985.
Scott, Janny. "Obama Chooses Reconciliation over Rancor." *New York Times*, March 19, 2008, A1.
Seale, Bobby. *Seize the Time: The Story of the Black Panther Party and Huey P. Newton*. New York: Random House, 1970.

Sexton, Jared. *Amalgamation Schemes: Antiblackness and the Critique of Multiracialism*. Minneapolis: University of Minnesota Press, 2008.
Shanks, Andrew. *Against Innocence: Gillian Rose's Reception and Gift of Faith*. London: SCM Press, 2008.
Shipley, Jesse Weaver. "Africa in Theory: A Conversation between Jean Comaroff and Achille Mbembe." *Anthropological Quarterly* 83, no. 3 (2010): 653–78.
Shulman, George. *American Prophecy: Race and Redemption in American Political Culture*. Minneapolis: University of Minnesota Press, 2008.
Skocpol, Theda, Ariane Liazos, and Marshall Ganz. *What a Mighty Power We Can Be: African American Fraternal Groups and the Struggle for Racial Equality*. Princeton, N.J.: Princeton University Press, 2006.
Smith, Jonathan Z. "Religion, Religions, Religious." In *Critical Terms in Religious Studies*, edited by Mark C. Taylor, 269–84. Chicago: University of Chicago Press, 1998.
Smith, Tom W. "Changing Racial Labels: From 'Colored' to 'Negro' to 'Black' to 'African American.'" *Public Opinion Quarterly* 56 (1992): 496–514.
Smith, Wilfred Cantwell. *The Meaning and End of Religion: A New Approach to the Religious Traditions of Mankind*. New York: Macmillan, 1963.
Snarr, C. Melissa. *All You That Labor: Religion and Ethics in the Living Wage Movement*. New York: New York University Press, 2011.
Spillers, Hortense. "Destiny's Child: Obama and Election '08." *boundary 2* 39, no. 2 (2012): 3–32.
Stall, Susan, and Randy Stoecker. "Community Organizing or Organizing Community? Gender and the Crafts of Empowerment." *Gender and Society* 12, no. 6 (1998): 729–56.
Stein, Sam. "Jesse Jackson: Obama Just Turned Crisis into Opportunity." *Huffington Post*, July 8, 2008. http://www.huffingtonpost.com/2008/03/18/jesse-jackson-obama-just-_n_92109.html?.
Stout, Jeffrey. *Blessed are the Organized: Grassroots Democracy in America*. Princeton, N.J.: Princeton University Press, 2010.
———. *Democracy and Tradition*. Princeton, N.J.: Princeton University Press, 2005.
Swarts, Heidi J. *Organizing Urban America: Secular and Faith-based Progressive Movements*. Minneapolis: University of Minnesota Press, 2007.
Taylor, Charles. *A Secular Age*. Cambridge, Mass.: Belknap Press, 2007.
Taylor, Diana. *The Archive and the Repertoire: Performing Cultural Memory in the Americas*. Durham, N.C.: Duke University Press, 2003.
Taylor, Verta. "Gender and Social Movements: Gender Processes in Women's Self-Help Movements." *Gender and Society* 13, no. 1 (1999): 8–33.

Touré. "No Such Place as 'Post-Racial' America." *New York Times*, November 8, 2011. http://campaignstops.blogs.nytimes.com/2011/11/08/no-such-place-as-post-racial-america/.
Truth and Reconciliation Commission. "Application in Terms of Section 18 of the Promotion of National Unity and Reconciliation Act No. 34 of 1995." 1999. http://www.justice.gov.za/trc/decisions%5C1999/99_snyman.html.
Van Peebles, Melvin. *Panther: A Novel*. New York: Thunder's Mouth, 1995
Vial, Theodore. *Modern Religion, Modern Race*. New York: Oxford University Press, 2016.
Walker, Corey D. B. "Barack Obama and the Crisis of the White Intellectual." *Counterpunch*, January 12–14, 2008. http://www.counterpunch.org/2008/01/12/barack-obama-and-the-crisis-of-the-white-intellectual/.
———. *A Noble Fight: African American Freemasonry and the Struggle for Democracy in America*. Urbana: University of Illinois Press, 2008.
Walzer, Michael. *Interpretation and Social Criticism*. Cambridge, Mass.: Harvard University Press, 1987.
Warren, Calvin L. "Black Nihilism and the Politics of Hope." *CR: The New Centennial Review* 15, no. 1 (2015): 215–48.
Warren, Mark R. *Dry Bones Rattling: Community Building to Revitalize American Democracy*. Princeton, N.J.: Princeton University Press, 2001.
Weate, Jeremy. "Achille Mbembe and the Postcolony: Going Beyond the Text." *Research in African Literatures* 34, no. 4 (2003): 27–41.
Weber, Max. *Economy and Society: An Outline of Interpretive Sociology*. Berkeley: University of California Press, 1978.
———. *The Sociology of Religion*. Boston: Beacon, 1963.
Weheliye, Alexander G. *Habeas Viscus: Racializing Assemblages, Biopolitcs, and Black Feminist Theories of the Human*. Durham, N.C.: Duke University Press, 2014.
Weil, Simone. *Gravity and Grace*. London: Ark, 1987.
West, Cornel. *The American Evasion of Philosophy: A Genealogy of Pragmatism*. Madison: University of Wisconsin Press, 1989.
———. *Prophesy Deliverance! An Afro-American Revolutionary Christianity*. Louisville, Ky.: Westminster John Knox Press, 2002. Originally published in 1982.
———. *Race Matters*. Boston: Beacon, 1993.
Westphal, Merold. "Derrida as Natural Law Theorist." In *Overcoming Onto-Theology*. New York: Fordham University Press, 2001, 219–28.
Wilderson, Frank B. III. *Red, White, and Black: Cinema and the Structure of U.S. Antagonisms*. Durham, N.C.: Duke University Press, 2010.

Wilmore, Gayraud S., and James H. Cone. *Black Theology: A Documentary History*. Maryknoll, N.Y.: Orbis, 1979.
Wilson, Lindy. "Bantu Stephen Biko: A Life." In *Bounds of Possibility: The Legacy of Steve Biko and Black Consciousness*, edited by N. Barney Pityana, Mamphela Ramphele, Malusi Mpumlwana, and Lindy Wilson, 15–77. Cape Town: David Philip, 1991.
Wise, Christopher. *Derrida, Africa, and the Middle East*. New York: Palgrave Macmillan, 2009.
Wolf, Susan. "Moral Saints." *Journal of Philosophy* 79, no. 8 (1982): 419–39.
Wood, Richard L. *Faith in Action: Religion, Race, and Democratic Organizing in America*. Chicago: University of Chicago Press, 2011.
Wood, Richard L., and Brad R. Fulton. *A Shared Future: Faith-Based Organizing for Racial Equity and Ethical Democracy*. Chicago: University of Chicago Press, 2015.
Wynter, Sylvia. "1492: A New World View." In *Race, Discourse, and the Origin of the Americas: A New World View*, edited by Vera Lawrence Hyatt and Rex Nettleford, 5–57. Washington, D.C.: Smithsonian Institution Press, 1995.
———. "Beyond the Word of Man: Glissant and the New Discourse of the Antilles." *World Literature Today* 63, no. 4 (1989): 637–48.
———. "On Disenchanting Discourse: 'Minority' Literary Criticism and Beyond." *Cultural Critique* 7 (1987): 207–44.
———. "Unsettling the Coloniality of Being/Power/Truth/Freedom: Towards the Human, After Man, Its Overrepresentation—An Argument." *CR: The New Centennial Review* 3, no. 3 (2003): 257–337.
Zerilli, Linda M. G. "The Turn to Affect and the Problem of Judgment." *New Literary History* 46, no. 2 (2015): 261–86.
Ziarek, Ewa Plonowska. "Bare Life on Strike: Notes on the Biopolitics of Race and Gender." *South Atlantic Quarterly* 107, no. 1 (2008): 89–105.
Žižek, Slavoj. "Holding the Place." In *Contingency, Hegemony, Universality: Contemporary Dialogues on the Left*, by Judith Butler, Ernesto Laclau, and Slavoj Žižek, 308–29. London: Verso, 2000.
———. *The Puppet and the Dwarf: The Perverse Core of Christianity*. Cambridge, Mass.: MIT Press, 2003.
———. *The Sublime Object of Ideology*. London: Verso, 1989.
———. *Tarrying with the Negative: Kant, Hegel, and the Critique of Ideology*. Durham, N.C.: Duke University Press, 1993.
———. *Violence: Six Sideways Reflections*. New York: Picador, 2008.

INDEX

academia, 7–8, 10–11, 66
aesthetics, 27, 67, 74, 106, 107, 108, 110, 112, 220
African National Congress, 164
Afro-pessimism, 15, 110, 136–38
Agamben, Giorgio, 63, 69, 85–91, 201
Alinsky, Saul, 114, 117–18, 122
Appiah, Anthony, 205
Aquinas, Thomas, 149–50
Asad, Talal, 63
Augustine, 55, 83, 122
Auschwitz, 69
authoritarianism, 39, 44, 127
authority: Baldwin on 40–44, 54–56; blacks', 99; Christ's, 211, 214; father's, 98; Newton's, 197; Oprah as, 203; religious authorities, 234–35; secularization and, 73; struggle and, 30, 37; theology and, 8, 10, 11, 121; tradition and, 64, 75; traditional, 200
Aztec religion, 93–94

Badiou, Alain, 65, 211–12, 215, 241n26, 258n34
Bandung Conference, 2
Baring, Edward, 85
Barth, Karl, 24, 148
Beckett, Samuel, 25
Benjamin, Walter, 71, 74, 109, 153, 249n14
Berlant, Lauren, 132
Best, Stephen, 100
Black, Claude, 129–30
Black Consciousness Movement, 163–66, 171–78
Black Panther Party, 58, 115–16, 129, 181–84, 188–97
Bloch, Ernst, 71, 74, 153–54

blues, 35–36
Boulaga, Eboussi, 60, 74
Boyarin, Daniel, 78–79, 212–13, 217, 230–31
Bretherton, Luke, 122–23
brotherhood, 100–1
Brown, Michael, 147, 148
Butler, Judith, 169–71, 176, 217, 224, 245n22

Camus, Albert, 241n18
Carmichael, Stokely, 182, 190, 192, 194, 196
Carter, J. Kameron, 142
Center for Third World Organizing, 125–27
Césaire, Aimé, 69
charisma, 49–50, 115, 148, 200–1, 261n42
charity, 65, 71, 113
Charles, Ray, 52
Cheng, Anne, 140–42, 227–28
children, 42, 54, 64, 98–99, 104–5, 111–12, 141, 201, 202, 260n12
Christ: authority of, 214; blackness of, 3, 240n10; Body of Christ, 26, 28, 30, 132, 146, 234; Cone on, 13, 24, 25, 28, 29–31, 33, 242n54; identifies with poor, 133; identities united in, 199, 212; Malcolm X on, 3; model for life, 204; Newton compared to, 183, 193, 194–95, 196; paradox, 13, 24, 26, 33, 35, 38, 234; Schillebeeckx on, 144. *See also* resurrection
Christocentrism, 143
church: Baldwin on, 44, 45, 49; black, 27, 146, 233–38; Black Panthers and churches, 181, 183, 191; community

281

church (*continued*)
  of singularities, 72; Cone on, 27–28, 30, 35, 36; Du Bois on, 102; hope and, 157; invisible, 26; Malcolm X on, 3; Newton on, 193; Obama on, 113, 209; organizing and, 116, 117, 118, 127–28, 130; undercommons as, 143. *See also* Christ: Body of Christ
Cleage, Albert, 1, 3, 202
Cleaver, Eldridge, 189, 192, 194–95
coalitions, 4, 117, 120, 125, 130
Coates, Ta-Nehisi, 202–3
colonialism, 2, 10, 62, 69–74, 80, 92–93, 110, 116
colorblindness, 38, 84, 138, 154–55
Columbus, Christopher, 92, 94
communion, 30, 41, 45, 47, 49, 52, 56, 82, 111
Cone, James, 24, 26–38, 66, 120, 128, 129, 133, 135, 148–49, 154, 190
contextual theology, 10–11, 36–38, 135–36, 148, 187
Cortes, Ernesto, 118–21
Crow, 139–40
Crusoe, Robinson, 79

death: Agamben on, 87–88; Baldwin on, 45, 56; Christ overcoming, 142, 146; of church, 237–38; Cone on, 29, 30, 34, 128; Du Bois on, 102, 104, 105; Mbembe on, 64, 65, 66, 69; Newton on, 193; Obama on, 97
deconstruction, 220–21
Defoe, Daniel, 79
Derrida, Jacques, 61, 62, 66, 71, 74, 82–85, 89–91, 216, 250n37. *See also* deconstruction
despair, 36, 130, 134, 141, 152, 158–60
disciplines, academic, 5, 9–11
diversity, 4, 8, 9, 89–90, 118, 124, 137–38, 147, 148. *See also* multiculturalism
Dolezal, Rachel, 156, 160
Du Bois, W. E. B., 101–6, 109, 177, 236
Duns Scotus, John, 67

Edelman, Lee, 141–42
Ehrenstein, David, 206
Éla, Jean-Marc, 60, 74

epistemic privilege, 50, 53, 66, 155, 187
equality, 29, 100–1, 117, 228
ethnicity, 126–27
evil, 34–35, 46, 110

Fard, Wallace, 202
Farmer, Paul, 204–5
fathers: accountable to community, 67; Baldwin on, 40–44, 46–51, 54–56; black fathers, 98–112 *passim*, 145; Cone on, 36; Malcolm X on, 4; Newton's, 193; Obama on, 97–98, 202, 207, 213. *See also* patriarchy
field Negro, 1–5, 17
Forman, James, 116
Foucault, Michel, 61, 62, 66, 87, 216
freedom: Baldwin on, 51, 53; Black Panthers on, 188, 191, 193, 195; Cone on, 28–33; liberalism and, 100–1; Obama on, 249n4; organizing and, 128; Rose on, 222; secularization and, 67
Freire, Paolo, 165, 176

Garner, Eric, 147, 148
Geuss, Raymond, 184–87, 265n24
Glaude, Eddie, 190, 233–34, 237–38
Guantanamo Bay, 69, 88

Ham, curse of, 80
Harney, Stefano, 143
Hartman, Saidiya, 99
Hegel, Georg Wilhelm Friedrich, 137, 166–70, 216, 219, 223–25
heteronormativity, 99, 107, 141
Hickman, Jared, 79
Hilliard, David, 191
homo sacer, 87, 201
hopelessness. *See* despair
house Negro, 1–5
humanism, 48, 190–91, 195, 196
Hutton, Bobby, 195

ideology. *See* idolatry
idolatry: Baldwin on, 40–59 *passim*; Geuss on, 187; hope and, 141, 142, 143, 146, 149, 159, 160; Iton on, 111; Malcolm X on, 3; naming as, 169; Newton on, 192, 196, 197; organizing and, 122, 149; privilege and, 7;

Schillebeeckx on, 144–46; secularism causing, 199; theology as critique of, 6, 9, 11, 12, 38; whiteness as, 8
Islam, 3, 213–14
Iton, Richard, 106–10

Jackson, Jesse, 178–79, 200, 211
Jay-Z, 111–12
Judaism, 23–24, 74, 78–79, 137, 212, 217, 218, 229–30
judgment, 56–59, 145, 152, 185–87, 192, 224, 245n24

Kantorowicz, Ernst, 87
Kelley, Robin, 179
Kidd, Colin, 80
Kierkegaard, Søren, 25, 38, 159
King, Jr., Martin Luther, 2, 28–29, 55, 56, 82, 108, 111, 114, 128, 148, 154, 178, 181, 195, 201, 202
Kripke, Saul, 166–68, 170

Lacan, Jacques, 61, 62, 66, 166–67, 177
Lasch, Christopher, 152
Latinos, 88, 120, 126, 130
Lear, Jonathan, 139–40
liberalism, 100, 114, 122
liberation theology, 22–23, 155–56
Lincoln, C. Eric, 237–38
Lofton, Kathryn, 203
Lorde, Audre, 99
love: Baldwin on, 40, 47–48; 51–59; Cone on, 30, 35; God object of, 149–50; Newton on, 193, 195–97; Rose on, 222, 223, 228, 229
Lumumba, Chokwe, 129

Magic Negro, 205–6, 214
Mahmood, Saba, 63
Malcolm X, 1–5, 28, 112, 128, 178, 181, 183, 188, 194, 195
Malcolm X Grassroots Movement, 129
Mandela, Nelson, 84–85
Marcus, Sharon, 174–77
Martin, Trayvon, 137, 147, 148, 158
Melamed, Jodi, 114
melancholia, 63, 99–100, 140–41, 145, 221, 227, 228
messianic, the, 103–6, 109–10, 112, 142, 153, 192, 202–5

method, theological, 11–12
Metz, Johann Baptist, 255n17
Milbank, John, 66–73
modernity, 4, 67, 87–88, 110, 145, 200, 220
Moltmann, Jürgen, 153–54
Montgomery bus boycott, 114–15
Moses, Bob, 115, 124, 196
Moten, Fred, 110, 143
Muhammad, Elijah, 41, 44, 46, 239n1
multiculturalism: ascendance of, 148, 183; black church and, 238; black theology and, 5; Obama's, 207, 209; organizing and, 118, 121, 127; racism and, 147; secularism and, 89–91, 138
Muslims, 3, 81, 178. *See also* Islam

Nas, 111–12
National Committee of Negro [later Black] Churchmen, 191, 236
National Union of South African Students, 164
nationalism, black, 1, 97, 116, 179, 189–92, 194
natural law, 85
negative theology, 6, 72; Baldwin's, 40, 47, 54–55, 57; Black theology as, 145; Malcolm X's, 3; revelation and, 169; Schillebeeckx's, 144, 145. *See also* idolatry
neoliberalism, 4, 22, 90, 114, 130, 137
nihilism, 254n12; black, 101, 117
Northern Negro Grass Roots Leadership Conference, 1
Northern Negro Leadership Conference, 1

Obama, Barack, 97–100, 111–13, 152, 154, 199–215
obedience, 3, 235
Oprah, 203–4
optimism, 110, 126, 128, 129, 131–32, 144, 152

Palestinians, 213–14
Pan-African Congress, 164
paradox, 24–38, 44, 86, 134, 138, 171, 234, 235
patriarchy, 38, 135, 174–75, 176, 190, 226–28. *See also* fathers

Paul, 199, 211–12, 214
pessimism, 126–27, 128, 130, 139–41.
  See also Afro-pessimism
Pinn, Anthony, 190
Plenty Coups, 139–40
police, 53, 57–59, 65, 116, 146, 181–83, 188, 194
Powell, Adam Clayton, 1
pragmatism, 103, 105, 190, 191, 216
prison, 8, 44, 57–58, 98, 111, 142–43, 146, 195, 196
privilege, 7, 38, 53, 65, 68, 152, 153, 155, 176, 227, 229
prophecy, 39–40, 41, 103, 233–34

Qu'ran, 3

rape, 174–76
resurrection, 64–66, 69, 142–43, 146, 254n47
revolution, 1–4, 103, 173, 192–93, 196
risk: Baldwin on, 54; Cone on, 29, 31–34; of naming, 171; of organizing, 228; Rose on, 221, 224. *See also* safety
Riverside Memorial Church, 116
Robeson, Paul, 108
Rock, Chris, 181

safety, Baldwin on, 43, 45, 46, 47, 49, 50, 53, 54. *See also* risk
salvation, 25, 27, 45, 47, 49, 52, 53, 57, 122, 148, 212
Schillebeeckx, Edward, 143–46
Schmitt, Carl, 44, 63, 86, 242n37
Seale, Bobby, 46, 183, 188, 189, 192, 194–95
secularization, 92–93, 143–45, 199, 233
sensuality, Baldwin on, 54–57
Shakur, Tupac, 179
Sharpton, Al, 149, 263n20
sin: Baldwin on, 45–47; original sin, 92, 209, 214
Smith, Wilfred Cantwell, 78
Snarr, Melissa, 121–24, 129
sociality, black, 101, 106, 138
Son of Man Temple, 191
South African Students' Organization, 165–66

Southern Christian Leadership Council (SCLC), 115
sovereignty, 2, 55, 86
Spillers, Hortense, 199
spirituals, 31, 35, 134
Stall, Susan, 123
Stoecker, Randy, 123
Stout, Jeffrey, 120, 190, 217
Student Nonviolent Coordinating Committee (SNCC), 115, 129, 189, 190, 192
supersessionism, 23–24, 30, 137, 138, 212, 213
Swarts, Heidi, 120
symbolic, the, 61–65, 68–74, 173, 174, 177

Tillich, Paul, 24
tradition, 25–26, 38, 100, 101, 234; black radical tradition, 110; black tradition, 3; Cone on, 27, 28, 35, 36; Du Bois on, 236; Judaism as, 218, 229, 230; Mbembe on, 64, 66, 74, 75; multiple traditions, 119, 190; philosophy of religion as, 76–78, 82, 93; prophecy and, 201; theology and, 8; traditional authority, 200; West on, 103
tragedy, 6, 25, 32, 46, 50
Transcendentalists, 47

Van Peebles, Mario and Melvin, 181–82
violence: Baldwin on, 41, 48, 56; blackness and, 147–48; charity and, 159; demystifying, 6; idolatry and, 11; Mbembe on, 63, 65, 68; racism and, 8; rape and, 174; Rose on, 219, 221, 225, 226, 227; secularism and, 70

Warren, Mark, 119–20, 127–28
Washington, Booker T., 177
Washington, Harold, 97, 208
Weber, Max, 200, 262n8
Weil, Simone, 52–53
West, Cornel, 25, 101, 103, 117, 120, 125, 190, 200, 201, 217
white supremacy, 2, 3, 4, 43, 77, 149, 154, 158, 180, 200, 235, 238
white tears, 158–59
whiteness: Baldwin on, 40, 51; Cone on, 32; defined, 7–8; Derrida on, 84;

heteronormativity and, 99; ideology and, 149; naming of, 180; philosophy of religion and, 77; renouncing, 7; transmission and, 99
Wilderson, Frank, 130
Winfrey, Oprah. *See* Oprah
Wolf, Susan, 262n14
Wood, Richard, 125–26

Wright, Jeremiah, 128, 202, 204, 209–11, 213
Wright, Richard, 41, 44, 46
writing, Baldwin on, 50–51, 52, 59

Young Jeezy, 111–12

Žižek, Slavoj, 163, 166–70

www.ingramcontent.com/pod-product-compliance
Lightning Source LLC
Chambersburg PA
CBHW030436300426
44112CB00009B/1024